THE CAMBRIDGE COMPAI

Saul Bellow is one of the most influential _
literature. Bellow's work explores the most important cultural and social experiences of his era: the impact of the Holocaust, the urban experience of European immigrants from a Jewish perspective, the fraught failures of the Vietnam War, the ideological seductions of Marxism and Modernism, and the changing attitudes concerning gender and race. This *Companion* demonstrates the complexity of this formative writer by emphasizing the ways in which Bellow's works speak to the changing conditions of American identity and culture from the postwar period to the turn of the twenty-first century. Individual chapters address the major themes of Bellow's work over more than a half-century of masterfully crafted fiction, articulating some of the most significant cultural experiences of the American twentieth century. It provides a comprehensive and accessible overview of a key figure in American literature.

Victoria Aarons is the O. R. & Eva Mitchell Distinguished Professor of Literature at Trinity University. She is the author of *A Measure of Memory* and *What Happened to Abraham*, both recipients of the Choice Award for Outstanding Academic Book; and the co-editor of *The New Diaspora: The Changing Landscape of American Jewish Fiction*, and *Bernard Malamud: A Centennial Tribute*. She is co-author of *Third-Generation Holocaust Representation: Trauma, History, and Memory*, and editor of *Third-Generation Holocaust Narratives: Memory in Memoir and Fiction*. Aarons has published over seventy scholarly articles and is on the editorial board of *Philip Roth Studies*, *Studies in American Jewish Literature*, *Women in Judaism*, and *Verbeia, Journal of English and Spanish Studies*. She serves as a judge for the Edward Lewis Wallant Award.

A complete list of books in the series is at the back of this book

THE CAMBRIDGE
COMPANION TO
SAUL BELLOW

THE CAMBRIDGE
COMPANION TO
SAUL BELLOW

VICTORIA AARONS
Trinity University, Texas

CAMBRIDGE
UNIVERSITY PRESS

CAMBRIDGE
UNIVERSITY PRESS

University Printing House, Cambridge CB2 8BS, United Kingdom

One Liberty Plaza, 20th Floor, New York, NY 10006, USA

477 Williamstown Road, Port Melbourne, VIC 3207, Australia

4843/24, 2nd Floor, Ansari Road, Daryaganj, Delhi – 110002, India

79 Anson Road, #06–04/06, Singapore 079906

Cambridge University Press is part of the University of Cambridge.

It furthers the University's mission by disseminating knowledge in the pursuit of education, learning, and research at the highest international levels of excellence.

www.cambridge.org
Information on this title: www.cambridge.org/9781107108936
10.1017/9781316266175

First published 2017

Printed in the United States of America by Sheridan Books, Inc.

A catalogue record for this publication is available from the British Library.

Library of Congress Cataloging-in-Publication Data
Aarons, Victoria, editor.
The Cambridge companion to Saul Bellow / edited by Victoria Aarons.
Cambridge ; New York : Cambridge University Press, 2017. |
Cambridge companions to literature | Includes bibliographical references and index.
LCCN 2016026624 | ISBN 9781107108936 (hardback)
LCSH: Bellow, Saul – Criticism and interpretation.
LCC PS3503.E4488 Z59 2017 | DDC 813/.52–dc23
LC record available at https://lccn.loc.gov/2016026624

ISBN 978-1-107-10893-6 Hardback
ISBN 978-1-107-52091-2 Paperback

CONTENTS

CONTENTS

CONTRIBUTORS

VICTORIA AARONS is O. R. & Eva Mitchell Distinguished Professor of Literature in the English Department at Trinity University and is the author of *A Measure of Memory: Storytelling and Identity in American Jewish Fiction* (1996), *What Happened to Abraham: Reinventing the Covenant in American Jewish Fiction* (2005), and most recently, co-editor of *The New Diaspora: The Changing Landscape of American Jewish Fiction* (2015) and *Bernard Malamud: A Centennial Tribute* (2016). She is co-author with Alan L. Berger of *Third-Generation Holocaust Representation: Trauma, History, and Memory* and editor of *Third-Generation Holocaust Narratives: Memory in Memoir and Fiction* (forthcoming, 2017). She is also the author of numerous essays in journals and scholarly collections, and she serves on the board of *Philip Roth Studies, Studies in American Jewish Literature, Women in Judaism: A Multidisciplinary Journal*, and *Verbeia, Journal of English and Spanish Studies*. Aarons is a judge for the Edward Lewis Wallant Award.

ALAN L. BERGER occupies the Raddock Family Eminent Scholar Chair for Holocaust Studies and is Professor of Judaic Studies at Florida Atlantic University, where he directs the Center for the Study of Values and Violence after Auschwitz. Among his books are *Crisis and Convenant: The Holocaust in American Jewish Fiction, Judaism in the Modern World, Children of Job: American Second-Generation Witnesses to the Holocaust*, and *Second-Generation Voices: Reflections by Children of Holocaust Survivors and Perpetrators*. He is co-editor of *Encyclopedia of Holocaust Literature, The Continuing Agony: From the Carmelite Convent to the Crosses at Auschwitz, Jewish American and Holocaust Literature: Representation in the Postmodern World, Jewish-Christian Dialogue: Drawing Honey from the Rock, Encyclopedia of Jewish American Literature*, and *Trialogue and Terror: Judaism, Christianity and Islam Respond to 9/11* (2012). He served as guest editor for a special issue of the *Saul Bellow Journal*: "Bellow and the Holocaust."

DAVID BRAUNER is Professor of Contemporary Literature at The University of Reading (UK), where he teaches courses in contemporary American and British fiction, Holocaust literature, and literature and ethnicity. He is the author of *Post-War Jewish Fiction: Ambivalence, Self-Explanation and Transatlantic Connections* (2001), *Philip Roth* (2007), and *Contemporary American Fiction*; and co-editor of *The Edinburgh Companion to Modern Jewish Fiction* (2015). His essays have appeared in a wide range of journals, including *The Journal of American Studies*, *The Yearbook of English Studies*, *Studies in the Novel*, *Modern Language Review*, *Canadian Literature*, *Studies in American Jewish Literature*, and *Philip Roth Studies*.

GUSTAVO SÁNCHEZ CANALES currently teaches English at The Universidad Autónoma de Madrid (Spain). His interests in research include contemporary Jewish American fiction, Holocaust literature, comparative literature, and literary theory. He has published numerous articles, book chapters, and reviews on the work of authors such as Philip Roth, Saul Bellow, Bernard Malamud, Chaim Potok, Cynthia Ozick, Allegra Goodman, Rebecca Goldman, Jonathan Safran Foer, and Michael Chabon, among others.

PHILIPPE CODDE is a visiting professor of American literature at Ghent University. He is the recipient of a BAEF Honorary Fellowship, Fordham University's Bennett *Fellowship*, and Ghent University's 2014 Arts and Humanities Teaching Award. He is the author of *The Jewish American Novel* (2007).

HILENE FLANZBAUM is the Allegra Stewart Chair of Modern Literature at Butler University, where she also directs the MFA program in Creative Writing. She is the editor of and a contributor to the *Americanization of the Holocaust* and the managing editor of *Jewish American Literature: A Norton Anthology*. She has published articles about Jewish American literature in *English Literary History*, *American Literary History*, *Studies in American Jewish Literature*, and the *Yale Journal of Criticism*, among others.

LEAH GARRETT is the Loti Smorgon Research Professor of Contemporary Jewish Life and Culture at Monash University. She has published extensively in Jewish literary studies, including *Journeys beyond the Pale: Yiddish Travel Writing in the Modern World* (1999), *The Cross and Other Jewish Stories by Lamed Shapiro* (2003), *A Knight at the Opera: Heine, Wagner, Herzl, Peretz and the Legacy of Der Tannhauser* (2011), and *Young Lions: How Jewish Authors Reinvented the American War Novel* (2015).

STEVEN G. KELLMAN, Professor of Comparative Literature, the University of Texas at San Antonio, is the author of *The Self-Begetting Novel, Loving*

Reading: Erotics of the Text, The Translingual Imagination, Switching Languages: Translingual Writers Reflect on Their Craft, and *Redemption: The Life of Henry Roth* (2005), which received the New York Society Library Award for Biography.

S. LILLIAN KREMER, University Distinguished Professor, Emerita, Department of English, Kansas State University, was a Fulbright Lecturer in Belgium and a guest lecturer in the Czech Republic, Italy, and Israel. She is the author of *Witness Through the Imagination: The Holocaust in Jewish American Literature*, *Women's Holocaust Writing: Memory and Imagination*, and editor and contributing author of *Holocaust Literature: An Encyclopedia of Writers and Their Work*, a two-volume reference work designated a *CHOICE* Best Reference Book, the American Library Association Dartmouth *Medal* Honorable Mention, and awarded the Judaica Bibliography Book Award by the Association of Jewish Libraries.

PAULE LÉVY is Professor of American Literature at the University of Versailles, France. She has widely published in the field of Jewish American literature. In addition to numerous articles, her book publications include *Figures de l'Artiste: Identité et écriture dans la littérature juive américaine de la deuxième moitié du XXe siècle* (2006), *American Pastoral: La Vie réinventée* (2012), and the edited volumes, *Profils américains: Philip Roth* (2002), *Ecritures contemporaines de la différence* (2003), *Mémoires d'Amériques* (2009), *Autour de Saul Bellow* (2010), and *Lectures de Philip Roth: American Pastoral* (2011).

TIMOTHY PARRISH, Professor of English, Virginia Tech University, is the author of *Walking Blues: Making Americans from Emerson to Elvis* (2001), *From the Civil War to the Apocalypse: Postmodern History and American Fiction* (2008), and *Ralph Ellison and the Genius of America* (2012). He is also the editor of *The Cambridge Companion to Philip Roth* (2007) and *The Cambridge Companion to American Novelists* (2013). He has published widely on contemporary American literature.

SUKHBIR SINGH is an eminent scholar and teacher of English, American, and Indian literatures at Osmania University, Hyderabad, India. He was awarded Junior and Senior UGC research fellowships, and Major and Minor Research Projects by the UGC; Senior Fulbright Visiting Fellowship at the University of Chicago (Divinity School), IL, by the United States Educational Foundation in India; and Pierce Loughran Visiting Scholarship by the W.B. Yeats Society of Ireland. He is currently on the International Board of Editors for the Anthology of American Literature for the Asian Students funded by the Luce Foundation in the United States. He was elected to the Board of Directors and Executive Council of the American Studies Research Center, Hyderabad.

LEONA TOKER is Professor in the English Department of the Hebrew University of Jerusalem. She is the author of *Nabokov: The Mystery of Literary Structures* (1989), *Eloquent Reticence: Withholding Information in Fictional Narrative* (1993), *Return from the Archipelago: Narratives of Gulag Survivors* (2000), *Towards the Ethics of Form in Fiction: Narratives of Cultural Remission* (2010), and articles on English, American, and Russian literature. She is the editor of *Commitment in Reflection: Essays in Literature and Moral Philosophy* (1994) and co-editor of *Rereading Texts/Rethinking Critical Presuppositions: Essays in Honour of H.M. Daleski* (1996), as well as of *Knowledge and Pain* (2012). She founded and is editor of *Partial Answers: Journal of Literature and the History of Ideas*, a semiannual academic periodical published by Johns Hopkins University Press.

MARTÍN URDIALES-SHAW is Senior Lecturer in the Department of English, French and German at the University of Vigo, Spain. He works on American Twentieth-Century literature, mainly specializing in the fields of Jewish American narrative, 1930s urban fiction, and, more recently, American popular culture, graphic novels, and Holocaust studies. His main publications include a monograph on Bernard Malamud's oeuvre, and articles on the works of Bernard Malamud, Henry Roth, Clifford Odets, Tillie Olsen, and Rudolfo Anaya.

CHRONOLOGY

1915   Solomon (Saul) Bellow is born on June 10 in Lachine, Quebec, Canada to Russian-born Abraham Belo (b. 1881), who held a variety of small-time jobs, including baker, bootlegger, and junk-dealer, and Lescha (Liza) Gordin Belo (b. 1883?). Family name is changed to Bellows.

1918   Bellows family moves to Montreal. Speaks French and Yiddish in the home.

1923   Bellow becomes ill with peritonitis and pneumonia. Hospitalized for six months at Royal Victoria Hospital.

1924   Bellows family moves to Humboldt Park, Chicago. Family name is changed to Bellow.

1930   Graduates Sabin Junior High.

1933   Graduates Tuley High School.

1933   Liza Bellow dies after battle with breast cancer. Bellow enrolls at the University of Chicago, where he remains for two years.

1935   Transfers to Northwestern University because of family's financial difficulties. Studies English literature and anthropology.

1936   Publishes short pieces in the *Daily Northwestern*.

1937   Graduates Northwestern with a BA in anthropology. Becomes an associate editor of the *Beacon*, Chicago's liberal magazine. Receives graduate fellowship in Department of Sociology and Anthropology at the University of Wisconsin, Madison.

1938   Returns to Chicago after two semesters at the University of Wisconsin. Marries Anita Goshkin. Teaches anthropology and English at Pestalozzi-Froebel Teachers College.

1940   Travels to Mexico City to interview Trotsky, who was assassinated before they could meet.

1941	Short story, "Two Morning Monologues," published in *Partisan Review*. Becomes a naturalized citizen of the United States.
1944	Publishes *Dangling Man*. Birth of first son, Gregory.
1945	Joins the Merchant Marine.
1946	Joins the faculty of the English Department at the University of Minnesota as an assistant professor. Meets Robert Penn Warren.
1947	Publishes *The Victim*. Embarks on first European trip.
1948	Receives Guggenheim Fellowship. Publishes "Spanish Letter" in *Partisan Review*. Travels to Paris with Anita and Gregory.
1949	Publishes "Sermon by Dr. Pep" in *Partisan Review* and "The Jewish Writer and the English Literary Tradition" in *Commentary*.
1950	Returns to America, relocating in Queens, New York.
1951	Publishes "By the Rock Wall" in *Harper's Bazaar*. Begins Reichian therapy.
1952	Translated I. B. Singer's "Gimpel the Fool" for Partisan. Assumes residency at Yaddo, artists' colony in Saratoga Springs, New York. Becomes friends with Ralph Ellison. Works at Princeton with Delmore Schwartz. Meets lifetime friend John Berryman.
1953	Begins teaching at Bard College. Meets Hannah Arendt. Second residency at Yaddo. Publishes *The Adventures of Augie March* to considerable acclaim.
1954	*The Adventures of Augie March* wins National Book Award for Fiction. Separates from Anita. Resigns position at Bard.
1955	Abraham Bellow dies of aneurysm. "A Father-To-Be" published in the *New Yorker*. Moves to Reno, Nevada.
1956	Marries Sasha (Sondra) Tschacbasov. Meets John Cheever at Yaddo. Moves to Tivoli, New York. Teaches at the New School for Social Research. Publishes *Seize the Day*.
1957	Birth of son, Adam. Meets Philip Roth at the University of Chicago. Fourth residency at Yaddo.
1959	Publishes *Henderson the Rain King*. Meets Alice Adams. Separates from Sondra.
1960	Meets Hebrew writer S. Y. Agnon in Israel. Founds magazine the *Noble Savage*, coedited with Keith Botsford and Jack Ludwig.
1961	Marries Susan Glassman.

1962	Begins professorship in the committee on Social Thought at the University of Chicago.
1963	Publishes "The Writer as Moralist" in *Atlantic Monthly*. Writes Introduction to *Great Jewish Short Stories*.
1964	Birth of son Daniel. Publishes *Herzog*.
1965	Receives National Book Award for Fiction for *Herzog* and the Formentor Prize.
1966	Separates from wife Susan.
1967	Travels to Middle East to cover the Six-Day War for *Newsday*.
1968	Publishes short story collection *Mosby's Memoirs*.
1969	Publishes *Mr. Sammler's Planet* serially in *Atlantic Monthly*.
1970	Publishes *Mr. Sammler's Planet* in book form.
1971	*Mr. Sammler's Planet* wins National Book Award for Fiction.
1974	Marries Alexandra Ionescu Tulcea.
1975	Publishes *Humboldt's Gift*, a novel based in large part on the poet Delmore Schwartz. Travels to Israel and interviews major Israeli novelists and political figures, including Prime Minister Yitzhak Rabin.
1976	Receives Pulitzer Prize for Fiction for *Humboldt's Gift*. Non-fiction collection *To Jerusalem and Back* appears serially in the *New Yorker* and then in book form. Receives Nobel Prize in Literature.
1977	Receives Gold Medal for Fiction of the American Academy and Institute of Arts and Letters. Teaches at Brandeis. Begins appointment as member of Prize Fellows Committee to select MacArthur grant recipients.
1980	Begins co-teaching with Allan Bloom in the Committee on Social Thought. Receives the O. Henry Award.
1981	Meets with Samuel Beckett in Paris.
1982	Publishes *The Dean's December*. Publishes story "Him with His Foot in His Mouth" in *Atlantic Monthly*.
1983	Publishes "In the Days of Mr. Roosevelt" in *Esquire*.
1984	Publishes "What Kind of Day Did You Have?" in *Vanity Fair*. Publishes the collection of stories *Him with His Foot in His Mouth*. Lachine Public Library renames as Saul Bellow Public Library.
1985	Brothers Maurice and Sam die. Separates from Alexandra.
1986	Participates in PEN International Conference in New York. American-Jewish novelist Bernard Malamud dies.
1987	Publishes *More Die of Heartbreak*.

1988   Receives Medal of Freedom from President Ronald Reagan. Travels to Italy and receives Scanno Prize in Abruzzo.

1989   Publishes *A Theft* and the novella *The Bellarosa Connection*. Receives PEN/Malamud Award and the Peggy V. Helmerich Distinguished Authors Award. Marries Janis Freeman. Begins work on two unfinished novels, *All Marbles Still Accounted For* and *A Case of Love*.

1990   Receives National Book Foundation's lifetime Medal for Distinguished Contribution to American Letters. Publishes story "Something to Remember Me By" in *Esquire*.

1991   Publishes *Something to Remember Me By: Three Tales*.

1992   Friend Allan Bloom dies.

1993   Publishes collection of non-fiction pieces *It All Adds Up*. Begins teaching appointment at Boston University.

1994   Travels to the Caribbean island of Saint Martin and becomes seriously ill after eating contaminated fish with ciguatera poisoning. Returns to Boston where he is hospitalized.

1995   Returns to teaching at Boston University. Last short story, "By the Saint Lawrence," appears in *Esquire*. Founds (with Keith Botsford) the new literary journal, *News from the Republic of Letters*.

1997   Publishes novella *The Actual*.

1999   Series of interviews with Philip Roth. Birth of daughter, Naomi Rose.

2000   Publishes *Ravelstein*, Bellow's final novel based on longtime friend and colleague, philosopher Allan Bloom, who taught at the University of Chicago's Committee on Social Thought.

2001   *Collected Stories* published, preface by Janis Freedman Bellow and introduction by literary critic James Wood.

2003   Library of Congress begins publishing collected works.

2005   Dies at his home in Brookline, MA, on April 5 at age 89. Following traditional Jewish rites is buried in Brattleboro Cemetery, Vermont.

VICTORIA AARONS

Introduction: Saul Bellow in His Times

Saul Bellow, recipient of the Nobel Prize in Literature (1976), remains one of
the major literary figures of the twentieth century. A defining voice of post-
World War II America, Bellow continues to be a celebrated icon of twentieth-
century letters, a writer whose penetrating prose has influenced writers and
readers in America and abroad since the late 1940s. Bellow's novels, beginning with *Dangling Man* (1944) and concluding with *Ravelstein* (2000), span
over half a century and reflect the erratic, mutating, and often torturous
political, cultural, and intellectual character of his times. Bellow's literary
oeuvre articulates some of the most significant cultural experiences of the
American twentieth century. His fiction represents and comments on some of
the century's major cultural events and issues: the urban experience of
European immigrants, especially Jewish immigrants; the socio-cultural
ascendance of an influential Jewish middle-class; the ideological seductions
of Marxism and Modernism; the tensions between residual European intellectual culture and emergent popular culture; the fraught failures of the
Vietnam War; the changing attitudes about gender and race; the "culture
wars" in 1990s America; and the underlying fault-lines of anti-Semitism.
Moreover, the span of Bellow's career witnessed the impact in America of the
Holocaust: as Bellow once put it, "a crime so vast that it brings all Being into
Judgment."[1] Bellow's fiction casts its moral gaze upon the spectacle of
a civilization in anxious flux, the spinning out-of-control of its impelling
desires.

Since the publication of his first novel, *Dangling Man*, extolled by Edmund
Wilson in the *New Yorker* as "one of the most honest pieces of testimony on
the psychology of a whole generation who have grown up during the
Depression and the war," Bellow's fiction came to define the literary possibilities for American cultural thought and expression.[2] Following the publication of his major, breakthrough novel, *The Adventures of Augie March*,
in 1953, Bellow would go on to occupy a prominent place in American
literature for over half a century. The American-Jewish novelist Jonathan

Rosen, in remembrance of Bellow, has said that his "presence in the world was like a kind of sheltering genius," an exacting intellectual who "elevated the role of the writer to the highest possible sphere."[3] The distinguished English novelist Martin Amis has called Bellow "The greatest American author ever."[4] J. M Coetzee has described Bellow as "perhaps *the* giant" of American fiction of the second half of the twentieth century.[5] Bellow is known as one of the three major post-World War II American-Jewish writers to raise the profile and secure a place for American-Jewish literary expression beyond the earlier writing of the immigrant tradition. Along with Bernard Malamud and Philip Roth, Bellow created a "new" Jewish voice and presence in American letters. To be sure, Bellow became one of the central Jewish voices writing in and about America in the post-World War II era, but he also rapidly came to be considered a major American literary presence in the second half of the twentieth century. In straddling his Jewish immigrant origins and his American upbringing, as Christopher Hitchens put it, "it mattered to him that the ghetto be transcended and that he, too, could sing America."[6]

Bellow embraced American life from the point of view of the astute observer of human folly, but also from that of determined transcendence. Solomon (Saul) Bellow, born in 1915 in Lachine, Quebec, to Russian Jewish émigrés Abram and Lescha Belo (later changed to Bellows), did not come to the United States until 1924. Despite, or perhaps because of, his early French-influenced and Yiddish-speaking years in Canada, Bellow's work epitomized a developing diversity of American life at a critical moment in American history, as the relative openness of American borders allowed for European immigration to the cities. The American city, especially Chicago and New York, was home to Bellow, the source of impetuous and seductive desire and heady exuberance, as his ardent protagonist Augie March, with intoxicating fervor, declares in the opening pages of the novel: "I am an American, Chicago-born."[7] Augie's unequivocal exuberance is a celebration of both place and identity, an opening for seemingly limitless possibilities.

Bellow's primary fictive landscape is urban America, the stage upon which his characters play out their most passionate impulses, escapades, and extravagances. As Bellow's protagonist Artur Sammler ironically puts it, America is "advertised throughout the universe as the most desirable, most exemplary of all nations."[8] It is here that Bellow's characters locate their passions and appetites. And it is in the city, the "soul of America," in Sammler's terms, that Bellow's protagonists expose their most persistent anxieties and obsessions, embracing intellectual and emotional fixations that compel the defining narratives of their lives (146). The city for Bellow is, as he puts it in the novel *Seize the Day*, a "carnival of the street," a shifting, undulating landscape upon which his characters define themselves as American Jews in the second half of the twentieth century.[9] They speak the language of urban America: gritty, performative, harsh, intense, antagonistic, and animated, breathing life into a cityscape that captures the noise of post-war life.

With fourteen novels, three collections of short stories, three plays, and two collections of essays, Bellow was a highly prolific writer over the course of his career and has been one of the most critically significant and culturally recognized American writers of the twentieth century. The Nobel Prize for Literature in 1976 recognized him "for the human understanding and subtle analysis of contemporary culture that are combined in his work."[10] Bellow is the only novelist to have received the National Book Award three times: in 1954 for *The Adventures of Augie March*, a novel that Philip Roth described as "the most important book published in English in the second half of the 20th century";[11] in 1965 for *Herzog*; and in 1971 for *Mr. Sammler's Planet*. In 1976 Bellow received the Pulitzer Prize for the novel *Humboldt's Gift*, and in 1988 he was awarded the National Medal of Arts by the Congress of the United States. In 1989 he received the PEN/Malamud Award, and in 1990 the Medal for Distinguished Contribution to American Letters by the National Book Foundation. As a further measure of Bellow's status in American letters, the acclaimed novelist Philip Roth was the first recipient of the PEN/Saul Bellow Award for Achievement in American Fiction, a prize named in Bellow's honor. Roth, upon receipt of the award, named Bellow along with William Faulkner as the two writers who formed "the backbone of 20th-century American literature" and asked, "How could I be anything but thrilled to receive an award bearing Saul Bellow's name?"[12]

Bellow's standing as a central figure in American letters and as a major voice of the twentieth century is further evidenced by the critical acclaim he has received both in America and abroad. As the English literary critic, essayist, and novelist James Wood puts it, "Bellow was one, to my mind, of the greatest of American prose stylists in the 20th century – and thus one of the greatest in American fiction."[13] Indeed, Bellow's influence and accomplishments, undiminished by time, reach into a new century and affect generations of writers who have followed, writers inspired by the power of his literary imagination and the weight of his ideas. As the novelist Ian McEwan has said, "It will be some time before we have the full measure of Saul Bellow's achievement."[14] Upon Bellow's death in 2005, McEwan in tribute wrote:

> Saul Bellow started publishing in the 1940s, and his work spreads across the century he helped to define. He also redefined the novel, broadened it, liberated

it, made it warm with human sense and wit and grand purpose ... We are saying farewell to a mind of unrivalled quality. He opened our universe a little more. We owe him everything.[15]

Undeniably, Saul Bellow is considered, along with Philip Roth and John Updike, to be one of the genuinely significant writers of his generation. Bellow, with subtle nuance and acute judgment, measures the intellectual and moral temper of his age. A writer of the mind, Bellow, through rich, candid, and uncompromising language, manages in his fiction to write simultaneously of the colloquy of the street and of the main ideas of the European intellectual tradition.

Bellow's current status as a major American novelist and intellectual arbiter of his time began with the early reception of his work. From Bellow's initial appearance as a novelist, readers recognized the originality and significance of his fiction. Initial reviews of Bellow's first novel, *Dangling Man*, were notably favorable. The writer Delmore Schwartz, whom Bellow would later make the subject of his novel *Humboldt's Gift*, wrote in the *Partisan Review* shortly after the publication of *Dangling Man*: "Here, for the first time ... the experience of a new generation has been seized and recorded."[16] Nathan L. Rothman in an early review applauded Bellow on the publication of *Dangling Man*, as "a writer of great original powers ... He writes with obvious style and mastery, with a sharp cutting to the quick of language, with a brilliance of thought."[17] *Dangling Man*, Rothman predicted, was "the herald of a fine literary career."[18] *The Victim*, Bellow's second novel, was greeted with no less enthusiasm for its depictions of the anxieties of American Jews in the direct aftermath of World War II, a novel that, as Richard Match said in the *New York Herald Tribune Book Review*, "rates as a subtle and thoughtful contribution to the literature of twentieth-century anti-Semitism."[19] It was with the publication of *The Adventures of Augie March*, however, that Bellow's career was firmly ensconced in the canon of American letters. The novelist Robert Penn Warren praised the novel as "by far the best one" written to date by Bellow, "a rich, various, fascinating, and important book, and from now on any discussion of fiction in America in our time will have to take account of it."[20] As Bellow himself said of *The Adventures of Augie March* in an October 19, 1953 letter to his longtime friend Samuel Freifeld, "I myself feel happier about this book than about anything I have ever done."[21] Lionel Trilling, in his review of the novel, calls *The Adventures of Augie March* a "remarkable achievement," a work that encompasses "a human reality at once massive and brilliant."[22]

One might consider the trajectory of Bellow's work in terms of the following general directions and preoccupations, and as responses to the historical, socio-political, and cultural conditions of his times. Early novels, such as *Dangling Man* (1944), *The Victim* (1947), and *Seize the Day* (1956), focus on alienated mid-twentieth-century man, estranged from self and others. The novels of Bellow's early literary maturity, *The Adventures of Augie March* (1953) and *Henderson the Rain King* (1959), involve themselves with the idea of "America" as a scene of self-creation and self-determination. Intellectual man and the ironies of self-projection emerge thematically in *Herzog* (1964), *Mr. Sammler's Planet* (1970), *Humboldt's Gift* (1975), *The Dean's December* (1982), and *Ravelstein* (2000). But these periodic directions only provide a skeletal framework within which Bellow's rich fictive conceits are stretched, reaching beyond – in fact, in defiance of – any one thematic parameter. Nonetheless, seen in these ways, Bellow's fiction can show us the intersecting, mutually dependent, and ironically complex conditions of American culture in the twentieth century.

Since his death in 2005, Bellow remains in the forefront of American fiction, and Bellow's work continues to receive sustained critical and scholarly attention. Ongoing scholarly interest in Bellow can be seen in the continuing publication of books, journal articles, and chapters in collections on his work. In 2000 the first major critical biography of Bellow was published by James Atlas (*Bellow: A Biography*). In 2010 Benjamin Taylor published a fascinating and important collection (*Saul Bellow: Letters*) of selected correspondence between Bellow and numerous literary, philosophical, and cultural figures. More recently, 2015 has seen two major publications devoted to Bellow: the first of two volumes of Zachary Leader's authoritative, comprehensive biography, *The Life of Saul Bellow: To Fame and Fortune, 1915–1964*; and Benjamin Taylor's edited collection of Bellow's non-fiction prose, *There Is Simply Too Much to Think About*. These major publications suggest the enduring influence of Bellow's work on American literature and thought. Perhaps the full extent of Bellow's influence and the impact of his work can only be seen in retrospect, as the intellectual, moral, and material landscape that he both shaped and predicted is being played out.

Rather than attempting a wide-sweeping, broad-brush account of Bellow's extensive literary career, this *Companion* hopes to engage readers in thinking through some of Bellow's most pronounced and influential moments as they shape his career-defining works. Moreover, the approaches taken to Bellow's work in this collection introduce student-scholars to some of the thornier questions raised by his critical assessment of the human condition. As Bellow put it, "The writer ... is invariably motivated by a desire for truth."[23]

As biographer Zachary Leader points out, "Bellow was a famed noticer and his novels and stories are packed with things perfectly seen."[24] Reading Bellow is not easy. His work challenges us to think hard about some of the most difficult and complex moments in history. It also requires readers to examine their own moral compass in assessing history, culture, and personal responsibility. Willis Salomon has remarked that "Bellow's novels often 'go big' with concepts, history, and the 'great books' he taught for years as a professor in the Committee on Social Thought at the University of Chicago."[25] In doing so, Bellow's novels question the very premises of human motivations and actions and place demands on readers to examine thoughtfully the impulses and justifications of their actions. Bellow's intellectual bent as a novelist, his consistent focus on embodied ideas, reveals itself often in characters whose most defining traits represent the follies of self-delusion.

To read Bellow is to engage explicitly in an ethical assessment of the worth of the human endeavor. Each of the chapters in this collection poses occasions for deep engagement in the enduring problems and ethical considerations that have defined Bellow's work throughout his career. This collection seeks to allow new Bellow readers an entry into this complex writer at the same time that it encourages longtime readers of Bellow to rethink their understanding of his work. For students introduced to Bellow for the first time, the essays in this *Companion* will explore some of Bellow's most persistent questions and show the way in which Bellow's key works provide a commentary on some of the most pressing contingencies of the second half of the twentieth century. For seasoned readers of Bellow, the essays in this volume are designed to continue the discussion of the concerns that have preoccupied scholars ever since Bellow's fiction became the subject of critical attention in the academy and beyond. In engaging Bellow's work through the perspectives taken in the individual chapters in this *Companion*, readers will see a map, not just of Bellow's career, but of the key concerns of twentieth-century American literature and culture: identity-formation and personhood; intellectual movements such as existentialism, Marxism, and psychoanalysis; race; the changing place of America in a globalizing world; anti-Semitism; genocide; gender; cultural pluralism; and aging and death. In constructing a critical anthology on Bellow's works, one can select from many different, equally compelling directions: the Jewish Bellow, the American Bellow, the comic Bellow, the intellectual Bellow, the Postmodern Bellow, the autobiographical Bellow, the political Bellow, and the like. This collection engages these different approaches in a dialogue, offering multiple perspectives by which readers can appreciate the diverse directions of Bellow's work and the range of contemporary critical thought. This collection includes distinguished critics who approach Bellow in the context of American literature and culture. Among these distinguished readers of Bellow are scholars from around the world, whose perspectives on Bellow are not specifically "American," suggesting the appeal of Bellow's work beyond America and the international resonance it has for many of his readers.

Part of Bellow's longstanding appeal stems from the ways his novels "talk to each other," changing and extending his conceptual reach with successive novels as, taken together, they speak to the changing conditions of American identity. The arrangement of this volume reflects the development of Bellow's fiction by following the arc of his career without being limited to a narrow chronology. The individual chapters address the major themes and directions of Bellow's work over more than a half-century of masterfully crafted fiction, its influences, its developing protagonists, its nuances, and its complexities of thought and feeling.

Notes

1. *Saul Bellow: Letters*, ed. Benjamin Taylor (New York: Viking, 2010), p. 439.
2. Edmund Wilson, "Doubts and Dreams: *Dangling Man* Under a Glass Bell," *The New Yorker* (April 1, 1944): 78.
3. Jonathan Rosen, "Dave Eggers et al., on Saul Bellow," *Slate Magazine* (April 8, 2005), www.slate.com/articles/arts/culturebox/2005/04/saul_bellow.5.html.
4. Robert Birnbaum, "Author Interview: Martin Amis," *Literary Theory* (December 8, 2003), http://www.identitytheory.com/martin-amis/.
5. J. M. Coetzee, "Bellow's Gift," *The New York Review of Books* (May 27, 2004), http://www.nybooks.com/articles/archives/2004/may/27/bellows-gift/.
6. Christopher Hitchens, "The Great Assimilator," *The Atlantic* (November 1, 2007): 1.
7. Saul Bellow, *The Adventures of Augie March* (1953; rpt., New York: Viking, 1969), p. 3.
8. Saul Bellow, *Mr. Sammler's Planet* (1970; rpt., New York: Penguin, 1984), p. 14.
9. Saul Bellow, *Seize the Day* (New York: Viking, 1956), p. 78.
10. "The Nobel Prize in Literature 1976," Nobelprize.org., Nobel Media AB 2013 (May 4, 2014), www.nobelprize.org/nobel_prizes/literature/laureates/1976/.
11. "Author Philip Roth Wins Saul Bellow Award," *USA Today* (April 1, 2007), http://usatoday30.usatoday.com/life/books/news/2007-04-01-roth_N.htm.
12. "Author Philip Roth Wins Saul Bellow Award."
13. James Wood, "The High-minded Joker," *The Guardian* (April 8, 2005), www.theguardian.com/books/2005/apr/09/saulbellow.
14. Ian McEwan, "Master of the Universe," *The New York Times* Editorials/Op-Ed (April 7, 2005), www.nytimes.com/2005/04/07/opinion/07mcewan.html?pagewanted=2&_r=0.
15. McEwan, "Master of the Universe."
16. Delmore Schwartz, "A Man in His Time," *Partisan Review*, 11.3 (1944): 348.

17. Nathan L. Rothman, "Introducing an Important New Writer," *Saturday Review of Literature* (April 15, 1944): 27.
18. Rothman, "Introducing an Important New Writer," p. 27.
19. Richard Match, "Anti-Semitism Hits a Jew," *New York Herald Tribune Book Review* (November 23, 1947): 10.
20. Robert Penn Warren, "The Man with No Commitments," *The New Republic* (November 2, 1953): 22–23.
21. *Saul Bellow: Letters*, p. 123.
22. Lionel Trilling, "A Triumph of the Comic View," in *A Company of Readers: Uncollected Writings of W. H. Auden, Jacques Barzun, Lionel Trilling*, ed. Arthur Krystal (New York: Simon & Schuster, 2001), p. 101.
23. Saul Bellow, "The Writer as Moralist," in *There Is Simply Too Much to Think About*, ed. Benjamin Taylor (New York: Viking, 2015), p. 159.
24. Zachary Leader, *The Life of Saul Bellow: To Fame and Fortune, 1915–1964* (New York: Alfred A. Knopf, 2015), p. 12
25. Willis Salomon, "Saul Bellow on the Soul: Character and the Spirit of Culture in *Humboldt's Gift* and *Ravelstein*," *Partial Answers: Journal of Literature and History of Ideas*, 14.1 (2016): 127–140.

I

PHILIPPE CODDE

Bellow's Early Fiction and the Making of the Bellovian Protagonist

Introduction

It is often said that great authors write only one book. The idea behind this expression is that the whole oeuvre of these writers is so consistent that it can really be considered a single work of art. This observation is certainly valid for Saul Bellow's novels, which constitute one of the most impressive post-World War II literary oeuvres. Even his earliest novels – *Dangling Man* (1944), *The Victim* (1947), and *Seize the Day* (1956) – already feature the typical Bellovian protagonist that became so characteristic of Bellow's most famous works: a male, Anglo-Saxon, Jewish, introspective, and slightly alienated intellectual who, possessed of clarity of vision and equipped with parodic self-irony, has wonderful conversations, but mainly with himself – think of the eponymous protagonists of *Henderson the Rain King* (1959) and *Herzog* (1964), Charlie Citrine in *Humboldt's Gift* (1975) or Albert Corde in *The Dean's December* (1982), to name only a few. As such, these early novels remain important not only because they launched Bellow as America's "philosophical novelist,"[1] but also because they can be seen as Bellow's creative laboratory, where the ideas and characters of his later novels were tested and refined.[2]

Dangling Man

While the early novels clearly anticipate Bellow's later work, there are also remarkable differences: inspired by the bleaker forms of European literature and philosophy, particularly French existentialism[3] and Fyodor Dostoyevsky's work, the early novels share none of the effervescence and buoyancy that characterizes Augie's drive to go at things "free-style"[4] in *The Adventures of Augie March* (1953) or Henderson's incessant desire to get more out of life – "*I want, I want, I want, oh, I want*"[5] – in *Henderson the Rain King*. In fact, in Bellow's early fiction, Henderson's "I want" still sounds like a rather desperate "I can't." This is perhaps most obvious in Bellow's literary debut, *Dangling Man*, a novel written near the end of World

War II and clearly inspired by Dostoyevsky's *Underground Man*, Albert Camus' *L'Etranger*, and especially Jean-Paul Sartre's *La Nausée*. Equally written in the form of a journal, the novel documents the life and times of the Jewish protagonist named Joseph (without a last name) who is dangling because his life is put on hold when he receives a draft call for the army. He quits his job as a clerk in a travel agency, but because his induction is indefinitely suspended, he spends his days waiting inanely, philosophizing about life, freedom, despair, and death, while wandering from one conflict to the next with the few people he meets during his period of isolation. In an interview, Bellow once stated that "each of us has to find an inner law by which he can live. Without this, objective freedom only destroys us. So the question that really interests me is the question of spiritual freedom in the individual."[6] In *Dangling Man*, Joseph is presented with a complete freedom, and the novel indeed investigates whether or not this freedom ends up destroying him.

In an oft quoted passage, Joseph makes it clear that he is tired of the traditional code of conduct and that he is looking for a new code that allows for personal feelings: "Today, the code of the athlete, of the tough boy ... is stronger than ever. Do you have feelings? ... Do you have emotions? Strangle them. To a degree, everyone obeys this code."[7] With all this spare time on his hands, Joseph has the freedom to invent a different value system. From the outset, however, it becomes clear that Joseph is not using his freedom very constructively: "I do not know how to use my freedom and have to embrace the flunkydom of a job because I have no resources – in a word, no character" (12). Too cowardly to face the choices that inevitably come with freedom, he longs for automatisms and turns his life into a concatenation of insignificant, repetitive non-events. When he does go out occasionally, his social contacts turn into such disastrous and painful conflicts that they paradoxically end up isolating him even more: he makes a scene at a restaurant when a former communist friend refuses to acknowledge him; he experiences a crisis at the Servatius party when he feels completely alienated from the other guests and understands he will never be able to create a "colony of the spirit" (39) with these people; at another party, he spanks his niece Etta for considering him insignificant; and he has similarly violent episodes with a German neighbor, with a bank clerk, and with his landlord – all events that make him feel like "a human grenade" (147). He becomes increasingly aware of his social isolation and alienation: "I, in this room, separate, alienated, distrustful, find in my purpose not an open world, but a closed, hopeless jail. My perspectives end in the walls" (92).

Separated from all other human beings, Joseph starts a dialogue with an inner voice that goes by the name of "*The Spirit of Alternatives*," a.k.a. "*But on the*

Other Hand" or *"Tu As Raison Aussi."* The Spirit of Alternatives keeps urging Joseph to take action and end the deadlock he finds himself in, but Joseph meekly complains "But with whom, under what circumstances, how, toward what ends?" (139). While he desperately wants to become "a whole man" (68) who uses his freedom creatively, he also understands that this can only be achieved by belonging to a community, a colony of the spirit, from which an incarcerated Joseph sees himself fatally excluded. He desperately wants to be a good man, but at the same time he realizes that "goodness is achieved not in a vacuum, but in the company of other men, attended by love" (92).

In the novel's rather depressing conclusion, Joseph decides to throw the towel into the ring and "to give myself up ... to surrender. I was done" (183). After seven months of dangling, he voluntarily joins the army, welcoming his surrender with the following words (also the ironic conclusion of the novel): "I am no longer to be held accountable for myself; I am grateful for that. I am in other hands, relieved of self-determination, freedom canceled. Hurray for regular hours! And for the supervision of the spirit! Long live regimentation!" (191). He gives up his freedom, gets rid of boredom by choosing the rigid regimentation of the army and by losing his individuality among the anonymous mass men in the army. Earlier in the novel he had stated "Death is the abolition of choice. The more choice is limited, the closer we are to death. The greatest cruelty is to curtail expectations without taking away life completely. A life term in prison is like that" (148). If one also considers his realization that the "final end" of any human quest is "the desire for pure freedom" (153–4), it becomes difficult to see Joseph's surrender of his freedom as anything but a failure. Thus, Bellow's first novel perfectly captures the angst, irresolution, and despair of the (post)war period. Thrown into an indifferent universe, Joseph fails to create his own values and therefore seeks solace in regimentation. As Ihab Hassan has stated, Bellow's book "leaves the ineradicable impression of a man who screams out in laughter to see his guts dangling from his belly."[8]

Bellow's first novel was written near the end of World War II, when rumors and news about the concentration camps were just starting to spread. Still, there are some subtle references in the novel not to the Holocaust as such, but to fascism and to Jewish victims of massacres. It took Bellow until 1970, however, with the publication of *Mr. Sammler's Planet*, to write about the topic of the Holocaust more openly. When interviewed about this in 1990, he admitted: "There are so many things I've not been able to incorporate ... things that got away from me, the Holocaust, for instance. I may even have been partly sealed against it, because somehow I couldn't tear myself away from my

American life. Jewish criticism is hard on me on this score."[9] In *Dangling Man*, Joseph does have a nightmare about a massacre of Jewish victims committed by the Rumanian fascists of the Iron Guard; he dreams that he enters "a low chamber with rows of large cribs or wicker bassinets in which the dead of a massacre were lying" (120). He also recalls a scene from his youth when he was confronted with anti-Semitism himself: when the father of a German friend of his said that Joseph was handsome, the mother replied with a snide: "*Mephisto war auch schön*" (70). He immediately recognized the age-old anti-Semitic slur that equated the Jews to the devil. In Bellow's defense, then, such issues clearly were already on his mind in his earliest work, even if he did not address the topic of the Holocaust explicitly. In fact, in Bellow's second novel, *The Victim*, published shortly after the war, anti-Semitism becomes the novel's main theme.

The Victim

The bleak atmosphere and the rather impassive protagonist of *Dangling Man* also feature in *The Victim* (1947). For this novel, Bellow clearly found his inspiration in Sartre's controversial essay *Anti-Semite and Jew* (1946). The protagonist, Asa Leventhal, a man as alienated from his wife, family, and friends as is Joseph, is accused by an anti-Semite of having destroyed the latter's life. As a result, the novel becomes a searing investigation of the issues of responsibility, anti-Semitism, and Jewish authenticity. At a party thrown by a mutual acquaintance, Leventhal observes the Gentile Kirby Allbee make an anti-Semitic comment directed at Leventhal's friend Harkavy. When the Jewish Harkavy sings a ballad at the party, the drunk Allbee rudely interrupts him by stating that "It isn't right for you to sing them. You have to be born to them." Instead, Harkavy should sing a Psalm or "any Jewish song. Something you've really got feeling for."[10] While the comment clearly angers Leventhal, he is as passive and fatalistic as Joseph in *Dangling Man*, so he simply shrugs off the nasty comment. Several months later, however, when Leventhal loses his job, he asks Allbee for an introduction to his superior, Rudiger, at *Dill's Weekly*. Leventhal then makes such a scene in Rudiger's office that he obviously does not get the position, but afterwards, Allbee is also fired. While Allbee sees this as a clear instance of revenge for his earlier anti-Semitic comments, Leventhal refuses to acknowledge his responsibility in the matter. The consequences for Allbee are devastating, however: he loses his job, his wife leaves him, and, when his wife dies shortly afterwards, Allbee ends up in the gutter and becomes a homeless bum. Out for justice, Allbee then increasingly foists himself upon Leventhal, accusing him, harassing him at work, haunting him day and night, until a numbed and resigned Leventhal even allows Allbee to take over his home.

While these events clearly turn Leventhal and Allbee into antagonists (Jew and anti-Semite), several critics have pointed out that Allbee also becomes Leventhal's dark double.[11] Leventhal experiences a "strange close consciousness of Allbee, of his face and body, a feeling of intimate nearness," and Allbee's eyes reflect "the look of recognition. Allbee bent on him duplicated the look in his own. He was sure of that" (143). There is even "the explicit recognition in Allbee's eyes which he could not doubt was the double of something in his own" (151). Both men consider themselves victimized by the other (Leventhal wonders "Why me?"; 70), so the novel's title actually refers to both of them, but given that they are doubles, the book is significantly not called *The Victims*.

Considered from this perspective, it becomes clear that Leventhal's conflict with Allbee is really an externalization of Leventhal's internal conflict – Allbee really becomes Leventhal's own Spirit of Alternatives in a physical form. In fact, Allbee and Leventhal become perfect illustrations of Sartre's definitions of the anti-Semite and the inauthentic Jew. Allbee's world view is the age-old anti-Semitic cliché – exemplified in *The Protocols of the Elders of Zion* – that the whole world is run by the Jews: "you must have connections" (127); "Jews have influence with other Jews" (236). Leventhal, however, corresponds to the cliché of the inauthentic Jew who depends on the anti-Semite for his own self-definition: as long as there are anti-Semites, there obviously are Jews, so this relieves the inauthentic Jew of defining his own identity. Hence, Leventhal is convinced that he is surrounded by anti-Semites: in a movie theater, he wants to attack a woman for uttering "some insult about the 'gall of Jews'" (133); he insists that his brother kick out his mother-in-law for her anti-Semitism; and even Williston, Leventhal's mentor, ends up being suspected of anti-Semitism by Leventhal. But in all of these cases, and despite his great indignation, Leventhal chooses to remain passive when confronted with real or imagined anti-Semitism. The reason why Leventhal never resists, and why he lets the anti-Semite determine his identity, is his own confusion about his Jewishness: by allowing the anti-Semite to define him, Leventhal acquires a firm sense of identity – that of the eternal Jew – whereas a rejection of this viewpoint would force him to define his own authentic Jewishness. As Michael Glenday points out, "Leventhal is the worst kind of Jew who uses his identity in an irresponsible, churlish and damaging way. Because he is weak as an individual he tries to aggrandise himself by hiding behind the powerful stereotypes of persecution."[12]

The search for an authentic definition of Jewishness that is not determined by the anti-Semite, then, becomes Leventhal's major objective in this novel.

On the one hand, he is the cliché of the self-hating Jew. At the party where Allbee verbally attacked Harkavy, part of Leventhal actually thought the attack was deserved because Harkavy kept flaunting his typically Jewish characteristics: "Harkavy attracted stares ... all his traits, the Jewish especially, became accentuated" (34). In other words, when in the presence of Gentiles, Leventhal is ashamed of his Jewishness; however, when in the presence of Jews, he also rejects the opposite response – that of total assimilation: he berates Disraeli, for example, for giving up his Jewishness in order to become British (116). Clearly, Leventhal has a split mind about his Jewishness: a split between authenticity and self-hatred, which is symbolized in his anti-Semitic double. Leventhal's decision finally to throw out his double after Allbee's dramatic suicide attempt, then, can be read as an overcoming of his self-hatred. Yet Bellow does not grant Leventhal such a positive ending. The novel's troubling conclusion displays Leventhal some time later during a chance meeting with Allbee, still obsessed with anti-Semitism and still trying to derive his self-definition from the views of the anti-Semite: "[W]hat's your idea of who runs things?" (264) he desperately asks Allbee. But Allbee does not even deign to give him an answer, and as the stage lights of the theater go out, Leventhal is symbolically left in the dark.

In Bellow's early post-war novel, the Holocaust is still not discussed openly, but Bellow's sketch of American anti-Semitism uses the Holocaust as an important backdrop; it is "deeply buried yet tightly woven into the fabric of the narrative, rarely explicit but always there, like a symptom."[13] There are, of course, the many anti-Semitic comments made by Allbee, which Leventhal meekly tries to counter: "I don't see how you can talk that way. That's just talk. Millions of us have been killed. What about that?" (131). In a time when the dead "get buried in layers" (173), Leventhal realizes that "Man is weak and breakable, has to have just the right amounts of everything – water, air, food; can't eat twigs and stones; has to keep his bones from breaking and his fat from melting" (88–9). The most conspicuous references to the Holocaust, however, can be seen in Bellow's remarkable use of gas imagery. Immediately after Allbee's anti-Semitic comments and Leventhal's reply that millions have been killed, "an eddy of exhaust gas caught him in the face" (133). Not coincidentally, when Allbee tries to kill himself, he does so by opening the gas in Leventhal's apartment. This happens just when Leventhal has a nightmare about seeing his wife on a train platform: "Over and over again he saw the station platform, the cars in the tunnel, and made out Mary's face in the crowd of passengers ... he imagined himself running on the platform. It was unendurable" (252). When he awoke from his nightmare, "[g]as was pouring from the oven" (254). Given that Allbee is Leventhal's double, an externalization of Leventhal's split mind, Allbee's suicide obviously entails the murder of Leventhal: "'You want to murder me? Murder?' Leventhal gasped. The sibilance of the pouring gas was almost deafening. 'Me, myself!' Allbee whispered despairingly" (254).

Seize the Day

After the 1953 publication of the energetic, freestyling, globetrotting *Augie March*, the 1956 publication of *Seize the Day* seemed a strange return to the claustrophobic settings and mentality of Bellow's earlier novels – the novel is situated entirely in the New York Hotel Gloriana and a nearby broker's office, and it deals with just a single day in Tommy Wilhelm's life. This is not as surprising as it may seem at first sight, however, because *Seize the Day*, though published only in 1956, was actually composed in 1951, before *Augie March*.[14] The novel's passive protagonist, Tommy Wilhelm, also bears a striking resemblance to Joseph and Leventhal, the anti-heroes of Bellow's earliest novels. Not surprisingly, Bellow called *Seize the Day* "victim literature, very much like *The Victim* itself."[15]

In Tommy Wilhelm, Bellow has created one of the keenest portraits of a loser, a man who has literally lost everything he cherished in life. Separated from his wife, he lives alone in a hotel room, surrounded by septua- and octogenarians. Like Allbee, Bellow's other "loser," he lives "in worse filth than a savage," drinking gin "as though it were tea."[16] Though burdened with a substantial alimony, he is deprived of all contact with his two children, and even his father, who rents a room in the same hotel, lives in "an entirely different world from his son's" (10). Thus alienated from wife, children, and father, Wilhelm seeks the company of Dr. Tamkin, a dubious, self-proclaimed psychologist who convinces Wilhelm to invest his final buck in lard. But the price of lard goes down, and Wilhelm becomes a financial loser as well.

Trusting the word of another dubious character, a talent scout, Wilhelm had quit his studies and had left for Hollywood, where he stayed for seven years "through pride and perhaps also through laziness" (7). His disillusion should have been no surprise, however, for a screen test had already shown that he lacked all talent as an actor. But Wilhelm left for Hollywood anyway, depending not so much on talent but "on luck" (15). Even the talent scout who lured him to Hollywood typecast him as "the type that loses the girl" (21). Hence, Wilhelm's life is a concatenation of losses, and what he does not simply lose, he is sure to throw away. He is aware that he is always choosing that which he *knows* is wrong: "He had decided that it would be a bad mistake to go to Hollywood, and then he went. He had made up his mind not to marry his wife, but ran off and got married. He had resolved not to invest money with Tamkin, and then had given him a check" (23). One of his most serious miscalculations in this respect had been his decision earlier in life to dodge his responsibility for his wife and child by the typical Bellovian escape mechanism: by volunteering for military draft.

At the outset of this short novel, Wilhelm is finally "tired of losing" (7). *Seize the Day* therefore describes – not unlike Bellow's previous novels – one fateful day in the life of a man whose "routine is about to break up" (4). His uneventful, diurnal routine in the company of the aged had provided Wilhelm with a sense of security after his series of losses, but now that even his routine is about to go, Wilhelm faces genuine "anxiety" (66). Like the man laughing because his guts are dangling from his belly, he can easily be provoked to laughter, but this is only the mirth of the desperate: "Wilhelm could not restrain himself and joined in with his own panting laugh. But he was in despair" (41). As in previous novels, this existential angst sends the Jewish protagonist on an internal quest for selfhood, a selfhood that should in turn allow him to connect meaningfully to a community.

Wilhelm's quest for selfhood – Like Joseph's and Leventhal's – is directly related to the dilemma between assimilation and authentic Jewishness. Whereas his father is a self-proclaimed upholder of "tradition," Wilhelm is "for the new" (14). This internal dilemma between the two alternative options available to the American Jew again finds its externalization in a form of doubling: originally named Wilhelm Adler, the protagonist changed his name to Tommy Wilhelm when he decided fully to embrace the tinsel values of worldly success in Hollywood: "In California he became Tommy Wilhelm" (24). His name change, however, was only a feeble substitute for the genuine change of personality he was unable to effect. He never managed to rid himself of a feeling of inner division, of literally being "of two minds" (73): "Wilhelm had always had a great longing to be Tommy. He had never, however, succeeded in feeling like Tommy, and in his soul had always remained Wilky" (25). As his alter ego, the fully assimilated actor Tommy Wilhelm, his father thinks him "the wrong kind of Jew" (86). Wilhelm's rejection of the name Adler is obviously also an attempt to discard his Jewish origins. But his father, though he claims to uphold traditions, clearly does not provide the alternative of authentic Jewishness, for he is remarkably short of pity and empathy. When his son comes pleading for "kindness, mercy" (73), the selfish father – who cannot even remember which year his own wife died – ruthlessly rejects him, convinced that Wilhelm is only after his money. He even advises Wilhelm to "carry nobody on your back" (55), to ditch his responsibility for his wife and children – advice that he clearly heeds himself when rejecting his son's plea for help. Wilhelm, however, is determined to better himself and longs for a new life: "let me do something better with myself. For all the time I have wasted I am very sorry. Let me out of this clutch and into a different life" (26). The object of his quest becomes precisely the sense of community and responsibility he sees lacking in his father.

Wilhelm reveals that, many years earlier, he had a vision which convinced him that "there is a larger body, and from this you cannot be separated" (84). Caught in the swarming masses in the subway, he was overwhelmed by a sense of community with his fellow beings:

> all of a sudden, unsought, a general love for all these imperfect and lurid-looking people burst out in Wilhelm's breast. He loved them. One and all, he passionately loved them. They were his brothers and his sisters. He was imperfect and disfigured himself, but what difference did that make if he was united with them by this blaze of love? And as he walked he began to say, "Oh my brothers – my brothers and my sisters," blessing them all as well as himself. (85)

Until now, he had rejected his vision as "another one of these subway things. Like having a hard-on at random." But on this "day of reckoning, he consulted his memory again and thought, *I must go back to that.* That's the right clue and may do me the most good. Something very big. Truth, like" (85; my emphasis). His quest consists, in other words, of a return to his feeling of community.

As in previous novels, this search for pertinence is occasioned by the omnipresent indifference he experiences in New York City, where all authentic values have been replaced by exchange values, by money. It is a world where "money, rather than man, is the measure of all things ... individuals have no intrinsic worth but are only valuable as commodities."[17] Appeals for sympathy get mistaken for base financial demands, and the city knows only one God: "They adore money. Holy money! Beautiful money! It was getting so that people were feeble-minded about everything except money. While if you didn't have it you were a dummy, a dummy! ... If only he could find a way out" (36). Wilhelm's vision in the subway has made it clear where his "way out" could possibly lead.

While Wilhelm's vision had already intimated the importance of community, Tamkin also points out that one needs to connect to other people; the self in isolation is a mere nothingness: "'What art thou?' Nothing. That's the answer. Nothing. In the heart of hearts – Nothing! So of course you can't stand that and want to be Something and you try" (70). "Every man realizes," therefore, "that he has to love something or somebody. He feels that he must go outward" (70). This insight corresponds to Wilhelm's assertion earlier in the novel that "a man is only as good as what he loves" (10). In *Seize the Day*, Bellow – notorious for his ambivalent endings[18] – does not provide an easy way out for his protagonist, or for himself as a novelist. There is, however, a marked difference when one compares the ending of *Seize the Day* to those of previous novels. Whereas previous novels showed characters who, in the end, turned out to be unable to change, the tearful ending of *Seize the Day* is paradoxically also the most sanguine ending. Wilhelm, who literally wanted to "go back" to his vision of the loveable, teeming masses, gets sucked up in a "great, great crowd, the inexhaustible current of millions of every race and kind pouring out, pressing round, of every age, of every genius, possessors of every human secret, antique and future" (115), and, against his will, he gets shoved into a Jewish funeral parlor. Faced with the corpse of a total stranger, Wilhelm suddenly breaks down and "sob[s] loudly" both for his own failures and for "another human creature" (117). While he had previously paid someone to pray for his mother when she died (turning grief into another commodity), now he cannot help mourning the death of a stranger, thus saying Kaddish for all of humanity, sinking "deeper than sorrow, through torn sobs and cries toward the consummation of his heart's ultimate need" (118). His earlier vision had identified his heart's ultimate need as a genuine community of real, authentic souls. That is why the critic Kulshrestha mentioned during an interview with Bellow that *Seize the Day*, "in spite of its make-up of a victim novel ... moves to a very unexpected transcendence, suggesting thus a relationship with and an advance on the victim-group." Bellow considered this "very shrewd, an excellent observation."[19]

Keith Opdahl remarks that "in the Jewish funeral home, he [Wilhelm] accepts his racial heritage."[20] Such a reading obviously provides a nice resolution of Wilhelm's division between two forms of Jewishness, with the new Tommy finally rediscovering his connection to the Jewish community. It is quite remarkable, however, that in later editions, Bellow altered one phrase to obfuscate the specific Jewish denomination of the funeral parlor: while earlier versions of the novel feature a description of a stained glass window with "the blue of the Star of David like velvet ribbon,"[21] in a later edition, this has become "with the blue of a great star fluid, like velvet ribbon" (116). This second description obviously makes the funeral less conspicuously Jewish. In fact, in the later edition, Bellow seems to have taken great care in keeping the location as universal and non-denominational as possible. Hence, the later edition seems to emphasize that Wilhelm connects to the whole of humanity, rather than only to the Jewish community, which, in itself, is central to the Jewish concept of *Mentshlekhkayt*.[22]

Though Bellow leaves Wilhelm at the end of his novel "in the center of a crowd" (118), the ending is obviously still very tentative, for Wilhelm's *feeling* of community does not as yet result in any real community, commitment, or responsibility. Far from "a pathetic display of total defeat,"[23] the ending is really "both a failure and a triumph."[24] Wilhelm is financially ruined and betrayed by virtually everyone he knows (even Tamkin split when the financial loss became too great). Hence, Wilhelm's sense of community concerns only a general, abstract humanity, and the novel ends where any truly affirmative novel would start. But, at least, there is a first sign of hope.

Bellow's early novels, then, perfectly capture the American climate of anxiety and despair in the immediate aftermath of World War II. They focus on the struggles of the solitary man who experiences an existential crisis resulting from his engagement with the city and with his Jewish identity. Each of these novels tells "the story of the hero's attempt to live with, survive within, the void that has opened at his feet."[25] As later novels such as *Henderson* and *Herzog* show, Bellow's protagonists become increasingly successful at surviving this void.

Notes

1. Cynthia Ozick, "Introduction," in Saul Bellow, *Seize the Day* (rpt. 1956; New York: Penguin, 2001), pp. ix–xxiv.
2. As Cynthia Ozick has suggested, "There are whole pages in *Dangling Man* that might have been torn out of *Seize the Day*. There are rolling tracts of dialogue in *The Victim* with telling affinities to *Ravelstein*." Cynthia Ozick, "Lasting Man," *The New Republic* (February 10, 2011).
3. See Philippe Codde, *The Jewish American Novel* (West Lafayette, IN: Purdue University Press, 2007).
4. Saul Bellow, *The Adventures of Augie March* (rpt. 1953; New York: Penguin, 1979), p. 7.
5. Saul Bellow, *Henderson the Rain King* (rpt. 1959; New York: Penguin, 1996), p. 12.
6. Bruce Cook. "Saul Bellow: A Mood of Protest" in *Conversations with Saul Bellow*, p. 18.
7. Saul Bellow, *Dangling Man* (rpt. 1944; London: Alison Press, 1984), p. 9.
8. Ihab Hassan, *Radical Innocence: Studies in the Contemporary American Novel* (Princeton: Princeton University Press., 1961), p. 299.
9. Keith Botsford, "Saul Bellow: Made in America," in *Conversations with Saul Bellow*, pp. 246–247.
10. Saul Bellow, *The Victim* (rpt. 1947; New York: Penguin, 1988), pp. 34–35.
11. See, for example, Cook, "Saul Bellow: A Mood of Protest" in *Conversations with Saul Bellow*, p. 15; Malcolm Bradbury, "Saul Bellow's *The Victim*." *The Critical Quarterly*, 5. 2 (1963): 122; Jonathan Baumbach, *The Landscape of Nightmare.*

Studies in the Contemporary American Novel (London: Weidenfeld and Nicolson, 1966), p. 41; Irving Malin, *Saul Bellow's Fiction* (Carbondale: Southern Illinois University Press, 1969), p. 118; Daniel Fuchs, *Saul Bellow: Vision and Revision* (Durham: Duke University Press, 1984), p. 43; S. Lillian Kremer, *Witness Through the Imagination: Jewish-American Holocaust Literature* (Detroit: Wayne State University Press, 1989), p. 38.

12. Michael K. Glenday, *Saul Bellow and the Decline of Humanism* (Basingstoke: Macmillan, 1990), p. 30.
13. Mark Shechner, *After the Revolution: Studies in the Contemporary Jewish American Imagination* (Indianapolis: Indiana University Press, 1987), p. 127.
14. Judy Newman, *Saul Bellow and History* (London: Macmillan, 1984), p. 11.
15. Chirantan Kulshrestha, "A Conversation with Saul Bellow," in *Conversations with Saul Bellow*, p. 90.
16. Bellow, *Seize the Day*, p. 37.
17. Julia Eichelberger, *Prophets of Recognition: Ideology and the Individual in Novels by Ralph Ellison, Toni Morrison, Saul Bellow, and Eudora Welty* (Baton Rouge: Louisiana State University Press, 1999), pp. 111 and 114.
18. See Mark Weinstein, "Bellow's Endings," in *Saul Bellow: A Mosaic*, eds. L. H. Goldman, Gloria L. Cronin, and Ada Aharoni (New York: Peter Lang, 1992), pp. 87–95; and Keith Opdahl, *The Novels of Saul Bellow: An Introduction* (University Park: Pennsylvania State University Press, 1967), p. 4.
19. Kulshrestha, "A Conversation with Saul Bellow," in *Conversations with Saul Bellow*, p. 98.
20. Opdahl, *The Novels of Saul Bellow*, p. 117.
21. Bellow, *Seize the Day*, p. 126.
22. Josephine Zadovsky Knopp, *The Trial of Judaism in Contemporary Jewish Writing* (Urbana: University of Illinois Press, 1975), p. 7.
23. Richard Lehan, *A Dangerous Crossing: French Literary Existentialism and the Modern American Novel* (Carbondale: Southern Illinois University Press, 1973), p. 119.
24. Keith Opdahl, *The Novels of Saul Bellow*, p. 97.
25. Frank D. McConnell, *Four Postwar American Novelists: Bellow, Mailer, Barth, and Pynchon* (Chicago: University of Chicago Press, 1977), p. 10.

2

HILENE FLANZBAUM

Seize the Day: Bellow's Novel of Existential Crisis

"Don't marry suffering," the shifty Dr. Tamkin advises Tommy Wilhelm, the hero of Saul Bellow's 1956 novella, *Seize the Day*. "Some people do," he warns, "They get married to it, and sleep and eat together, just as husband and wife. If they go with joy, they think it's adultery" (94). Yet Tommy appears to have little choice: Suffering has found him. At the age of 44, Tommy is unemployed, estranged from his wife and children, at war with his father, and soon-to-be homeless. In *Seize*, the reader follows Tommy through a single day when either his bad decisions or bad luck (which *is* it?) culminate in one of the more memorable and puzzling scenes in American literature: the protagonist at a stranger's funeral "where he had hidden himself in the center of a crowd by the great and happy oblivion of tears" (114).[1]

A first reading of *Seize* mystifies, for, at its conclusion, the book's central crises remain unresolved. Still unemployed, broke and unloved, Tommy has few prospects for improvement. Why, then, does Bellow describe his "oblivion of tears" as "happy"? Are these cathartic tears that ease Tommy's suffering, or are we witnessing his final collapse? If the text had a tomorrow, would we find Tommy homeless and mad on the streets of New York City? Even as they worry about Tommy's future, however, readers struggle to overcome their annoyance with the needy protagonist. Does Tommy merit our sympathy? Isn't his father, the fastidious Dr. Adler, who refuses to help him, heartless? His estranged wife taking advantage of him? And what about the cunning and unreadable Dr. Tamkin – doesn't he too exploit Tommy's weakness?

More pragmatic readers, however, may side with Tommy's father, agreeing that he should have known better than to trust the devious Tamkin: Tommy must bear responsibility for the mess he has made of his life. A man of 44 years of age can blame no one but himself, they argue. Hasn't he quit his job over an imagined slight by his boss? Hasn't he initiated the affair that enraged his wife and led to his exile from home and children? Surely Tommy's father is right when he turns his back on this sad sack that "makes too much of his troubles," concluding that Tommy "ought not to turn(ed) them into a career" (42). Tommy, this reader decides, is an over-emotional, self-pitying loser who courts every disaster this nasty world serves him.[2]

Even those more sympathetic to Tommy question his judgment. As he makes them, Tommy knows his decisions are wrong. About his abrupt plan to quit school and go to California to make it in motion pictures, Tommy recalls that "after much thought and hesitation and debate he invariably took the course he had rejected innumerable times. He had decided it would be a bad mistake to go to Hollywood and then he went" (19).

Such a "mistake," however, hardly makes him unique. Like any gambler, who, against all odds, puts fifty bucks on number 17 and spins the wheel, Tommy prays for unrealistic outcomes. This kind of magical thinking permeates the American psyche. A half-century before Internet millionaires, get-rich quick schemes of a different sort circulated. Hollywood legend had it that fifties' mega-star Lana Turner had been "discovered" on her lunch break from a secretarial job. There she sat, drinking a soda at Schraft's (the Burger King of its day), when a producer took one look at her and supposedly said, "I'm gonna make you a star." It is impossible to say how many young men and women, Hollywood hopefuls, ventured – and continue to venture – out to California on the basis of such improbable endings; suffice it to say that the number surely approaches the number of people that rushed to California in 1849, or who buy lottery tickets today. Our national mythos supports belief in such miracles: Risk itself is embedded deeply in the American success story. Without risk, we are taught, there will be no reward.

The backbone of the economy itself – the stock market – operates only because Americans wager that they can win. Although these victories are not uncommon or particularly unrealistic, winning in the stock market requires capital, knowledge, discretion, and time. The market can provide an opportunity to make money, but even in the most bullish times, such fortunes are rarely made overnight.[3] Tommy spins the wheel on Wall Street too, and yet with little to invest, bad judgment, and no time, he loses his last dollar. But the sympathetic reader argues that Tommy has tried to make a living the hard way. He *has* taken some irrational risks, certainly, but he has also labored hard and long as a traveling salesman for the Rojac corporation. The sacrifice and toil that brought second-generation Americans economic security should have been Tommy's fate too. Not to be. Like Arthur Miller's tragic hero, Willy Loman – who also spends day after day on the road, and ends up lonely and estranged from his children – Tommy realizes neither riches nor economic security.[4] Rather than an American success story, then, *Seize* narrates economic failure – an antidote to Horatio Alger and Dale

Carnegie stories, or any happy capitalist narrative that promises wealth, quickly obtained or otherwise.

To add to Tommy's troubles, he goes broke while all around him, everyone else prospers. "There's money everywhere," he says, and the cagey Dr. Tamkin urges Tommy to get in the game: "With all this money around you don't want to be a fool while everyone else is making" (6). Here, Bellow describes the American fifties, when the stock market rose to unprecedented heights; kitchens filled with new appliances, suburbs rose out of cornfields, and shiny supermarkets replaced neighborhood grocers.[5] A rising tide, the author warns, does not lift all boats. That Bellow has chosen to focus on an individual who cannot swim with the affluent, places Tommy firmly in the large literary camp of American dissenters; thus, on this level, *Seize* reads like other canonical texts that describe the soul-killing properties of capitalism. Perhaps his closest literary ancestor would be "Bartleby the Scrivener," the notorious dissenter who also meets his demise on Wall Street, the metonymy of American capitalism. As Cynthia Ozick notes in the introduction to the 1996 edition, "one can imagine that if Melville had allowed Bartleby a voice ... Wilhelm's own torrent of yearning ... would have emerged"(xxiii).

In his own decade, Tommy stands among several notorious literary misfits. Holden Caulfield's nervous breakdown in the best-selling *Catcher in the Rye* had been published in 1951, five years earlier than *Seize* – and although Holden's problems are not economic, he looks at the adults around him and understands that making money is an unholy enterprise; in film, James Dean's *Rebel Without a Cause* (1955) broke box-office records. Dean's character, James Stark, has no interest in becoming the domesticated subject his father has. Finally, Allen Ginsberg's "Howl," published in the same year as *Rebel Without a Cause*, bears surprising similarities to *Seize*. For instance, when Tamkin describes one of his mentally ill patients who howls from his window like a wolf, Tommy thinks that for once Tamkin sounds genuine (63). Finally, Sal Paradise, the idealistic adventurer of Jack Kerouac's anti-capitalist manifesto, *On the Road*, joins this rebellious group in 1957.

Tommy differs, however, from his fellow literary travelers because, like Loman, he has little romantic appeal. He wears no leather jacket; rides no motorcycle; unlike Holden, his rebellion cannot be attributed to immaturity. He hasn't the courage to rebel. If only he had the backbone to escape the capitalist juggernaut, and, like Paradise, hit the road. Middle-aged, and heir to no great Whitmanian instinct, Tommy falls to pieces. His rapid downward spiral recalls earlier literary characters who also fall victim to a hostile universe. One thinks perhaps of George Hurstwood in Dreiser's "Sister Carrie" or the protagonist of Jack London's short story, "To Build

A Fire," who decides, against all good instinct, to venture into sub-zero temperatures and eventually freezes to death while his sturdier dog runs to safety.[6]

In *Seize*, motifs of literary naturalism prevail. Bellow litters the text with images of animals, persistently designating their behaviors to that of humans. The Hollywood agent, Maurice Venice, is oxlike, and Bellow many times describes Tommy as a hippopotamus in a world of scavengers. Those who prey on him are avian. Tamkin is a "rare, peculiar bird, with those pointed shoulders, that bare head, his loose nails, almost claws and those brown soft deadly, heavy eyes" (78). His nails are "clawlike" (58). On Tommy's wide back, his wife too – given the gender expectations of fifties' culture – also gets to feast.[7] After meeting old man Rappaport, "the Rockefeller of the chicken industry," Tommy has "a queer feeling" about the means of the old man's fortune. The wooden buildings the animals live in "look like prisons," and the animals are "cheated" into laying eggs. Bellow, of course, suggests here that, metaphorically at least, Tommy is one of the chickens "that has been slaughtered to feed the greedy around him" (82), for Tamkin describes the stock market as a place where "people go … with murder in their hearts. They want to make a killing" (65).

In the world of *Seize*, one feasts or is feasted upon; the chicken may wish it were born a fox, but so be it. Genetic determinism, Bellow tells us, seals Tommy's destiny, for "From one grandfather he had inherited such and such head of hair … from another, broad thick shoulders, an oddity of speech from one uncle … From his mother, he had gotten sensitive feelings, a soft heart, a brooding nature, a tendency to be confused under pressure" (22). It is precisely these characteristics that make him unfit for capitalist culture. Not a predator, he will be prey: he "can't change his lungs, his constitution, or temperament" (21). The slowest gazelle will be eaten – must be eaten, if the cycle of nature is to continue. Those who survive this world are tougher than Tommy – less emotional, more cynical, and more prepared to feast on the weaknesses of others. To blame Tommy for his problems, then, is to blame him for what he cannot control – we do not condemn the gazelle for not being faster. And yet sympathy for such creatures would be misspent energy. After all, this is the way of the world.

In *Seize*, the naturalist jungle appears as the city, which is particularly inhospitable to the sensitive souls who are stuck inside it. In New York, Tommy feels "the end of the world" approaching, with its "complexity and machinery, bricks and tubes, wires and stones, holes and heights. It is impossible to tell the sane from the mad." Such language again recalls Ginsberg's "Howl," which also inquires into the relation between sanity and madness. Tommy feels the pains of humanity so strongly that he is overwhelmed in a crowd (79) and finds city life untenable. "I miss the country," he mourns to his father, "There's too much push here. It works me up too much. I take things too hard" (41).

II

In the twenty-first century, Saul Bellow's centrality in the Jewish-American literary canon is so established that it may amaze contemporary readers to discover that in the first several decades of its reception *Seize* attracted few critical discussions that dealt with its ethnic dimensions. It is useful to remember, however, that in the mid-1950s, neither the topics of race nor of ethnicity seemed to be on anyone's mind. In the decade of euphoria that followed victory at war – but at the same time harbored McCarthyism and the paranoia of the Cold War – conversations about hyphenate identities were rare; if had at all, they transpired in hushed voices. As Section I of this chapter indicates, *Seize* can be – and was – quite fruitfully read as a novel in the mode of American dissent, with little ethnic inflection. On one level, this may have been at least partially desirable to Bellow, who in an early draft of the book hung a Star of David over the casket that appears in the final scene, but removed it from the final manuscript.[8] In this vein, the reader may notice that Bellow labels no character as Jewish. The references to religion are muted enough to be overlooked if one lacks familiarity with certain signals and codes.

By the 1970s, however, as the discussion of ethnicity moved front and center, critics easily located and thoroughly discussed Jewish motifs; similarly, Bellow is understood today not only as a major American novelist of the twentieth century, but also distinctly a product of Jewish culture.[9] Thus, in the last quarter century, *Seize* has been read as a text rich with Jewish references and themes. It is important to note that reading Jewishness in this text not only sharpens the discussion of American themes; it also locates the deeper philosophical dimensions of the text.

A crucial discussion that has evolved in the wake of ethnic criticism involves the timing of Tommy's "day of reckoning," (2) as Bellow calls it. With this allusion, the author invokes Yom Kippur, the Jewish "day of reckoning." In fact, the aged Mr. Rappaport asks Tommy if he has tickets yet for the high holy days. Here, the informed reader knows that he refers to the autumn holidays of Rosh Hashanah (the Jewish New Year) and Yom Kippur (the Jewish day of atonement). The eight days between these two holidays are called the "The Days of Awe."[10] On these fateful days God decides "who will live and who will die ... who will be inscribed in the book of life for another year and who will perish; who will die by fire and who by flood."[11] Scripture tells us that by the time Yom Kippur arrives, God will have made these decisions. Unlike Catholic ritual, for instance, where forgiveness is granted by clergy, Jewish theology holds that no human being can grant God's pardon. For those who sincerely atone, merely asking is enough, for the liturgy grants pardons but then teaches, "For the crimes against God, you are forgiven; *but for the crimes you have committed against another human being, you must make amends.*"

It is impossible to overstate the importance of the second half of that statement, both to Jewish theology and to Bellow's text.[12] The Talmud teaches the importance of what we do in this life, here on earth. About abstractions, Jews can speculate; about deeds, however, Jews have rules to follow. The first and most important of these rules is to establish good relationships with humans. In modernity, Jewish thinkers argued that God appeared here on earth – in things – and, more importantly, in people and the transactions between them. In each human interface, we are changed – to either negative or positive affect. Thus, it becomes one's ethical duty to enact divinity in our relationships. Most important of all, what Jewish theologians have preached for over a thousand years: one need not *believe* as a Jew to be Jewish; one needs to *act* as a Jew.

Oddly, in Bellow's world, no one acts in accordance with any of the values that Jewish philosophers fostered. In *Seize*, the seemingly most sympathetic character, Tamkin, exploits him to make a profit. Knowing that Tommy longs for family feeling and genuine conversation, Tamkin poses as a benevolent father figure. While part of Tommy realizes that the doctor is an impostor, he craves the emotional connection that Tamkin seems to offer. "That the doctor cared about him" pleases Tommy: "This is what he craved: that someone should care about him, wish him well. Kindness, mercy, he wanted" (69). Tommy gives Tamkin a check, suspecting that he will lose the money on the market but hoping that he will receive compassion instead.[13]

As the only character in the novella who demonstrates genuine feeling, Tommy acquires nobility. In *Seize*, humans show no compassion toward troubled souls; the individuals portrayed are so distant from religion that mercy can only be bought. At the site of his mother's grave, Tommy "pays a man to say a prayer for her. He was among the tombs and wanted to be tipped for the El molai rachamin ... Thou God of Mercy" (108).[14] Similarly, he wonders of his wife, "Have you forgotten that we slept so long together? Must you now deal with me like this, and have no mercy?"(109).

In *Seize*, assimilation to American culture appears here in its most tragic incarnation. For Tommy, his father's adoption of American values has been heartbreaking. Dr. Adler has grown wealthy; at the same time, he will have nothing to do with the suffering of others – not even his own child. As an adult, Tommy returns to the home of his father to seek what he has always lacked: compassion. Adler, however, frozen in his American personality, reacts as if Tommy only wants his money – because money, Bellow seems to say, is the only thing people want in the United States. The Americanized Dr. Adler "behaves towards Tommy as he had formerly done with his patients, and it was a great grief to Tommy. Couldn't he see? Couldn't he feel?" Tommy grieves, "Had he lost his family sense?"(8). For Bellow, then, becoming American requires more than accumulating wealth; it necessitates the loss of family feeling – or perhaps any emotional expenditure at all. This puts Tommy at a great disadvantage, for he cannot acquire the most important of Anglicized assets: the repression of emotion, or, as Bellow calls it, "reserve."

From the first line of the novel, Bellow alerts us to this valuable cultural capital: "When it came to concealing his troubles, Tommy Wilhelm was not less capable than the next fellow. So at least he thought"(1). Although Tommy tries to convince himself that he is capable of emotional and verbal restraint, he can only pretend. A few pages later, he admits that, "He was wrong to suppose that he was more capable than the next fellow when it came to concealing his troubles. They were clearly written on his face" (11). He chides himself for this weakness, admitting, "I am an idiot, I have no reserve. To me, it can be done. I talk. I must ask for it. Everyone wants to have intimate conversations, but the smart fellows don't give out, only the fools" (35). In other words, "reserve" – the ability to subdue, submerge, or otherwise disguise emotional vehemence – is the key to mastering American fortunes.

Such a discussion is read fruitfully in an ethnic context. Tommy rightly believes that he disgusts his father because "he is the wrong kind of Jew" (83). In this juxtaposition, Bellow, of course, is ironic: as the son of an Eastern-European immigrant, he has no doubt heard such formulations before. The "right kind of Jew" does not draw attention to himself. Like Tommy's father, he embodies Puritan perfection, wherein cleanliness pairs with Godliness, and financial success signals God's grace. Neat and trim, his hair perfectly combed, his fingernails spotless, he is also financially independent. A "master of social behavior" (35), Adler says nothing that makes others uncomfortable. He has pulled himself up by his bootstraps and understands that ignoring the pain of others provides no impediment to American achievement. He "carries no one on his back" (51) and advises his son to do the same.

But Tommy bears a heavy burden, and he is messy both in physique and with his emotions. While he has dirt under his fingernails and wrinkles in his suit, those superficial flaws point to larger ones.[15] In fact, the reader learns that the obstacle to Tommy's success is that he cannot disguise his suffering. In the old country, people suffered and were allowed to complain. In the new world of hope and dreams and streets paved with gold, everyone is happy – and if they are not (which is more than likely), it is their patriotic duty to keep quiet about it.

In a masterstroke of irony, Bellow has Tommy choose a stage name that recalls the most famous Wilhelm of his time – Wilhelm Reich, the psychoanalyst who contributed to the popularity of Primal Scream therapy (a "therapy" that the Jews who descended from Eastern Europe used without any instruction). As a young man, Bellow had briefly followed Reich's teachings, and some critics have supposed that Tommy's descent into weeping that closes the novel is his own "primal scream" – and is either comic or revelatory – depending upon their own feelings about Reich.[16] In the latter interpretation, Tommy's collapse can be read as a crucial step forward: after this nervous breakdown, some argue, Tommy will have a clean slate; he will let go of his traumatic past and move forward. Yet we would be mistaken if we did not understand Bellow's allusion as ambivalent. Just as Bellow came to view Reichian therapy as excessive, he surely portrays Tommy's reactions as over the top, inspiring one critic to refer to the scene in which he clutches his own throat as typical of the histrionics of Yiddish opera in the earlier twentieth century.[17]

Whatever one holds about the breakdown, however, Bellow seems clear that emoting in public, as Tommy does, is not advisable. Survival in America, he admonishes, depends upon *not* behaving this way. On the other hand, certain parts of one's Jewish inheritance should not be abandoned. In one of his more meditative moments, Tommy remembers his grandfather's name for him: "Velvel" – the Yiddish equivalent of William – (his birth name), but also the Yiddish word for "wolf" which again suggests the fierce and primal nature of his human emotions and desires. Velvel, Tommy believes, names his soul. Thus, in Tommy's quest to ease his own suffering he must find a world where the expression of such raw feeling is permitted and the expression of grief not taboo. In America, is it only at funerals where the expression of suffering does not paint you as an oddball and a loser?

Perhaps there is one other place – the world of art. For why else does one read literature if not for the emotional release that Tommy's weeping affords the reader? Within the text, Tommy also looks for catharsis through literature. He cannot remember much of his education except for his textbook of British Poetry and Prose. "Yes, he had read," Tommy thinks, "and this was one accomplishment he could recall with pleasure" (10). Several times in the novella, lines from John Milton's great elegy "Lycidas" float through

Tommy's mind: "How pure this was to say! It was beautiful. Such things had always swayed him" (10).[18] He even labors to understand Tamkin's absurd poem, believing that it too might offer sustenance. In one late chapter of the novella, Tommy remembers his early marriage with tenderness, thinking in particular of his wife reading him Keats' elegy to a young shepherd boy, "Endymion" (85). Tommy would lose himself in poetry if the world would permit it, but economics interrupts his reverie in the form of Mr. Rappaport's "old hand press(ing) against his thigh," demanding to see the numbers on the big board: "What's my wheat? Those damn guys are blocking the way, I can't see" (99).

If only Tommy *could* opt out of the world's "business," which allows time for neither grief nor poetry; or if only he had been born ten years later; or was more thick-skinned, or clear-headed; if only this final scene of weeping does preface his turn around. Yet even if none of Tommy's hopes can be realized, *Seize* pushes readers toward their own authentic selves, providing a corrective to those who show neither mercy nor kindness toward those who suffer in their midst. Tommy's downfall on Wall Street is our own, for chasing dollars leaves one like Rappaport – withered and half-blind. At last, Tommy recognizes his most inner self and is comforted by such knowledge: "I labor, I spend, I strive, I design, I love, I cling, I uphold, I give way, I envy, I long, I scorn, I die, I hide, I want" (111). If nothing else, then, Bellow's schlemiel finds his own humanity and points us toward our own. We could do worse, the author insists, than to recognize the Tommy that resides inside each of us.

Notes

All citations are taken from *Seize the Day*, introduction by Cynthia Ozick. New York: Penguin, 1956.

1. A number of critics have described Tommy Wilhelm as a "schlemiel," a Yiddish word used to describe an unfortunate soul or a chump. See Janis P. Stout, "Suffering as Meaning in Saul Bellow's *Seize the Day.*" *Renascence*, 39.2 (1987): 365.

2. Robert Baker in "Bellow Comes of Age," *Chicago Review*, 11.1 (Spring 1957) points out that Tommy is in essence gambling away his last few dollars, while Julia Eichelberg ("Renouncing 'The World's Business' in *Seize the Day*," *Studies in American Jewish Literature*, 17 (1998)) points out that "Rather than investing in a company's stock, which would at least theoretically enable that company to produce more of something, Tamkin and Wilhelm are engaging in the kind of 'investment' that generates income but produces nothing of real value, process in which anyone's gains must from another investor's loss."

3. Sarah Blacher Cohen, in *Saul Bellow's Enigmatic Laughter* (Urbana: University of Illinois Press, 1974), argues that "Denied a well-earned promotion at the Rojac

Corporation, Wilhelm has imprudently resigned, only to enact his own version of Death of a Salesman." This is also expounded on in Gordon Bordewyk, "Saul Bellow's Death of a Salesman." *Saul Bellow Newsletter*, 1 (1981): 18–21.

4. Willy Loman, is the protagonist of Arthur Miller's well-known, much-performed, and Pulitzer Prize-winning "Death of a Salesman" (1949).

5. The early 1950s, during which Bellow was writing this novel, coincided with the lowest unemployment rates in the second half of the twentieth century. The historic Dow Jones industrial average shows that the 1950s had the highest rate of return in any decade of its existence: www.stockpickssystem.com/histor ical-rate-of-return/. The S&P also showed historical peaks in total returns and dividend distribution rates during those years: www.simplestockinvesting.com /SP500-historical-real-total-returns.htm.

6. I refer to George Hurstwood of Theodore Dreiser's 1900 novel, *Sister Carrie*, whose fate is sealed after an unexpected wind blows the door of a safe shut; and to "To Build a Fire," (1908). In his 2015 biography, *The Life of Saul Bellow* (New York: Knopf), Zachary Leader provides a thorough examination of the effects of naturalist writings on the writer. See especially pp. 137–149.

7. For instance, Jennifer Holt, *The Ideal Woman* (Turlock: California State University Stanislaus Indiana University Approved Rooms for Women Official Rental Contract, 2006), delineates the gender constructs that appeared in the 1950s and writes "Women were considered domestic caregivers, with sole responsibility for the home and child rearing, while men 'brought home the bacon.'"

8. See Emily Budick, "Yizkor for Six Million: Mourning the Death of Civilization in Saul Bellow's *Seize the Day*" in *New Essays on Seize the Day*, ed. Michael Kramer (Cambridge: Cambridge University Press, 1998), p. 94.

9. It is fair to say that the subject of Bellow as Jewish writer has been well plumbed by critics. Here is the briefest of lists: Gregory Johnson, "Jewish Assimilation and Codes of Manners in Saul Bellow's 'The Old System,'" noted in various other critical texts, L. H. Goldman, *Saul Bellow's Moral Vision: A Critical Study of the Jewish Experience* (New York: Irvington, 1983), and Eugene Goodheart, "The Jewish Writer in America." *Review*, 116.1 (2008): 93–107.

10. Cynthia Ozick, Introduction to *Seize the Day*, by Saul Bellow (New York: Penguin Books, 2003), p. xii. Ozick notes that Wilhelm's day "is the day before Yom Kippur, the Day of Atonement, comprising the most solemn hours of the Jewish liturgical calendar."

11. From the liturgy of the Day of Atonement: "On Rosh Hashanah it is inscribed/And on Yom Kippur it is sealed/How many shall die and how many shall be born/Who shall live and who shall die/Who at the measure of days and who before/Who by fire and who by water/Who by the sword and who by wild beasts/Who by hunger and who by thirst/Who by earthquake and who by plague/Who by strangling and who by stoning/Who shall have rest and who shall go wandering/Who will be tranquil and who shall be harassed/Who shall be at ease and who shall be afflicted/Who shall become poor and who shall become rich/Who shall be brought low and who shall be raised high."

12. As the Talmud teaches, "Yom Kippur does not forgive transgressions between a man and his fellow – until (or unless) he seeks forgiveness from him (directly)" (Mishnah Yoma 8:9).

13. The importance of Dr. Tamkin has been a point of contention among critics. While some, like Cronin, believe that he "is portrayed as a grotesque, a devil, a 'magician,' a 'confuser of the imagination,' a 'faker,' a 'deceiver,' and a 'hypnotist' who beguiles and mesmerizes the innocent with his reductive modern assumptions about life and human nature. Tamkin is a physical grotesque whose twisted body reflects his twisted mind" (Gloria L. Cronin, "Saul Bellow's Quarrel with Modernism in *Seize the Day*." *Encyclia: The Journal of the Utah Academy of Sciences, Arts, and Letters*, 57 (1980): 97), others believe his character is more nuanced: Mohragh writes that Tamkin "'remains a most problematic and controversial figure' insofar as he is 'an unabashed liar and manipulator'" and yet "a source of authentic values and redeeming ideas" (Gilead Mohragh, "The Art of Dr. Tamkin: Matter and Manner in Seize the Day." *Modern Fiction Studies*, Special Bellow Issue, 25.1 (Spring 1979): 103–116). Yet others have gone so far to pronounce that his presence is resoundingly positive, leading Wilhelm toward a meaningful existence: Richmond writes, "It is apparent that Saul Bellow has created Dr. Tamkin as the archetypal figure of the shaman, a primitive charlatan who, nevertheless, had a kind of medicine-power in the psychologic sense. See Lee J. Richmond, "The Maladroit, the Medico, and the Magician: Saul Bellow's Seize the Day" *Twentieth Century Literature* 19.1(Duke University Press: Hofstra University, 1973): 21–22.

14. Yet another demonstration of Tommy's distance from religion, as well as the many unlearned Jews in the United States, it became common practice for the poor men of Jewish learning to walk among cemeteries hoping to be paid by mourners for saying prayers for the dead.

15. There is some indication that Mr. Perls is a Holocaust survivor. For a reading of *Seize the Day* as Holocaust text, see Budick, "Yizkor for Six Million."

16. Eusebio Rodriguez, *Critical Essays on Saul Bellow* (Boston: G.K. Hall, 1979), pp. 91, 99. Rodriguez draws comparisons to Reichianism: "'Tommy Wilhelm embodies a form of armoring that constitutes the masochistic.' The masochist as Reich defines one: 'Subjectively, a chronic sensation of suffering which appears objectively as a tendency to complain; chronic tendencies to self-damage and self-deprecation ("Moral Masochism") and a compulsion to *torture others* which makes the patient suffer no less than the object.'" He goes on to say: "A Reichian parable of hope for modern urban man, *Seize the Day* ends at the moment when the doors of perception fling open, and Wilhelm realizes his heart's ultimate need, a feeling of brotherhood and a love for all mankind."

17. For a more detailed discussion of *Seize* as Yiddish opera, see Michael Kramer's "Introduction" to "New Essays on *Seize the Day*."

18. John Milton's elegy written for a drowned friend, "Lycidas," was first published in 1637; John Keats' elegy, "Endymion," was first published in 1818.

3

STEVEN G. KELLMAN

Bellow's Breakthrough: *The Adventures of Augie March* and the Novel of Voice

The word "breakthrough" is so routinely coupled with Bellow's third novel that it almost seems to constitute part of the book's formal title: *The Adventures of Augie March: A Breakthrough*. By 2015, ten years after Saul Bellow's death, Louis Menand was able to say: "As everyone has said, Bellow not least, 'Augie March' was the breakthrough book."[1] Back in 1958, Leslie Fiedler published a long, magisterial overview of the contemporary flowering of American Jewish fiction and the movement of Jewish authors from the margins of American literary culture to its center, which he titled "The Breakthrough: The American Jewish Novelist and the Fictional Image of the Jew." Fiedler presents Bellow as the culmination of that breakthrough, particularly in his creation of "the most satisfactory character ever projected by a Jewish writer in America: Augie March."[2] In 1964, when Irving Malin and Irwin Stark published their influential anthology *Breakthrough: A Treasury of Contemporary American-Jewish Literature*, they argued that: "It is not so much that the Jew has caught up with America. America has at long last caught up with the Jew."[3] And, excerpting its sixth chapter in their collection, they offered *The Adventures of Augie March* as a prime exhibit of that breakthrough.

In reference books and literary histories, the word "breakthrough" became virtually indispensable to discussions of Bellow's bravura performance, as when Daniel Fuchs declared that: "*The Adventures of Augie March* was Bellow's breakthrough novel from the point of view of reversing Modernist aestheticism and the sense of alienation and victimization that much twentieth-century literature embodied, including his own. It was a breakthrough into anti-Modernism, a real switch."[4] Ben Siegel echoes the claim, contending that Bellow's third novel "was clearly his major breakthrough work."[5] Surveying contenders for the title "Great American Novel," Lawrence Buell states that: "Bellow's *The Adventures of Augie March* (1953) became his breakthrough book owing to its surge of Whitmanian, Twainian, and Dreiserian energy in exfoliating Augie's wanderings and musings as a

32

prototypically hyphenated American in and around Chicago."[6] And in 2011, when the Chicago Public Library adopted *The Adventures of Augie March* for its One Book, One Chicago reading program, Julia Keller explained the selection to readers of the *Chicago Tribune* by noting that: "'Augie March' was the breakthrough, the novel that was so lusty, so filled with verbal fireworks, that it probably made readers sit up and grasp the arms of their chairs."[7]

Amid the near-universal invocation of "breakthrough" to describe *The Adventures of Augie March* (1953), it is reasonable to ask: Break from what? Through to what? In addition to marking the emergence of American Jewish literature into mainstream culture, *Augie March* was a personal quantum leap in the career of Saul Bellow. It received the National Book Award and, through its both critical and commercial success, abruptly thrust its author out of pinched obscurity. It made him a literary celebrity and solvent. His first novel, *Dangling Man* (1944), had sold barely 1,550 copies, and his second, *The Victim* (1947), only 2,257 copies,[8] so the 30,000 copies that *Augie March* managed to sell[9] marked a significant improvement in Bellow's prospects as a professional writer. Publication of the spectacularly best-selling *Herzog* in 1964 would make him rich and famous. Bellow recalled that at the time he began writing *Augie March*: "I had, earlier, published two small and correct books."[10] *Dangling Man* would occupy a mere 140 pages in the 2003 Library of America edition that includes it along with the 235 pages of *The Victim*. That same volume also includes all 614 pages of *The Adventures of Augie March*, a novel that originally filled 22 notebooks and 1100 manuscript pages.[11] Though Bellow intended *Augie March* to sprawl across two volumes, his publisher, Viking, forced him to pare the text down to a single plump tome.

The third novel marked a dramatic departure from the tightly constructed, spare prose of *Dangling Man* and *The Victim*, short works that David Mikics calls "constricted exercises in modernist angst, adroit and deliberately airless." And the ebullience of *Augie March*, which Mikics describes as "a constantly surprising all-night party in book form, a riposte to the staid *New Yorker* fiction of its day," constituted a rejection of the alienation and desolation that characterize not only the two earlier books but much of Modernist fiction. "It rushed out of me," Bellow recalled about the torrent of words that formed *Augie March*. "I was turned on like a hydrant in summer."[12] The characteristically Bellovian urban metaphor of a hydrant suggests not only verbal profusion but also a spontaneous overflow of powerful prose: "The book just came to me," Bellow claimed. "All I had to do was be there with buckets to catch it."[13] The inspiration for *Augie March* came to him so forcefully that he put aside forever another work-in-progress,

The Crab and the Butterfly, a dour account of two men in a hospital room. With the high energy prose of his new project and the high spirits of its protagonist, Bellow was escaping the crimped, angst-ridden universes of Franz Kafka and T. S. Eliot.

Liberated from the ideal of artistic concision, he felt free to create the kind of novel that Henry James, in his Preface to *The Tragic Muse*, calls "large loose baggy monsters." In defense of his copious new novel's imperfections, Bellow explained to Bernard Malamud that, in his opinion: "A novel, like a letter, should be loose, cover much ground, run swiftly, take risk of mortality and decay. I backed away from Flaubert, in the direction of Walter Scott, Balzac and Dickens"[14] With his third novel, Bellow rejected the formal fastidiousness of such Modernists as Ford Madox Ford, Ernest Hemingway, and Virginia Woolf. *Augie March* happened to be published the same year as Samuel Beckett's *L'Innommable*, but, though the two novels differ radically in style and tone, each, rejecting narrative continuity, heralds the advent of the Postmodern in its own way.

Emphasizing its "open, expansive, metaphoric, and encyclopedic style,"[15] at odds with the well-wrought urns created by the disciples of Flaubert, Robert Shulman locates *Augie March* instead within the comic, open-form tradition of François Rabelais, Robert Burton, Laurence Sterne, and James Joyce. An eventful, exuberant bildungsroman that follows the progress – or at least trajectory – of its picaresque young protagonist through the Depression to the end of World War II, it is episodic rather than tightly plotted. Its original title, *Life Among the Machiavellians*, eventually morphed into *From the Life of Augie March* and finally into *The Adventures of Augie March* – not only in homage to *Adventures of Huckleberry Finn*, but also in recognition of the adventitiousness of what happens to Augie throughout. The hyperbolic oddness of the many odd jobs Augie takes on – newspaper vendor, florist, Santa's elf, soda jerk, shoe salesman, pet groomer, butler, paint salesman, book thief, coalyard weigh-master, bookkeeper, union organizer, author's assistant, ship's purser, black marketeer, among many others – underscores the apparent randomness of his experience. Like Zelig and Forrest Gump, he is a shape-shifter who shows up in unlikely places, even in the presence of an historical figure, Leon Trotsky.

"Saying 'various jobs,'" Augie explains, "I give out the Rosetta stone, so to speak, to my entire life."[16] Discussions of *Dangling Man* and *The Victim* often make reference to novels by Bellow's French Existentialist contemporaries Jean-Paul Sartre and Albert Camus. As much as Joseph in *Dangling Man* and Asa Leventhal in *The Victim*, Augie March is a protean figure whose existence precedes his essence; pure potential, he lacks a core identity beyond the sum total of his varied experiences. Nevertheless, while not oblivious to what he calls the "rock-depth of heavy trouble, where, I guess the greater part of human beings have always spent most of their silent time,"[17] Augie lacks the *douleur de vivre* of Sartre's Antoine Roquentin and Camus's Meursault. The fortuitousness of everything and the superfluousness of the individual leave him elated, not despondent. When his childhood friend Jimmy Klein, working as a store detective, catches Augie red-handed stealing books, Jimmy muses: "A train could hit you and you'd think it was just swell and get up with smiles, like knee-deep in June."[18] Locating the breakthrough Bellow achieved through *Augie March* in a more confident, assertive, expansive mood, Ihab Hassan, who calls the book "this trend-busting novel,"[19] declares: "It is not unfair to say that in his first two novels Bellow had not yet discovered the dramatic equivalent of *joy*."[20] For Christopher Hitchens, who indeed discovers joy in *Augie March*, it is "a farewell to the age of Bellow's uncertainty, an adieu to the self of his two earlier novels, *Dangling Man* (1944) and *The Victim* (1947)."[21]

It is also a departure from the literature of alienation that set the tone for much mid-century writing in Europe and North America. "I am a person of hope,"[22] declares Augie toward the end of a novel that restores Emersonian optimism to a literature that had become colored by the power of blackness, as well as a Whitmanesque egalitarianism to a Modernist culture that had congealed into hieratic gestures. Despite his indigent origins, Augie is not intimidated by the wealthy Renlings, who want to adopt him, or the heiress Thea Fenchel, who wants to marry him. And he is not too proud to befriend the hoodlums who hang out in William Einhorn's pool hall, or Stoney, the hobo who rides the rails with him from Cleveland to Detroit. Cherishing the inherent dignity of every human being, Augie asks: "What did Danton lose his head for, or why was there a Napoleon, if it wasn't to make a nobility of us all."[23] What Augie calls "this universal eligibility to be noble"[24] informs the entire novel. Like Whitman, he is "no stander above men or women or apart from them"[25] and mixes freely with the unshod as well as the silk-stockinged.

Remaining open to possibility, Augie is reluctant to commit himself to any one of the many women who flit in and out of his story. Sophie Geratis, one of the hotel workers Augie tries to recruit for the CIO (Congress of Industrial Organizations), even offers to divorce her husband to marry him, but when he declines, Sophie complains: "Nothing is ever good enough for you to stick to."[26] Bellow's refusal to stick to a single narrative line results in a novel that, unlike *Dangling Man* and *The Victim*, takes a fresh turn with each succeeding episode. Though most reviewers found Bellow's break away from his earlier claustral fiction exhilarating, Norman Podhoretz, for one, remained wary. While respecting *Augie March* as a radical departure from Bellow's previous two "disciplined, abstract, subjective and somber" novels, Podhoretz faulted the author for trying too hard to be free-wheeling: "Mr. Bellow can't spurt out the images fast enough; the book is almost bursting at the seams in an effort to be exuberant."[27]

The child of immigrants from Eastern Europe, Augie March is – famously – "an American, Chicago born," and the opening sentence of the novel describes Augie's birthplace as "that somber city."[28] Though most of the story takes place in Chicago, Augie, a vagabond, also ventures into Ohio, Michigan, Pennsylvania, New York, Texas, Mexico, the Atlantic Ocean, France, Italy, and Belgium. Supported by a Guggenheim grant, Bellow himself began writing *Augie March* in Paris, but later sections were written in Salzburg, Florence, Rome, Positano, Sorrento, London, New York, Seattle, Portland, and Princeton. Though *Augie March* is a contender for the title Great Chicago Novel, its author boasted that: "Not a single word of the book was composed in Chicago."[29] Augie's mobility, reflecting Bellow's restlessness, produces a spacious narrative that breaks the unity of place found in *Dangling Man* and *The Victim*.

Delmore Schwartz began his contemporaneous review of *Augie March* by announcing that: "Saul Bellow's new novel is a new kind of book."[30] It brought something new to Bellow's nascent literary career, but more broadly, and importantly, it was a breakthrough for Jewish writers and for post-war American fiction in general. However, what Bellow himself found most invigorating about writing his breakthrough novel was the malleable, hybrid style that he improvised for it. "What I found was the relief of turning away from mandarin English and putting my own accents into the language," he recalled in 1991:

> My earlier books had been straight and respectable. As if I had to satisfy the demands of W.H. Fowler. But in *Augie March* I wanted to invent a new sort of American sentence. Something like a fusion of colloquialism and elegance. What you find in the best English writing of the twentieth century – in Joyce or E.E. Cummings. Street language combined with high style.[31]

Bellow's "own accents" were in part the intonations of his first language, Yiddish. Its presence is felt not only in occasional Yiddish words (*"macher"*;[32] *"schmuck"*;[33] *"meshuggah"*[34]) that in 1953 were just beginning to penetrate the general American vocabulary. It is in the profusion of statements phrased as questions and in the syntactical inversions characteristic of Yiddish. "Against you I got nothing,"[35] a cousin called Five Properties assures Augie. And there is a definite Yiddish twist when Cousin Anna insists: "Don't forget to tell them it's now extra the Saturday afternoon paper!"[36] Bellow even coins an amalgam of Yiddish and French, *accoucherka*, when Augie recalls how Grandma Lausch, an immigrant from Odessa who claims knowledge of French, German, Polish, Russian, and Yiddish, berates him for hanging out with "that piss-in-bed *accoucherka*'s son."[37] Leslie Fiedler notes that Bellow's language is "enriched by the dialectic and intellectual play of Jewish conversation."[38] In 1953, it was a breakthrough to insert that conversation into mainstream American literature.

But Bellow's use of language is remarkable not only for its Yiddishisms. Though Jewish, Augie grows up in a Catholic Polish neighborhood, but he is early on attracted to wider linguistic horizons. After climbing up on the roof and gazing at the panorama of Chicago, he marvels at how his native city "exhausted your own imagination of details and units, more units than the cells of the brain and bricks of Babel."[39] As narrator, Augie, a self-defined "listener by upbringing,"[40] projects a voice that has absorbed the many languages of the Babel he inhabits – scattered bits of Czech (*"piva"*[41]), French (*"C'est la moindre des choses"*[42]), German (*"Ich kann nicht anders"*[43]), Hebrew (*"Ribono shel olam!"*[44]), Italian (*"Lasciar le donne?"*[45]), Latin (*"lacrimae rerum"*[46]), Russian (*"Bozhe moy!"*[47]), Spanish (*"Es el amo del águila!"*[48]), and Yiddish (*"Gedenk, Augie, wenn ich bin todt!"*[49]). Bellow's supple style accommodates not only the varied languages Augie hears, but also varied registers of the English language, from the vernacular to the inkhorn. William Einhorn, the shady businessman who takes Augie on as a protégé, combines the argot of the hoodlums in the pool hall he owns with the fustian of a self-anointed neighborhood monarch when he warns Augie, who has just participated in an armed robbery, about where he could end up if he continues his criminal ways: "Those sad and tragic things are waiting to take you in – the clinks and clinics and soup lines know who's the natural to be beat up and squashed, made old, pooped, farted away, no-purposed away."[50] Augie himself is a child of Chicago's mean streets, but he actually reads the books he is commissioned to steal, and by the time he tells his story, he can slip an allusion to Greek philosophy ("But a man's character is his fate, says Heraclitus,"[51] into his very first paragraph. Erudite references to paragons of Western culture such as Thucydides, Montesquieu, Plotinus, Tolstoy, and Chaucer coexist with savvy remarks about Al Capone, John Dillinger, and Jake "the Barber" Factor.

Most critics have hailed the stylistic and cultural range of *Augie March*, its ability to telescope high and low, the respectable and the raffish, within a single sentence, as a breakthrough, but Ihab Hassan, for one, was bothered by discrepancies. "The voice is Augie's, the style Bellow's," he argued, "and it is the disparity between what Augie *can* see and Bellow *must* render that forces the style of the novel so heavily upon our attention."[52] Yet there are two Augies – the comic, bumbling, young ingenu whose misadventures take him from Chicago to Europe ("My own figure for the shape of the book," wrote Bellow, "is that of a widening spiral that begins in the parish, ghetto, slum and spreads into the greater world"[53]) and the older, seasoned narrator who can articulate his experiences with a sophisticated intellectual vocabulary. Bellow's ambition was to invent a flexible sentence that could accommodate both, to orchestrate a polyphony that, marked *allegro*, captures the vivacity of his narrator/protagonist, what Augie calls "the *animal ridens* in me, the laughing creature, forever rising up."[54] It is characteristic of Augie to employ an elegant Latin phrase to describe his own rambunctious, irreverent self.

And it is hard to avoid the conclusion that, with *The Adventures of Augie March*, Bellow, freeing himself from the dolor of his first two books, tapped the *animal ridens* in himself. The third novel is a bravura literary performance, and its author takes obvious delight in deploying his bounteous verbal resources. Augie's opening declaration that "I am an American" announces Bellow's goal of creating a modern American epic, before leading his anti-hero through a wide variety of experiences and more than six hundred pages. For John Milton, who took on the challenge of forging an "answerable style"[55] commensurate with his cosmic ambition, the poet's task, finding fit words to "justify the ways of God to men,"[56] is as formidable as Adam's or Satan's, and the completed poem is testimony to the poet's transcendent skills. Like an epic bard, Bellow flaunts his literary gifts through striking similes that establish not only comparisons but also the ingenuity and playfulness of the author. Augie produces a fusillade of recondite analogies to explain philanderers such as his brother Simon: "They come playing the god like bloody Commodus before the Senate, or run with jockeys and wrestlers like Caracalla, while knowing that somewhere the instrument of their downfall is beginning to gather thought to thought about them, like loops on the knitting needle."[57] The description of Augie carrying crippled Einhorn on his back into a brothel echoes the description in another epic, *The Aeneid*, of "Aeneas, too, who carried his old dad Anchises in the burning of Troy."[58]

Moreover, as if composing a Greek epic, Bellow revels in hyphenated epithets. The cold, foreboding Atlantic Ocean, in which Augie sets sail after enlisting in the Merchant Marine, is not Homer's "wine-dark sea" – "It wasn't," explains Augie, "any apostle-crossed or Aeneas-stirred Mediterranean, the clement, silky, marvelous beauty-sparkle bath in which all the ancientest races were children."[59] And, spending a night in a Detroit jail, Augie employs multiple hyphens to contemplate the darkness that is the common ambience of all human beings – "the mud-sprung, famine-knifed, street-pounding, war-rattled, difficult, painstaking, kicked in the belly, and grief and cartilage mankind, the multitude, some under a coal-sucking Vesuvius of chaos smoke, some inside a heaving Calcutta midnight, who very well know where they are."[60]

Furthermore, Bellow's epic imagination overflows repeatedly with an outpouring of catalogs. He takes delight in describing, through Augie, the panoply of humanity encountered in the elevator at Chicago City Hall:

> In the cage we rose and dropped, rubbing elbows with bigshots and operators, commissioners, grabbers, heelers, tipster, hoodlums, wolves, fixers, plaintiffs, flatfeet, men in Western hats and women in lizard shoes and fur coats, hothouse and arctic drafts mixed up, brute things and airs of sex, evidence of heavy heeding and systematic shaving, of calculations, grief not-caring, and hopes of tremendous millions in concrete to be poured or whole Mississippis of bootleg whisky and beer.[61]

And, less like Homer than Whitman hearing the varied carols that America is singing, Augie enumerates the motley array of immigrant children who attend the city college with him: "In the mixture there was beauty – a good proportion – and pimple-insolence, and parricide faces, gum-chew innocence, labor fodder and secretarial forces, Danish stability, Dago inspiration, catarrh-hampered mathematical genius; there were waxed-eared shovelers' children, sex-promising businessmen's daughters – an immense sampling of a tremendous host, the multitudes of holy writ, begotten by West-moving, factor-shoved parents."[62]

In *Augie March*, Bellow adopted excess rather than economy as his aesthetic principle. Many critics have complained about the book's longueurs, particularly the belabored late episode in which Augie and Thea go off to Mexico to hunt lizards with an eagle named Caligula. Claiming that "The first two hundred pages of 'Augie March' are the best writing Bellow ever did,"[63] Louis Menand implies that the last four hundred pages are a letdown. Fifty years after the novel's publication, Joan Acocella, reviewing a new edition, noted that: "The novel runs out of steam in its last quarter or so, but that is often the case with a bildungsroman (see 'Huckleberry Finn,' 'My Antonia'), because it is the quest that is romantic, and no ending of that, no fall into adult life, will seem a worthy conclusion."[64] More than forty years after his breakthrough, Bellow himself came to scorn the very freedom and amplitude that have continued to impress readers about his third novel. "It seems to me now one of those stormy, formless American phenomena – like Action Painting," he wrote Martin Amis in 1995. "It *was* necessary to invent a way to cope with the curious realities of American life, and I did obviously *invent* something. But the book I now find disconcertingly amorphous, sound and fury signifying not too much."[65]

Amis offered a very different take on Bellow's novel: "*The Adventures of Augie March* is the Great American Novel," he proclaimed. "Search no further. All the trails went cold forty-two years ago."[66] One measure of a literary breakthrough is the extent to which a book affects other writers. E. L. Doctorow credited his reading of *Augie March* with his own liberation as a novelist: "But Bellow was important to me – I'd read *The Adventures of Augie March* in college, and it was in the nature of a revelation, the freedom in that narrative – that there were no rules for the writing of a novel except as you made them up."[67] Bellow's third novel turned John Updike into an admirer; he insisted that the book established Bellow as "our most exuberant and melodious postwar novelist."[68] Furthermore, Philip Roth lauded *Augie March* as a transcendent achievement. "For me as a writer," Roth stated, at the ceremony in which he received the Saul Bellow Award, "*The Adventures of Augie March*, published by Bellow in 1953, remains the most inspiring American novel I have ever read."[69]

Notes

1. Louis Menand, "Young Saul: The Subject of Bellow's Fiction." *The New Yorker*, 91.12 (May 11, 2015): 76.
2. Leslie Fiedler, "The Breakthrough: The American Jewish Novelist and the Fictional Image of the Jew," *Midstream*, 4 (1958), p. 35.
3. Irving Malin and Irwin Stark, eds. *Breakthrough: A Treasury of Contemporary American Jewish Literature* (Philadelphia: The Jewish Publication Society of America, 1964), p. 2.
4. Daniel Fuchs, "Identity and the Postwar Temper in American Jewish Fiction." In Josephine G. Hendin, ed. *A Concise Companion to Postwar American Literature and Culture* (Malden: Blackwell, 2004), p. 241.
5. Ben Siegel, "The Visionary Exuberance of Saul Bellow's *The Adventures of Augie March*." In Alfred Bendixen, ed. *A Companion to the American Novel* (Malden: John Wiley & Sons, 2015), p. 55.
6. Lawrence Buell, *The Dream of the Great American Novel* (Cambridge, MA: Harvard University Press, 2014), p. 162.
7. Julia Keller, "'Adventures of Augie March' is new One Book, One Chicago pick." *Chicago Tribune* (August 17, 2011), http://articles.chicagotribune.com /2011–08-17/entertainment/chi-belows-augie-march-one-book-one-chicago-pick -20110817_1_augie-march-saul-bellow-somber-city.
8. Zachary Leader, *The Life of Saul Bellow: To Fame and Fortune, 1915–1964* (New York: Knopf, 2015), p. 329.
9. James Atlas, *Bellow: A Biography* (New York: Random House, 2000), p. 207.
10. Saul Bellow, "John Berryman, Friend," *New York Times Book Review* (May 27, 1973): 263.

11. Atlas, p. 186.
12. Saul Bellow, "I Got a Scheme!: The Words of Saul Bellow," *The New Yorker*, 81 (April 25, 2005): 74–75.
13. Atlas, p. 147.
14. Saul Bellow, *Letters*. Benjamin Taylor, ed. (New York: Viking, 2010), p. 128.
15. Robert Shulman, "The Style of Bellow's Comedy," *PMLA*, 83.1 (1968): 109.
16. Saul Bellow, *The Adventures of Augie March: Novels 1944–1953* (New York: Library of America, 2003), p. 413.
17. Bellow, *Augie March*, p. 487.
18. Ibid., p. 689.
19. Ihab Hassan, *Radical Innocence: Studies in the Contemporary American Novel* (Princeton: Princeton University Press, 1961), p. 304.
20. Hassan, *Radical Innocence*, p. 303.
21. Christopher Hitchens, "The Great American Augie," *The Wilson Quarterly*, 25.1 (2001): 24.
22. Bellow, *Augie March*, p. 986.
23. Ibid., pp. 413–414.
24. Ibid., p. 414.
25. Walt Whitman, "Song of Myself," sect. 24. In Walt Whitman, *Leaves of Grass: Norton Critical Edition*, eds. Sculley Bradley and Harold W. Blodgett (New York: Norton, 1973), p. 52.
26. Ibid., p. 899.
27. Norman Podhoretz, "The Language of Life," *Commentary*, 15 (January 1953): 378.
28. Bellow, *Augie March*, p. 383.
29. Saul Bellow, "How I Wrote Augie March's Story." *New York Times Book Review* (January 31, 1954): BR3.
30. Delmore Schwartz, Review of *The Adventures of Augie March*. *Partisan Review*, 21.1 (1954): 112.
31. Saul Bellow, "A Second Half Life." *It All Adds Up: From the Dim Past to the Uncertain Future* (New York: Viking, 1994), pp. 317–318.
32. Bellow, *Augie March*, p. 627.
33. Ibid., p. 634.
34. Ibid., p. 660.
35. Ibid., p. 662.
36. Ibid., p. 402.
37. Ibid., p. 394.
38. Leslie Fiedler, "Saul Bellow," *Prairie Schooner*, 31 (1957): 104.
39. Bellow, *Augie March*, p. 906.
40. Ibid., p. 463.
41. Ibid., p. 645.
42. Ibid., p. 927.
43. Ibid., p. 656.
44. Ibid., p. 930.
45. Ibid., p. 946.
46. Ibid., p. 856.
47. Ibid., p. 392.
48. Ibid., p. 797.

49. Ibid., p. 423.

50. Ibid., p. 516.

51. Ibid., p. 383.

52. Hassan, *Radical Innocence*, p. 310.

53. Bellow, *Letters*, p. 102.

54. Bellow, *Augie March*, pp. 994–995.

55. John Milton, *Paradise Lost*. William Kerrigan, John Rumrich, and Stephen M. Fallon, eds. *The Complete Poetry and Essential Prose of John Milton* (New York: Modern Library, 2007), p. 518.

56. Milton, *Paradise Lost*, p. 295.

57. Bellow, *Augie March*, p. 649.

58. Ibid., p. 521.

59. Ibid., p. 944.

60. Ibid., p. 582.

61. Ibid., p. 426.

62. Ibid., p. 425.

63. Menand, "Young Saul," p. 74.

64. Joan Acocella, "*Augie March* Books." *The New Yorker*, 79.29 (October 6, 2003): 117.

65. Bellow, *Letters*, p. 510.

66. Martin Amis, "The American Eagle: *The Adventures of Augie March* by Saul Bellow." *The War Against Cliché: Essays and Reviews, 1971–2000* (New York: Hyperion, 2001), p. 447.

67. Pamela Paul, *By the Book: Writers on Literature and the Literary Life from The New York Times Book Review* (New York: Henry Holt, 2014): 276.

68. Jack De Bellis, *The John Updike Encyclopedia* (Westport: Greenwood Press, 2000), p. 66.

69. Philip Roth, "Acceptance Speech by Philip Roth for the Saul Bellow Award," PEN America (May 31, 2007). www.pen.org/nonfiction/acceptance-speech-philip-roth-saul-bellow-award.

4

GUSTAVO SÁNCHEZ CANALES

Bellow's Cityscapes: Chicago and New York

In plain English, the pleasure Chicago gives is a remission from the pain of New York. As a center New York is a fraud and an abomination.
(Bellow, *Letters*, 255)[1]

I didn't ride around the city on the cars to make a buck or to be useful to the family, but to take a reading of this boring, depressed, ugly, endless, rotting city.
(Bellow, "Something to Remember Me By," 200)[2]

In 2013 Victoria Aarons edited a special issue of the *Saul Bellow Journal* in which I contributed a comparative analysis of James Joyce's Dublin and Saul Bellow's Chicago. The editor of this issue said in her "Foreword: Saul Bellow's Urban Landscapes" that a major point made in this essay was that "the city is a character in itself."[3] In effect, the city plays a crucial role in Bellow's novels, to the extent that the behavior of virtually no protagonist can be fully understood unless it is studied in light of his or her relationship with the city – whether it be New York or Chicago: "The city is, indeed, the dramatic force in Bellow's novels; it is on the streets of Bellow's urban landscapes that his characters, in close and often stifling proximity, must confront themselves in themselves and in others."[4] I would add that this oppressive relationship between the individual and the city enables the novelist to address the question of the alienating effects of the modern metropolis on the individual.[5]

Typically, Bellow depicts intellectual urbanites who, in order to protect themselves from the outside world, have become self-marginalized individuals in search of some peace of mind. To this end, Sherryl Booth claims that "[t]hroughout [*The Dean's December*], images of rectangles consistently suggest isolation, sickness, and death."[6] This description can be extended to other novels such as *Dangling Man* (1944) – set in Chicago – and *Herzog* (1964) – set in New York City. An entry made in the protagonist's diary dated December 18 says that "Joseph suffers from a feeling of strangeness, of not quite belonging to the world, of lying under a cloud and looking up at

43

it."[7] At the outset of the novel *Herzog*, the narrator points out that "[c]onsidering his entire life, he realized that he had mismanaged everything – everything. His life was, as the phrase goes, ruined. ... *Grief, Sir, is a species of idleness.*[8]

In spite of the boredom and apathy initially displayed by many characters such as Joseph and Herzog, Bellow advocates through his protagonists human beings' ability to prioritize their freedom, independence, and personal integrity to the detriment of a number of false values that contemporary society apprizes. Before the Bellovian characters eventually come to terms with themselves, they have a high price to pay: "Suffering internal fracture and a profound sense of estrangement, continually riddled with self-doubt, Bellow's characters set out in search of an authentic self – hoping to discover the freedom of real being."[9] Arguably, what Ellen Pifer is actually pointing to here is Bellow's concern with the idea that the modern world threatens to dissipate the individual's inner self. Should one not be careful, one could end up getting annihilated. When it comes to exploring the pernicious effects of the city on the individual's soul, Gloria L. Cronin suggests that "[t]he subjects raised are by now familiar to Bellow readers. The exhaustion of the inner life, the failure of the poetic sensibility, the bankrupting of Western humanism, the destructive rationalism of modern technology, the diminishment of private life by the crisis mentality and the Heraclitan search for 'the essence of things.'"[10] Luckily, Bellow's protagonists' "Heraclitan search for 'the essence of things'" helps them finally come to terms with themselves far away from the city. Augie, Henderson, Herzog, and Corde are probably the clearest examples of this behavior.

In this chapter, I will focus on the relationship that several Bellovian protagonists have with New York and Chicago. A key issue common to most of – if not all – the novels addressed in the present chapter is that Bellow underscores his concern at the deterioration of the human being's inner self and the dangers inherent in living in a big metropolis. For this reason, at the end of this chapter I will attempt to show many of his protagonists' need to escape from the city and flee to a natural environment as the only way to truly reach some peace of mind.

****

In *Bellow: A Biography* (2000), James Atlas refers to Chicago as "Bellow's great theme."[11] The novelist's authorized biographer adds that his novels are "a virtual reconstruction of the city, neighborhood by neighborhood and street by street."[12] Atlas's statement is illustrative of Bellow's mixed feelings toward his hometown, as subtly expressed in an interview he granted to Joyce Illig in the early 1970s: "What abides in

Chicago is the people of the city, many of whom I've known from childhood. These are intrinsically interesting to me."[13] Bellow's "reconstruction of the city," as described by Atlas, is often performed on two different levels. When Bellow describes the Chicago of his childhood up to the years of his early youth, the description sometimes bears quasi-idyllic overtones. However, when he describes Chicago in the present time, he depicts it as an alienating place that threatens the individual's integrity. Conversely, his depiction of New York is mostly to denounce the city's present state of chaos, violence, and danger. (His definition of New York as "a fraud and an abomination" [included in the epigraph that opens this chapter] supports this assumption.) Below, I will look in more detail at the two levels on which his approach to the city operate.

Bellow's Chicago "has remained his home"[14] and "represented stability – a rare thing in his life."[15] Since most of his memories of childhood and youth are centered around his hometown, his sentimentality flourishes when he recalls those times. For this reason, in Bellow's Chicago novels there is often a contrast between an awful present and a past bordering on an Arcadia-type world. This contrast is partly due to the fact that the Chicago of the Golden 1920s, the 1930s, and the 1940s was an ethnically and culturally enlivened city, as we find in the description of Augie's and Simon's freshman year back in the 1930s. Although this decade is commonly known as the "Depression years," Bellow shows that Chicago was a land of opportunity: *"They filled the factory-length corridors and giant classrooms with every human character and germ, to undergo consolidation and become, the idea was, American. In the mixture there was beauty – a good proportion – and pimple-insolence, and parricide faces, gum-chew innocence, labor fodder and secretarial forces, Danish stability, Dago inspiration, catarrh-hampered mathematical genius."[16]

Chicago was a "city in progress," a thriving place where many opportunities opened up for immigrants such as Bellow and his family. This climate of a prosperous economy is well depicted in the following extract from *Humboldt's Gift* (1975): "my name was linked with Humboldt's, for, as the past receded, *the Forties began to be valuable to people fabricating cultural rainbow textiles*, and the word went out that in Chicago there was a fellow still alive who used to be Von Humboldt Fleisher's friend, a man named Charles Citrine."[17] In this sense, James Atlas's explanation about the Chicago of those years is most apropos:

the novel's great strength is its evocation of Chicago, a 'home-world' that stirs Citrine to rhapsodic reminiscences of the Humboldt Park he knew: *the old*

> *Chicago of ice wagons and planters made out of boilers on the Poles' front lawns; the pool halls and funeral parlors and Hungarian restaurants; the nickel-plated kitchen ranges and giant stoves with "a dome like a little church."*[18]

In the aforementioned interview with Joyce Illig, Bellow elaborates on the idea of Chicago as a prosperous city. Probably, the most important reason lies in its precocious industrial development:

> *In Chicago, things were done for the first time, which the rest of the world later learned and imitated.* Capitalist production was pioneered in the stockyards, in refrigerator cars, in the creation of the Pullman, in the creation of farm machinery, and with it also certain urban and political phenomena which are associated with the new condition of modern democracy. *All that happened there. It happened early.*[19]

The more the reader delves into Bellow's world, the more clearly one perceives the contrast between the Chicago Bellow sees out of his window and the city of his childhood/youth years, suggested by Bilton's remark that "[t]hroughout his fiction, Bellow constantly evokes a central, acutely painful distinction between his rooted Jewish upbringing and the restless urban milieu outside his window."[20] The cultural vitality of "provincial Chicago" in the first half of the twentieth century pointed out above contrasts with the kind of city it eventually became.[21] Below, I will focus on Chicago and New York as an epitome of modern America that crushes individual freedom and uniqueness. In *Humboldt's Gift* the well-known phrase "moronic inferno" used by the narrator summarizes what the city provokes within the Bellovian protagonist.[22]

In his Chicago-set first novel *Dangling Man*, Bellow introduces his protagonist Joseph, a 27-year-old employee who is waiting to be inducted into the army. Joseph feels overwhelmed by the alienating outside world. The novel, written during World War II and published in 1944, shows the boredom, apathy, and frustration experienced by a hopeless youth who is unable to cope with (his) life. He initially spends a great deal of his time confined to his room, where he tries to come to terms with himself. In *Dangling Man*, one of Bellow's most claustrophobic narratives, Joseph, who feels "rooted to [his] chair,"[23] refers to Chicago like this: "In a city where one has lived nearly all his life, it is not likely that he will ever be solitary; and yet, in a very real sense, I am just that. I am alone ten hours a day in a single room."[24]

This pattern of the modern city – no matter whether it is Chicago or New York – as an alienating place which could annihilate the human being's individuality is repeated not only throughout Bellow's early novels – *Dangling Man* and *The Victim* (1947) – but also throughout his middle novels – *Herzog* and *Mr. Sammler's Planet* (1970) – and later novels such as *Humboldt's Gift* and *The Dean's December* (1982). For example, the opening paragraph of *The Victim*, set in New York, helps establish the framework within which the conflicting relationship between Asa Leventhal and Kirby Allbee develops. According to Victoria Aarons, "[f]or Asa Leventhal, the central character of this novel, New York City is transformed into a Kafkaesque world of phobic disorientation. ... The landscape of Bellow's post-Holocaust America is aggressive and menacing, and it is against this landscape – psychic and terrestrial – that Leventhal finds himself frighteningly exposed as a Jew."[25] Aarons' statement is especially true at the outset of the novel, where the oppressive atmosphere exerted by the city of New York on its inhabitants as depicted by the narrator embodies the tense relationship between the presumed victimizer and the presumed victimized:[26]

> *On some nights New York is as hot as Bangkok.* The whole continent seems to have moved from its place and slid nearer the equator, the bitter gray Atlantic to have become green and tropical, and the people, thronging the streets, barbaric fellahin among the stupendous monuments of their mystery, *the lights of which, a dazing profusion, climb upward endlessly into the heat of the sky.*[27]

This sense of oppression is even more intense in *Herzog*, a novel where these kinds of claustrophobic scenes abound. Early in the narrative, it is explained that Herzog is going through a traumatic divorce with Madeleine, which, among other things, has affected his writing negatively. Depicted as someone who is in dire need of coming to terms with himself, Herzog displays a disavowal of New York in a typically Bellovian manner: "The Avenue was filled with concrete-mixing trucks, smells of wet sand and powdery grey cement. Crashing, stamping pile-driving below, and, higher, structural steel, interminably and hungrily going up into the cooler, more delicate blue. ... *He had to get out to the seashore where he could breathe.*"[28] Like Moses Herzog, Bellow never hid his distaste for New York. Actually, when asked for his opinion about the Big Apple, his answer could not have been more straightforward:

> I had the good luck to miss New York in the sixties ... as if I knew intuitively that it was going to go mad. It did go mad. This was no place for a writer. This was a place for performers, virtuosi exhibitionists, self-advertisers and promoters, people in the publicity game who describe themselves also as writers. It was no place for a writer. In fact, it was quite depressing for a writer.[29]

The images of Chicago and New York in, respectively, *Dangling Man* and *The Victim* or *Herzog* that Bellow projects are those of two cities that threaten to annihilate the contemporary individual. A similar picture is offered in *Mr. Sammler's Planet*. Also set in New York, *Mr. Sammler's Planet* approaches the radicalism that pervaded the United States of the late 1960s. In Aarons' words, "Bellow's New York in the late 1960s and early 1970s is a place of debauchery, depravity, criminality, profligacy, self-indulgence, and grasping excess."[30]

Artur Sammler is a 70-year-old Polish refugee who observes bare reality through one eye. His sense of helplessness in his encounter with a huge black pickpocket can be interpreted as the human being's vulnerability in his relationship with the modern world. Sammler is the archetypal Bellovian character who feels oppressed by the chaos of the big metropolis. The following extract is one of the most palpable examples of this feeling: "*Buses were unbearable, subways were killing*. Must he give up the bus? He had not minded his own business as a man of seventy in New York should do. ... *On the streets, he was tense, quick, erratically light and reckless, the elderly hair stirring on the back of his head.*"[31] The hostile urban atmosphere initially presented in this novel gets even worse in his next two novels, *Humboldt's Gift* and *The Dean's December*. Chicago's late 1960s and early 1970s radicalism is summarized in *Humboldt's Gift* in the violence with which Charlie's Mercedes-Benz has been battered and in *The Dean's December*[32] where such violence is graphically embodied in Rick Lester's dreadful murder.

In *Humboldt's Gift*, Charlie's Mercedes is a symbol of the American consumer society in which the individual lives. That his car has been smashed with a baseball bat underscores Bellow's denunciation of the violence perpetrated by society. When Bellow depicts the city as an extremely violent place, he sometimes resorts to humor as a coping strategy.[33] In this sense, Ben Siegel's explanation is most apropos: "Easily the novelist most successful in capturing contemporary life's realistic and grotesque aspects has been Saul Bellow."[34] Bellow's comic approach to the intellectual – present throughout his works – is acutely epitomized in Charlie Citrine's project, "a very personal overview of the Intellectual Comedy of the modern mind."[35]

Accompanied by a Mafioso-type individual called Rinaldo Cantabile, Charlie Citrine is led through the streets of Chicago and its underworld.[36] Chicago's underworld is embodied in the Russian Bath, "[t]hat old joint"[37] on Division Street:

> These Division Street steam-bathers don't look like the trim proud people downtown. Even old Feldstein pumping his Exer-cycle in the Downtown Club at the age of eighty would be out of place on Division Street. Forty years ago Feldstein was a swinger, a high roller, a good-time Charlie on Rush Street. *In spite of his age he is a man of today, whereas the patrons of the*

Russian Bath are cast in an antique form. . . . Things are very elementary here.
You feel that these people are almost conscious of obsolescence, of a line of
evolution abandoned by nature and culture.[38]

In *Humboldt's Gift* – Cantabile and his acquaintances – and in
The Adventures of Augie March (1953) – who can forget the
Einhorns? – Bellow gives a detailed account of city life where writers,
criminals, hoodlums, and gangsters coexist. It is in this context that Peter
Hyland's statement makes most sense: "Chicago provides the battle-
ground on which Bellow's protagonists struggle to find or hold on to
their identity, to identify some spiritual value within the vast metropolitan
clutter of objects and people that constantly threatens to crush them."[39]
Hyland's claim, which specifically refers to the pernicious effect Chicago
exerts on the individual, also applies to the city of New York. His statement addresses what is arguably the key central issue of *Humboldt's Gift*:
America's inability to treat its poets as it should, and, in this sense,
New York is a symbol of that modern malaise. Siegel insists that Charlie
Citrine – like Bellow himself – disavows living in the city of skyscrapers:
"New York . . . dilutes its boredom with culture. So anything significantly
revealing of the boring human condition, Charlie is convinced, will more
likely befall him in his hometown."[40] Humboldt embodies the struggle
between the artist's creative powers and the city's crushing influence on
the individual in general and the artist in particular: "Centering on a live
writer and a dead poet, Bellow tries to define the artist's role in a society
lured away by its massive material substance from its cravings for mind
and beauty."[41]

From a purely aesthetic perspective, Charlie has a romantic conception
of art. He is convinced that the poet should seek beauty and purity.
Probably more clearly in *Humboldt's Gift* than in his previous novels,
Bellow here ponders the role the artist plays in the modern world from
several angles: the poet's – i.e., Humboldt's – agony in the midst of this
earthly world; the separation of American culture from that of the Old
World; and the interrelation between the spiritual realm and the
material world. The story of Humboldt sails between the Scylla of the
spiritual world and the Charybdis of the sensible world.[42] Significantly,
while Charlie Citrine eventually survives in a world where money and
power exert an iron-like control over the individual, Von Humboldt
Fleisher does not. In this respect, it is worth pointing out that by presenting a figure such as Humboldt – modeled on Bellow's friend, the
ill-fated poet Delmore Schwartz[43] – Michael Yetman believes that "the
true artist is doomed by the very purity of his vision (its moral clarity, its

closeness to truth, etc.) to isolation and if not failure, rejection, at best misunderstanding, distortion."[44]

In *Delmore Schwartz: The Life of an American Poet* (1979), James Atlas touches on Schwartz's approach to life from a Bellovian standpoint. Basically, this approach to life consists of a constant struggle between the human being who refuses to give up on his individuality, and society, which threatens to end with it: *"It was not in Delmore's nature to be subdued or docile*, and as late as 1951, in an essay entitled 'The Vocation of the Poet in the Modern World', *he was still proclaiming the heroic character of the poet's role in rejecting 'the seductions of mass culture and middle-brow culture."*[45] Atlas adds that James Joyce "was his model for the artist in the modern world ... Because the Jew 'is an exile from his own country and an exile even from himself' ... 'yet he survives the annihilating fury of history'".[46] Delmore-Humboldt, a Jew himself, fails to survive "the annihilating fury of history." Humboldt's inability to survive is a key issue that enables Charlie Citrine to reflect on the loss of individuality, a problem which – as in his poet friend's case – could bring about the human being's own destruction. According to Charlie, the only way to retrieve the individual's almost already annihilated integrity is to recuperate the power of the imagination[47]: "Bellow believes that his faith in the imagination is not shared by contemporary society, which is materialistic and hostile to those who suggest ways of knowing that cannot be scientifically explained."[48]

Bellow takes up this inherently romantic theme in *The Dean's December*. In this novel Albert Corde, a former journalist and currently a dean, expects to retrieve the world of ideas, of poetry and critical observation. Corde's temporary stay in Bucharest permits him to take up the necessary distance to ponder not only his university's present state of affairs but also his own life in Chicago. As in the case of *Humboldt's Gift, The Dean's December* is an epitome of the decline of the post-industrial era.

After thinking about the individual's relationship with society, Albert Corde reaches the conclusion that evil not only exists in the outside world – what he calls the "inner city slum" – but in "the slum of innermost being."[49] He is also convinced that contemporary society has been going through a spiritual confusion bordering on insanity. This insistence leads him to analyze one of the most pressing problems for him: the planet's lead poisoning: "Corde's meditation upon the city is actually a meditation upon the spiritual malady of modern civilization and an exploration of the soul."[50] The dean regards lead poisoning as the embodiment of a more serious malaise: the end of thought. This issue, first introduced in *Humboldt's Gift* – Charlie Citrine tells his girlfriend Renata that "[t]he ideas of the last few centuries are used up"[51] – is further developed by Albert Corde with the aim of addressing his worry about the deterioration of human life in modern cities such as Chicago. He touches on the need to escape from the city and flee to the countryside – the classical Bellovian civilization/nature dichotomy – as a way to come to terms with oneself. The dichotomous nature of reality enables the protagonist to explore his soul: "Cities represent the American *idea*, the ideals of Liberalism, and while words are not the idea itself, words can revive dead ideas worth perpetuating, living for and acting upon."[52]

In effect, living in the city eventually becomes unbearable for most of Bellow's protagonists. For this reason, the only way out for them is to come to terms with themselves away from the city. In the case of Joseph in *Dangling Man*, his liberation is paradoxically to be found when he is inducted: "Long live regimentation."[53] In many other cases reconciliation with life takes place within a more natural environment. For example, in *Henderson the Rain King* (1959) Bellow's homonymous protagonist ends up with a lion cub on a plane that has landed somewhere in Newfoundland. (The implications of the name of this island should not be ignored. The name "Newfoundland," derived from the English phrase "New Found Land" and translated from the Portuguese "Terra Nova," suggests new beginnings or the chance to start over.) This is Henderson's last thought: "I guess I felt it was my turn now to move, and so went running – leaping, leaping, pounding, and tingling over the pure white lining of the gray Arctic silence."[54] As regards Herzog, whose peace of mind occurs when "he had no messages for anyone. Nothing. Not a single word," he is last seen in his Ludeyville countryhouse in the Berkshires.[55]

Much the same as in *Henderson the Rain King*, *Herzog*, and *Humboldt's Gift*, in *The Dean's December* the protagonist comes to terms with himself in a natural environment. In effect, when Corde and his wife Minna return to the United States, they do not go straight back to Chicago but stop at the Mount Palomar observatory (California). It is there, while they are looking up at the starry sky and the surrounding nature, that they realized "[e]very-thing overhead was in equilibrium, kept in place by mutual tensions. What was it that *his* tensions kept in place?"[56] This is exactly the answer to the Bellovian problematic relationship with the urban space: one needs to discover the close connection between the individual and creation.

Although in other stories the end does not take place within a natural scenario, there is usually a reference to nature. For instance, in the last scene of *Seize the Day* (1956) – a story set in New York – Wilhelm ends up attending the funeral of a person he does not know. Under this unusual circumstance, "[t]he flowers and lights fused ecstatically in Wilhelm's blind, wet eyes; the heavy sea-like music came up to his ears."[57] In the last scene of *Humboldt's Gift* the "flower motif" is also present. Charlie Citrine realizes that a flower has bloomed on Humboldt's tomb, which seems to show Bellow's vision of life as something cyclical. In this way, he could be advocating the idea that the human being lives on somehow after bodily death: "I'm a city boy myself. They must be crocuses."[58] According to Ted R. Spivey, "[t]his statement prepares us for the next problem of what can now be called the Bellow questing protagonist, a problem taken up in *The Dean's December, the problem of how to go beyond the modern urban consciousness and, like Wordsworth and Goethe, once again become integrated with nature.*"[59] Spivey's claim – especially the words in italics – is, in this regard, very suggestive, and so is Allan Chavkin's, for whom the influence of romantic poetry in Bellow's novels is especially clear in *Humboldt's Gift* and *The Dean's December.*[60] And, much the same as the romantics, Bellow invites his readers to ponder their inner selves in light of a (more) natural world and, therefore, far away from the urban space.[61]

Notes

1. *Saul Bellow: Letters.* Ed. Benjamin Taylor. New York: Viking, 2010.
2. *Something to Remember Me By: Three Tales.* New York: Viking, 1991.
3. Victoria Aarons (ed.), "Foreword: Saul Bellow's Urban Landscapes," *Saul Bellow Journal,* 26.1–2 (Winter/Fall 2013): v.
4. Victoria Aarons "Saul Bellow." *The Cambridge Companion to American Novelists.* Ed. Timothy Parrish, 2013: 230–240, 236.
5. See Malcolm Bradbury, *Saul Bellow* (London & New York, Methuen, 1982), p. 41; James Atlas, *Bellow: A Biography* (New York, Modern Library, 2000), p. 318; S. Lillian Kremer, "Cities on his mind: Urban Landscapes of Saul Bellow's Fiction," *Saul Bellow Journal,* 26.1–2 (Winter/Fall 2013): 1; Gustavo Sánchez-Canales, "A tale of two cities: A Comparative Analysis of James Joyce's Dublin and Saul Bellow's Chicago," *Saul Bellow Journal,* 26.1–2 (Winter/Fall 2013): 127; John Clayton, *Saul Bellow: In Defense of Man* (Bloomington: Indiana, 1979).
6. Sherryl Booth, "'Living your own experience': The Role of Communities in Saul Bellow's *The Dean's December.*" *Saul Bellow Journal,* 10.1 (1991): 13–24, 15.
7. Saul Bellow, *Dangling Man.* New York: Vanguard, 1944: 30.
8. Saul Bellow, *Herzog.* New York: Viking, 1964: 9 (emphasis in the original).
9. Ellen Pifer, *Saul Bellow: Against the Grain.* Philadelphia: University of Pennsylvania Press, 1990: 6.
10. Gloria L. Cronin, "Art vs. Anarchy: Citrine's Transcendental." *Indian Journal of American Studies,* 15.1 (1985): 33–43, 33.
11. Atlas, James. *Bellow: A Biography.* New York, Random House, 2000: 318.
12. Ibid.
13. Joyce Illig. "An Interview with Saul Bellow." *Conversations with Saul Bellow.* Ed. Gloria L. Cronin and Ben Siegel, 1994: 104–112, 109.
14. Peter Hyland. *Saul Bellow.* New York: St. Martin's Press, 1992: 4.
15. Atlas, *Bellow: A Biography:* 322.

16. Saul Bellow, *The Adventures of Augie March*. New York: Viking, 1953: 125 (emphasis mine).
17. Saul Bellow, *Humboldt's Gift*. New York: Viking, 1975: 9 (emphasis mine).
18. Atlas, *Bellow: A Biography*: 435 (emphasis mine).
19. Illig in Cronin and Siegel, 1994: 110 (emphasis mine).
20. Alan Bilton, "The Colored City: Saul Bellow's Chicago and Images of Blackness." *Saul Bellow Journal*, 16.2–17.1-2 (2001): 104–128, 104.
21. Atlas, *Bellow: A Biography*: 319.
22. *Humboldt's Gift*, 35
23. *Dangling Man*, 13.
24. Ibid., 10.
25. Victoria Aarons. "'Not enough air to breathe': The Victim in Saul Bellow's Post-Holocaust America." *Saul Bellow Journal*, 23.1-2 (2007–2008): 23–36, 24.
26. See Victoria Aarons, "'Washed Up on the Shores of Truth': Saul Bellow's Post-Holocaust America," in *A Political Companion to Saul Bellow*, eds. Gloria L. Cronin and Lee Trepanier (The University Press of Kentucky Press, 2013), pp. 129–152. In this article, Aarons acutely points out that "[i]n many ways, the Holocaust forms an absent presence in Bellow's fiction – it lives not only as historical fact, but also in its immediacy" (p. 133).
27. Saul Bellow, *The Victim*. New York: Vanguard, 1947: 1 (emphasis mine).
28. *Herzog*: 38 (emphasis mine).
29. Illig in Cronin and Siegel, 1994: 106 (emphasis mine).
30. Aarons, "*Saul Bellow*," 231.
31. Saul Bellow, *Mr. Sammler's Planet*. New York: Viking, 1970: 5–6 (emphasis mine).
32. Sherryl Booth, "'Living your own experience': The Role of Communities in Saul Bellow's *The Dean's December*," *Saul Bellow Journal*, 10.1 (1991): 13–24; Allan Chavkin, "Recovering the World That Is Buried Under the Debris of False Description," *Saul Bellow Journal*, 1.2 (1982): 47–57; Stevan Marcus, "Reading the Illegible: Modern Representations of Urban Experience," *The Southern Review*, 22.3 (1986): 443–64; Gustavo Sánchez-Canales, "The Romantic Spirit in Saul Bellow's *The Dean's December*," *Estudios Ingleses de la Universidad Complutense*, 11 (2003): 111–122.
33. Sarah Blacher Cohen, *Saul Bellow's Enigmatic Laughter* (Urbana: University of Illinois Press, 1974); Cohen, Sarah Blacher, "Comedy and Guilt in *Humboldt's Gift*," *Modern Fiction Studies*, 25.1 (1979): 47–57; Newman, Judie, "Saul Bellow, *Humboldt's Gift*: The Comedy of History," *Durham University Journal*, 72 (1979): 79–87.
34. Ben Siegel, "Artists and Opportunists in Saul Bellow's *Humboldt's Gift*." *Contemporary Literature*, 19.2 (1978): 143–164, 143.
35. *Humboldt's Gift*: 73.
36. Gustavo Sánchez-Canales, "A tale of two cities," pp. 139ff.
37. *Humboldt's Gift*: 55.
38. Ibid., 78 (emphasis mine).
39. Peter Hyland, *Saul Bellow*. New York: St. Martin's Press, 1992: 7.
40. Siegel, "Artists and Opportunists," p. 150.
41. Ibid., 145.

42. Fredrica K. Bartz, "The Role of Rudoph Steiner in the Dreams of *Humboldt's Gift*," *Ball State University Forum*, 24.1 (1983): 27–29; Faye Kuzma, "'We flew on': Flights of Imagination in *Humboldt's Gift*," *Michigan Academician*, 25.2 (1993): 159–177; Ellen Pifer, *Saul Bellow Against the Grain* (Philadelphia: University of Pennsylvania Press, 1990), pp. 135ff; Herbert J., "*Humboldt's Gift* and Rudolf Steiner," *Centennial Review*, 22.4 (1978): 479–489. Interestingly, Ellen Pifer says that "[i]t is hunger for news of the soul that impels Citrine to study Steiner," p. 135.

43. James Atlas, *Delmore Schwartz: The Life of an American Poet* (New York: Farrar, Straus, Giroux, 1979).

44. Michael G. Yetman, "Who Would Not Sing for Humboldt?" *ELH*, 48.4 (1981): 935–951, 940.

45. Atlas, *Delmore Schwartz*: 302 (emphasis mine).

46. Ibid., 302.

47. In a conversation with Artur Sammler, his niece Margotte tells the old Polish refugee: "Modern civilization doesn't create great individual phenomena any more" (Saul Bellow, *Mr. Sammler's Planet* [1970], New York & London: Penguin Books, 1985), p. 16.

48. Allan Chavkin, "Bellow and English Romanticism," *Studies in the Literary Imagination*, 17.2 (1984): 7–18, 9.

49. *Dean's December*: 199.

50. Allan Chavkin, "*The Dean's December* and Blake's *the Ghost of Abel*," *Saul Bellow Journal*, 13.1 (1995): 22–26, 22.

51. *Humboldt's Gift*: 250.

52. Anne Weinstein, "*The Dean's December*: Bellow's Plea for the Humanities and Humanity," *Saul Bellow Journal*, 2.2 (1983): 30–41, 40.

53. *Dangling Man*: 191.

54. *Henderson the Rain King*: 341.

55. *Herzog*: 348.

56. *Dean's December*: 306.

57. *Seize the Day*: 118.

58. *Humboldt's Gift*: 487.

59. Ted R. Spivey, "Death, Love, and the Rebirth of Language in Saul Bellow's Fiction." *Saul Bellow Journal*, 4.1 (1985): 5–18, 10 (emphasis mine).

60. Chavkin, "Bellow and English Romanticism"; Saul Bellow, *The Dean's December* (New York & London: Penguin Books, 1982); M. A. Quayum, "*The Dean's December*," in *Saul Bellow and American Transcendentalism* (New York, Peter Lang, 2004), pp. 221–269; Gustavo Sánchez-Canales, "The Romantic Spirit"; James Stanger, "The Power of Vision: Blake's System and Bellow's Project in *Mr. Sammler's Planet*," *Saul Bellow Journal*, 12.2 (1994): 17–36.

61. M. A. Quayum, "*The Dean's December*."

5

VICTORIA AARONS

Bellow and the Holocaust

In a remarkably candid letter written in 1987 to the American-Jewish novelist Cynthia Ozick, Saul Bellow remarks on the reprehensible failure, in the
aftermath of the Holocaust, of American-Jewish intellectuals to respond
directly to the Nazi genocide of Europe's Jews. There is no denying the
fact, Bellow writes, that American-Jewish writers in particular "missed
what should have been for them the central event of their time, the destruction of European Jewry."[1] The response from American-Jewish intellectuals
to the Holocaust, Bellow argues, lacked the moral directness necessary to
speak on behalf of the collective conscience of the civilized world. Bellow's
censuring of this silence in the face of the devastation condemns the way that,
not only Jewish writers, but American intellectuals at large – voices of critical
analysis, commentary, and principled action – averted their gaze from one of
the defining events of the erosion of civilized life in the twentieth century.
As Bellow confessed,

> We ... should have reckoned more fully, more deeply with it. Nobody in America
> seriously took this on ... [I]n the matter of higher comprehension – well, the
> mental life of the century having been disfigured by the same forces of deformity
> that produced the Final Solution, there were no minds *fit* to comprehend ... and
> every honest conscience feels the disgrace of it.   (*Letters*, 438–439)

In speaking of the failure of his own moral and intellectual position, Bellow
admits,

> I was too busy becoming a novelist to take note of what was happening in the
> Forties. I was involved with "literature" and given over to preoccupations with
> art, with language, with my struggle on the American scene, with claims for
> recognition of my talent ... with anything except the terrible events in Poland.
> Growing slowly aware of this unspeakable evasion I didn't even know how to
> begin to admit it into my inner life. Not a particle of this can be denied ....
> I can't even begin to say what responsibility any of us may bear in such a matter,
> in a crime so vast that it brings all Being into Judgment.   (*Letters*, 439)

In large part, a modernist preoccupation with art as its own activity, Bellow confesses, prevented him and others from rising to the necessity of the intellectual's public moral duty.

For Bellow, then, the failure of the intellectual to lay claim to the burden of moral testimony in the wake of the legislated, systematic attempts to eradicate European Jewry was not only a failure of conscience but also an abdication of responsibility, an inexcusable neglect of the intellectual's obligation to reckon with the consequences of ethnic hatred and rampant global political ambition in the fraught years of the twentieth century. Bellow sees this failure as a willful blindness, and the growing recognition of the implications of such reticence in the face of atrocity – especially of post-war American-Jewish writers as well as his own personal negligence – seems to have left Bellow in a state of continuing residual unease. And so, some forty-plus years after the end of the war, the liberation of the concentration camps, and the enacted (if insufficient) efforts of reparation and asylum for those victims who survived the carnage, Bellow's attempts to grapple with the Holocaust and his literary and moral "place" in such discussions remains a source of unresolved restlessness: "Since the late Forties I have been brooding about it and sometimes I imagine I *can* see something. But what such brooding may amount to is probably insignificant. I can't even begin to say what responsibility any of us may bear in such a matter" (*Letters*, 439). And yet, despite his own nagging sense of evasion, Bellow wrote three works of fiction, spanning the same four decades that saw him "brooding" over the failure of his own and others' moral reckoning with the Holocaust, that speak not only to the devastating events of the Nazi genocide, but to the tentacles of apprehension and unease that persisted – and continued to persist – in its wake. The perspectives Bellow proposes in these three books and in their connections offer various ways of thinking about the Holocaust in the context of the mercurial and brutal twentieth century.

The novels *The Victim* (1947) and *Mr. Sammler's Planet* (1970) and the novella *The Bellarosa Connection* (1989) show Bellow at differing and evolving stages in his thinking about the effects of the Holocaust and its implications for topics as seemingly various as anti-Semitism, the assimilationist culture of American Judaism, the history of enlightened liberalism, and the possibility of a progressive, discerning American intellectual readership. Bellow comments in these narratives on the Jew as victim amidst not only war-torn Europe but also the tense landscape of America. In these novels, Bellow stages the cityscape of New York as simultaneously the most cosmopolitan, sophisticated, open city in the world, but also one in which the threat of persecution surfaces in an ominous atmosphere of dread and in the claustrophobic despair of the heat and glare of the city, the encroaching wills of the crowds, their "overwhelming human closeness and thickness ... innumerable millions, crossing, touching, pressing."[2]

The basic storyline of *The Victim* (following the publication of Bellow's first novel, *Dangling Man*, in 1944) centers on Asa Leventhal and his antagonist and double, the anti-Semite Kirby Allbee, who pursues Leventhal relentlessly through the claustrophobic, heat-drenched streets of New York City. Allbee's complaint against Leventhal involves the inflated, histrionic accusation that Leventhal, in retaliation for an offhand comment Allbee made at a party regarding the Jews, got him sacked from his job. For this, Allbee wants reparation and thus insinuates himself in Leventhal's life. *The Victim* is essentially a character study; plot here is subservient to character, as it generally is for Bellow. And thus we see Asa Leventhal unraveling, becoming increasingly anxious about Allbee's demands and the possibility of his own responsibilities and obligations. Leventhal comes to believe that he deserves Allbee's predatory accusations and that his insinuations and demands may, in fact, be justified: fearing that "'I did it on purpose, to get even ... not only because I'm terrible personally but because I'm a Jew' ... 'He made me believe what I was afraid of,'" Leventhal thought (103, 107). Leventhal comes to believe that, because of something in his nature, he deserves the assault upon him in the figure of Allbee. In this novel, Allbee comes to embody the metonymic representation of anti-Semitism in his pursuit of the Jew, Allbee who regards Leventhal with a gaze "of naked malice," hating him for what he has as well as his very constitution, his complexion as the Jew, his Jewish "traits" (196, 34). Allbee is, for Leventhal, the face of dread and inevitability: "Something would have to happen," Leventhal uneasily calculates, "something that he could not foresee" but that lies in wait for him (205). Leventhal is, in Bellow's calculation, an American Jew in the fraught years in the direct aftermath of the Nazi genocide, who suffers not only from the fear of the effects of anti-Semitism, but also from a permeating sense of survivor guilt. Leventhal is, as he admits, "lucky ... [he] had gotten away with it" (33). His uneasy admonition suggests that he, lucky to have been born in America rather than Europe, narrowly escaped what might have been his fate. And since he, unlike millions of others, survived, he projects their fear and vulnerability on himself, believing himself to have been singled out because he is a Jew, threatened by anti-Semitic persecution, for "revenge," "singled out to be the object of some freakish, insane process ... and he was filled with dread" (26).

In *The Victim*, the oppressive closeness of "the people, thronging the streets" of Bellow's undulating urban landscape is made menacing by the portentous peril of annihilation that threatens to erupt from the "shimmer of fumes" in the urban backdrop, the "redness in the sky, like the flame at the back of a vast baker's oven ... gaping fierily over the black of the Jersey shore," the "clouds heavily suspended" atop the chimneys of the "factories beginning to smolder," inviting "the hard encircling rumble of trucks and subterranean trains" (1, 14, 28, 40). Such markers of annihilation, perceptible totems of the Nazi extermination industry, suggest the continuing threat of murder and destruction. The specter of the Holocaust exists eerily amid the noise and confusion of Bellow's urban landscape, a harbinger of anti-Semitism and its relentless presence amid the disguises of the tenets of the post-war American ethos – liberalism, equality, and enlightened reason. Even the tarnished symbol of freedom here stands atilt, exhausted and flattened, ready to topple: "The Statue of Liberty rose and traveled backwards again; in the trembling air, it was black, a twist of black that stood up like smoke" (45). It is against this foreboding and volatile backdrop that the novel's central character, Asa Leventhal, navigates uneasily and apprehensively, the very air he breathes heavy with recent history, "strange . . . savage things. They hung near him all the time in trembling drops, invisible, usually, or seen from a distance. But that did not mean that there was always to be a distance, or that sooner or later one or two of the drops might not fall on him" (84). Bellow's Leventhal represents American-Jewish unease about persisting anti-Semitism represented in the very texture of the urban landscape of New York and also the plight of the Jew in America in the fraught post-war years.

Some twenty years hence, Bellow returned to the subject of the Holocaust in the novel *Mr. Sammler's Planet* (1970). Once again, the novel's center stage is "the charm, the ebullient glamor" of New York City, symbol of an America "[a]dvertised throughout the universe as the most desirable, most exemplary of all nations."[3] But life in post-war America runs parallel to "the breath of wartime Poland" during the Nazi occupation, to mass graves, to the fear and threat of exposure, to flight and death, the legislated, institutionalized "state of madness" marked by the Holocaust (*Mr. Sammler's Planet*, 5, 89). In *Mr. Sammler's Planet*, Bellow locates his protagonist Artur Sammler, a seventy year old Polish Holocaust survivor, amidst the cityscape of New York in 1969, the summer of the moon landing and a time of political and social unrest. While the novel is largely a meditation on America in the late 1960s – where "certain forms of success required an element of parody, self-mockery, a satire-on-the-thing itself" (70) – it also harkens back to the events in Europe that brought Sammler to this "planet." To be sure, Sammler navigates the streets of New York with no little trepidation. From the European refugee's eyes, "New York makes one think about the collapse of civilization, about Sodom and Gomorrah, the end of the world . . . things . . . falling apart" (304). Having endured and barely survived the "madness" and brutality of the civilized world, Sammler, a refugee in Manhattan, exists uneasily with "the breath of wartime Poland passing over ... damaged tissues" (147, 5). He "survives" uneasily, suspiciously, his critical gaze cast apprehensively over the debauchery, corruption, fraudulence, and collective self-delusion he witnesses all around him. Sammler, having been left for dead in a mass grave – "fired upon ... Bodies upon his own body. Crushing. His dead wife nearby somewhere. Struggling out much later from the weight of corpses" (92) – and then hiding in forests, in swamps, in the uncertain sanctuary of a mausoleum – "In the tomb of a family called Mezvinski he was, so to speak, a boarder" (89–90) – emerges into the spectral light of Manhattan, a survivor, "a symbolic character. He, personally, was a symbol ... judge and a priest. And of what was he a symbol? He didn't even know" (91). Here Sammler becomes the ironic spokesperson for Bellow, soliloquizing on the state of the enlightened world in the second half of the twentieth century, a state of pathological justifications, desperate explanations, an intellectual wasteland in the midst of false rationalizations, the moving parts of institutional political chaos, "the collapse of civilization" (304). The events and repercussions of the Holocaust exist in a kind of parallel universe in Bellow's reflective novel. For, however geographically and temporally distanced Sammler is from the anguished events of his past, the Holocaust is the defining lens through which Sammler navigates the world as well as the lens through which he is viewed by others.

Bellow engages the Holocaust more directly in *Mr. Sammler's Planet* than in *The Victim*. Here, too, Holocaust markers litter the New York landscape: the "grinding subway" and the claustrophobic sensation of "being sealed in by bodies" harkens back to Leventhal's disorienting experience of living in New York in the immediate years following the end of the war (*Mr. Sammler's Planet*, 6). Not entirely unlike the experience of the anguished Asa Leventhal, Bellow's protagonist in *The Victim*, the world in which Artur Sammler uncomfortably dwells is off kilter, highly suspect, and populated with the imposition of others who make demands upon his frayed emotional resources. Both men, indeed, have been betrayed by history, the long history of persecution against the Jews and the more proximate conditions of anti-Semitic reactiveness and scapegoating. For both protagonists, too, America is something of a failure, shown in both novels to be excessive in its propagandizing, over-blown, fraudulent untruth to itself. However, the events of the '30s and '40s in Europe are given a different inflection in *Mr. Sammler's Planet* than they are in *The Victim*. Bellow's approach to the Holocaust in this 1970 novel is more direct, less circumspect, symbolic, and guarded. Bellow can return to the Nazi devastation in direct references to bodies and graves, deceit and treachery. He can present it straightforwardly as an assault on decency and morality, if only in Sammler's assessment of his condition. The Holocaust is "bad news," Sammler sardonically acknowledges, "for humankind" (90). And, in this way, Bellow's later protagonist is a more self-ironic, self-aware, and perspicacious recipient of the novelist's critically observant judgment. Bellow is, with the publication of *Mr. Sammler's Planet*, more a novelist of ideas, more open in his alignment with his literary spokesperson. At an important moment in the unfolding of the novel, Sammler will contest Hannah Arendt's theory of the banality of evil, arguing that "The banality was only camouflage. What better way to get the curse out of murder than to make it look ordinary, boring, or trite? With horrible political insight they found a way to disguise the thing ... There was a conspiracy against the sacredness of life. Banality is the adopted disguise of a very powerful will to abolish conscience" (18). The direct engagement of the Holocaust by Bellow, as represented in his protagonist Sammler, allows for a return to the atrocities with less ambiguity and caution and more explicit condemnation.

Once again, in this novel we find an apprehensive protagonist, but this one is older, more self-aware, ironic, and discerning: Artur Sammler, survivor, Polish refugee relocated in Manhattan, a man who literally scrambled out of a mass grave meant for his death and who later risked capture, hidden in a mausoleum and in the Zamosht Forest amid the Polish partisans, "one of the doomed who had lasted it all out" (*Mr. Sammler's Planet*, 140). With his second Holocaust novel, Bellow moves from Asa Leventhal, a frightened, deeply phobic victim of veiled, oblique, American anti-Semitism, to Artur Sammler, a tangible, material victim of the atrocities of Nazi anti-Semitic fervor, a survivor, though by his own admission, "He hadn't even done that, since so much of the earlier person had disappeared. It wasn't surviving, it was only lasting. He had lasted" (*Mr. Sammler's Planet*, 91). Sammler stands as a direct victim of Nazi hatred and the systematized assault on Europe's Jews. Yet Asa Leventhal is, as the title of Bellow's 1947 novel would have it, *the* victim, a Jew existing in the tremulous wake of war, on another continent, to be sure, but for the American Jew, reeling from the specter of having barely escaped, one who, at least provisionally, "got away with it" (*The Victim*, 16).

For Asa Leventhal in *The Victim*, the Holocaust and its continuing threat can only be acknowledged and alluded to indirectly. Leventhal fearfully anticipates what has already happened to Sammler. But Sammler's past, the carnage he witnessed, while more unmediated and performed, is still largely contained behind the closed doors of his West Side flat, in his meditative contemplation of the events whose meaning he obsessively ponders: "The roots of this, the causes of the other, the source of events, the history,

the structure, the reasons why ... The soul ... sat unhappily on superstruc-
tures of explanation, poor bird, not knowing which way to fly"
(*Mr. Sammler's Planet*, 3–4). In Leventhal the Holocaust is secreted, existing
in his simmering dread, barely articulated to himself. Leventhal defensively
and wildly reacts. With Sammler, the articulation of the events of the
Holocaust is, largely, personal, familial. That is, while known, the specifics
are contained within the family: his damaged daughter, Shula-Slawa (Slawa,
the name given to her while hiding in a convent in Poland), whose fractured
name reflects the discomfort with and, ultimately, the impossibility of either
escaping the past or embracing a new identity; and his nephew Elya Gruner,
his protector and benefactor, and the paradigm of American-Jewish
assimilation still under the cloud of history.

By the time of the 1989 publication of Bellow's novella, *The Bellarosa
Connection*, however, the Holocaust is, tangentially, "behind us" and thus
can be spoken of with more distance, through a lens of gathered time and
perspective. When Bellow wrote *The Bellarosa Connection*, discussions of
the Holocaust had become increasingly institutionalized within the culture of
public discourse, yet, at the same time, conveniently buried, as we find with
Bellow's ironic literary construct of the Mnemosyne Institute in Philadelphia,
founded by the novella's narrator, as if memory can be contained and thus
controlled within its walls. The narrator of *The Bellarosa Connection* tells
the story of Harry Fonstein, a Jewish refugee from Nazi-occupied Poland
who escaped with false papers through the aid of the legendary Broadway
producer Billy Rose. Ensconced in the safety of America after his ordeal,
a very grateful Fonstein wants to locate his benefactor Rose to express his
gratitude. Rose, however, deflects Fonstein's wish to meet him, preferring to
avoid any entanglement, any lingering responsibility for the man he helped
save – "I don't like things from the past being laid on me," Billy Rose tells
Fonstein's wife and emissary – leaving Fonstein without the stage for the
"concluding chapter" of his journey.[4] When beseeched by Sorella, Fonstein's
wife, to spend just "fifteen minutes alone with my husband ... A handshake,
and he'll say thanks," Fonstein's rescuer wants no part of this affective
business: "Remember, forget – what's the difference to me?" he insists
(*The Bellarosa Connection*, 58, 53). For Billy Rose, life is all "show biz,"
all glitz, a transitory business (65). And here, Bellow seems to ask these
troubling questions: What value has remembering? How much time elapses
before experience becomes memory? When does the Holocaust become mere
memory? When, that is, does the Holocaust become history? How does
memory of the Holocaust play out in hyper-capitalist America?

With *The Bellarosa Connection*, Bellow once again returns to the
Holocaust as his subject and as the motivating event of the novel's action.

As Ezra Cappell suggests, with the publication of *The Bellarosa Connection*, "Bellow does not create an allegory of suffering as he had forty years earlier in *The Victim*; instead, he tells the American story of the Holocaust and the missed opportunities for salvation and redemption ... the harrowing American story of those who failed to think through the essential reality of a post-Holocaust world."[5] Here, again, "America," the immigrant's hoped for refuge, is the stage upon which the action is set. And as in *Mr. Sammler's Planet*, we are introduced to a refugee protagonist from Nazi-occupied Poland. But in *The Bellarosa Connection*, the Holocaust is history, and Bellow moves to the issue of the Holocaust as memory, the events resurrected by the novella's narrator, founder of Philadelphia's Mnemosyne Institute, at the time of the narrative retired from the memory business but very much still engaged in it in his rendition of the story of Harry Fonstein, escapee from the German death trap. "In Auschwitz," the narrator acknowledges, Fonstein "would have been gassed immediately" because of an unfortunate orthopedic impediment causing him to wear a boot (*The Bellarosa Connection*, 4). Speculating on Fonstein's narrowly escaped fate, the narrator conjectures that "Some Dr. Mengele would have pointed his swagger stick to the left, and Fonstein's boot might by now have been on view in the camp's exhibition hall – they have a hill of cripple boots there, and a hill of crutches and of back braces and one of human hair and one of eyeglasses" (*The Bellarosa Connection*, 4). The novella's narrator, a distant relative of Fonstein, not related by blood but rather by the vagaries of marriage (Fonstein was the nephew of the narrator's stepmother), unveils the story of Fonstein's history and his thwarted desire to thank the man through whose largess he was enabled to escape. Fonstein's life is, at the time of the narration, past history, existing only in the storied memory of Bellow's narrator who, by his own admission, "would like to forget about remembering" (2). The novella might be thought of, as Gustavo Sánchez Canales suggests, as moving "between the Scylla of remembering the Shoah ... and the Charybdis of forgetting it."[6] As Holocaust scholar Alan L. Berger proposes, *The Bellarosa Connection* is "an extended meditation on the appropriate role of post-Auschwitz memory ... that remembering the Shoah is the litmus test of Jewish authenticity while seeking to survive as a Jew after Auschwitz."[7]

The story that the narrator, himself the son of Russian Jews from New Jersey, tells is one of fortuitous good fortune and disenchantment. Most of Fonstein's family were killed by the Germans. Fonstein and his mother were secreted out of Europe with false papers, a rescue operation orchestrated by the notorious New York celebrity and gangster Billy Rose. As the caprice of show business would have it, "[y]esterday a hit man, today working against the Nazis" (*The Bellarosa Connection*, 13). Bellow's narrator is told the story of Fonstein's propitious adventure by his father, an immigrant, who, according to the narrator, "had a passion for refugee stories ... He hoped it would straighten me out to hear what people had suffered in Europe, in the real world" (5). The remainder of Fonstein's lucky life lived in America is devoted to tracking down the man who saved him so that he can thank him for his foresight and presumed altruism. But in these endeavors both Fonstein and his wife, who will take up the request on his behalf, are foiled, for the legendary Billy Rose, the man of the grand gesture, wants no part of such gratitude. For him, the escape mission was one more successful stunt, pulled off "on a spurt of feeling for his fellow Jews and squaring himself to outwit Hitler and Himmler and cheat them of their victims" (13). Billy Rose, no more than a "little Jewish promoter [who] took it into his queer head to organize a Hollywood-style rescue," was responsible for Fonstein's destiny (28). But this is where his "altruism" ends. "Very few of us," the narrator reminds us, "bother about accountability or keep spread sheets of con-science" (50). For Billy Rose, the past is the past; it has lost its currency. As he tells Fonstein's wife, "I don't like things from the past being laid on me. This happened one time, years ago. What's it got to do with now ... If your husband has a nice story, that's his good luck. Let him tell it to people who go for stories. I don't care for them" (58–59). Here Billy Rose's act of conscience is a mere fleeting flight of fancy, a theatrical escapade, a derring-do per-formed in the American way, where "Nothing is real that isn't a show" (65). Billy Rose, Bellow seems to suggest, can afford to be cavalier about his rescue mission in a way that Fonstein, whose life depended on it, cannot. It is this contrast that lies at the heart of *The Bellarosa Connection*.

Billy Rose emerges in this novella as the representative of American entre-preneurial showmanship, but also of American indifference. Like Billy Rose and his smuggling operation, America brought the Jews to Ellis Island and then "washed your hands of [them], never gave a damn about the future of [the] refugee" (*The Bellarosa Connection*, 46). Bellow suggests that such inattention, moments in which compassion and responsibility might simply be in vogue, is, after all, the American way. "There's nothing in this country that you can't sell, nothing too weird to bring to market and found a fortune on," including the lives of the dispossessed, Bellow's narrator insists (25). What is the point, the narrator queries, in brooding on the past, a messy business. As he says,

> First those people murdered you, then they forced you to brood on their crimes.
> It suffocated me to do this. Hunting for causes was a horrible imposition added
> to the original "selection," gassing, cremation. I didn't want to think of the

history and psychology of these abominations, death chambers and furnaces ... Such things are utterly beyond me, a pointless exercise.   (28)

It is revealing to read this passage in light of Bellow's correspondence with Cynthia Ozick, with which we began this chapter. For such "brooding" is what Bellow seems to have been engaged with over the course of these years (*Letters*, 439). In *The Bellarosa Connection*, Bellow turns his critical focus explicitly to America's lack of responsible reckoning, to the ways in which America failed to account for the devastation of European Jewry and its intervention during the war years and its assistance in the years that followed the war, the responsibility it had toward those Jewish refugees seeking new life on its shores. And if Billy Rose, in all his glitz and largess, is the embodiment of American excess and exhibitionism, then the narrator comes to embody the American-born Jew without a sense of history or collective consciousness. Bellow asks us to see his narrator, the spokesperson for the novella, as a metonymy for American sensibilities, the voice of willed innocence, a Jew, in contrast to his European ancestors, who

grew up under a larger range of influences and thoughts ... the children of a great democracy, bred to equality, living it up with no pales to confine us ... Were we giddy here? No doubt about it. But there were no cattle cars waiting to take us to camps and gas chambers ... One can think of such things – and think and *think* – but nothing is resolved by these historical meditations. To *think* doesn't settle anything. No idea is more than an imaginary potency.

(*The Bellarosa Connection*, 24)

Instead, Bellow suggests, one replaces critical evaluation and moral reckoning with historical amnesia; the narrator's advice to Fonstein, "given mentally – was: Forget it. Go American" (29).

In these three novels, we find a shift in the attitudes brought to bear, not on the actual events of the Holocaust, but, rather, on the perspective through which the past is negotiated and the place of that particular past in a changing American cultural consciousness. The three protagonists of Bellow's Holocaust novels come to suggest three different postures of such negotiation: first, there is the anxious and aggrieved Asa Leventhal, an American Jew in the years immediately following the war, an imagined victim; next, there is the survivor Artur Sammler, an experienced and disenchanted observer of the human project, no longer an "ordinary human being," but a "symbol" of public reverence for "the survivor," an identity he disdains (*Mr. Sammler's Planet*, 91); and, finally, Bellow gives us Fonstein, the Jewish refugee from Hitler's tyranny who sees himself as proof of America's righteous intervention in freeing the camps, its grand gesture in rescuing the preyed-upon Jew in a public act of self-appointed

guardianship. In all three narratives, America becomes the site of negotiations and renegotiations, the stage upon which an assessment and
calculation of responsibility is measured. What, Bellow's characters
seem to ask, is the appropriate response to this catastrophe? Wherein
lie our personal and collective responsibilities? How should Americans
see themselves, especially American Jews, in relation to the events of the
Holocaust? Such questions are rooted in American exceptionalism, the
conflicted ideological amalgamation of liberty, egalitarianism, individualism, populism, and capitalism and its accompanying high-minded
repudiation of the xenophobia, chauvinism, fanaticism, and madness of
others. In Bellow's Holocaust novels, the reality of genocide is juxtaposed
with these "defining" cultural values. Thus, Bellow moves in these narratives from the Jew as scrutinized, targeted outsider to embraced,
celebrated sufferer/survivor, to assimilated, reinvented, and largely
ignored shareholder, a product of American capitalist and commercial
entrepreneurialism.

What happens in the years between 1947 and 1989, those intervening
decades in which Bellow wrote *The Victim*, *Mr. Sammler's Planet*, and
The Bellarosa Connection? There exists, to be sure, a shift in political
postures and America's collective thinking about the events having taken
place in Europe in the 1930s and 1940s. Certainly between 1947 and 1989,
some of the darkness and traumatic reverberation felt in the years immediately following the end of the war lifts. And while America in the wake of war
celebrates victory, the effects on American Jews is perhaps more
complicated. The period in American history spanning these decades is
tumultuous: the victory and end of World War II, the too-soon celebrated
triumph of American empire-building, the Civil Rights Movement, the
Vietnam War, the fluctuating economy, the disenchantment with
global expansionism, the vagaries of narcissistic self-interest and self-
indulgence – these all place demands on memory and the value we place on
remembering. Events recede even as they are replaced. And the disposition
and character of memory in the face of self-interest and the myriad possibilities and patterns of self-deception are points of departure throughout
Bellow's literary career, concerns in which he was deeply invested. What
and how we remember, and the place of memory in American culture, are
very much at the center of Bellow's novels. In this regard, it is fundamental to
Bellow's project that America is the epicenter of transformation, of refa-
shioning, of posturing and reconstructions; New York, as Harry Fonstein
discovers, "is a collective fantasy of millions" (*The Bellarosa Connection*,
17). Here all business is, in the capitalist economy, as Billy Rose would have

it, "show biz." And memory too can be commodified; as the narrator of
The Bellarosa Connection tells us, "Memory is my field" (17).

In these three novels, Bellow shifts his focus. *The Victim* is set against the
looming sinister and threatening presence of the Holocaust in the backdrop,
represented by an ominous urban landscape littered with late-industrial
infernos of smokestacks, fiery chimneys, the endless reverberations of trains,
and American anti-Semitism that determines, to a significant degree, the
fraught condition of his central character. With the publication of
Mr. Sammler's Planet, enough time seems to have passed so that the
Holocaust is history and the victim in many ways can be exonerated.
The path is clearer, and thus Bellow can leave New York temporarily and
go back in the memory of the survivor, Artur Sammler, to the devastation of
Europe much more directly, to the mass graves, the death of millions, that
hover uneasily over Asa Leventhal's New York in *The Victim* and to which
Leventhal can only obliquely and hesitantly refer: "millions of us have been
killed. What about that?" (*The Victim*, 131). In *The Bellarosa Connection*,
the events of the Holocaust have receded into the past and thus they can be
reconstructed to contribute to American identity, self-interest, opportunism,
and self-absorption, a defensive adaptation to forgetfulness. Memory, after
all, is messy, calls to account past wounds.

If Sammler is the recipient of Leventhal's fears, a past he fortuitously
averted, then Fonstein is the projection of Sammler into the future of
America. For Harry, like Sammler, is a survivor, a Jew who emerged from
Nazi-terrorized Europe, saved from the gas by the wily Billy Rose, while
others were murdered. If the essential question for Bellow concerns how one
ought to live after the Holocaust, then, as we move from Leventhal's reluc-
tance to acknowledge the Holocaust, to Sammler's meditations on the failure
of the civilized world, to Fonstein's frustrated efforts to be recognized, we are
directed by Bellow to face the implications of the Holocaust head on – no
obfuscations, no self-serving evasions. "The Jews could survive everything that
Europe threw at them," Fonstein's wife poses to the equivocating narrator of
The Bellarosa Connection: "But now comes the next test – America. Can they
hold their ground, or will the USA be too much for them?" (*The Bellarosa
Connection*, 65). Bellow seems to ask: Have we learned anything from the
Holocaust? Have time and circumstance provided any sort of perspective on
the events of history and our own obligations to that particular past? Having
found ourselves, as Sammler puts it, "in the middle of the thing," in the
inescapable knowledge of the events, "[h]ow," Sammler asks, "did [such]
business finish?" (*Sammler*, 274). The answer to Sammler's pressing question
about the nature of obligation, alluded to at the close of the novel with the
reference "to do what was required" in the latter half of the twentieth century,

is taken up again and given purchase in *The Bellarosa Connection* (*Sammler*, 313). The question embedded in *The Victim* is whether it is possible for a Jew to live free of fear in a post-Holocaust world. *Mr. Sammler's Planet* offers a provisional answer by posing the Jew as an icon of surviving the depredations of civilization. Finally, *The Bellarosa Connection* contains Bellow's clear admonition about "what retention of the past really means" in the context of post-Holocaust Jewish life (*The Bellarosa Connection*, 102). At the novella's close, Bellow's narrator comes to discover the failure in his well-taught "New World version of reality," which denies his responsibility, as an American Jew, to history and to the value of memory (88). What the narrator comes to realize is that "You pay a price for being a child of the New World," and that price is a willed amnesia, and "When you think nothing, consciousness is driven out. Consciousness being gone, you are asleep," and this condition of unconsciousness, in Bellow's thinking, is akin to the death of the self, "something essential" (90, 96). Thus, as S. Lillian Kremer argues, Bellow's narrator undergoes, at the novella's close a "metamorphosis from historic amnesiac to advocate for perpetuation of historic memory."[8] Thus, the novella ends with the Jewish prayer to remember those departed, "Yiskor Elohim," a prayer "to remember your dead," but also a prayer for remembrance, for in the absence of memory the dead die again, the past lies buried, and loss is irrevocable (*The Bellarosa Connection*, 102).

Notes

1. Saul Bellow, *Letters*, ed. Benjamin Taylor (New York: Viking, 2010), pp. 438–439.
2. Saul Bellow, *The Victim* (rpt. 1947; New York: Penguin, 1988), p. 164.
3. Saul Bellow, *Mr. Sammler's Planet* (rpt. 1970; New York: Penguin, 1984), pp. 73, 14.
4. Saul Bellow, *The Bellarosa Connection* (New York: Penguin, 1989), pp. 58, 60.
5. Ezra Cappell, "Sorting the Vital from the Useless: Holocaust Memory in Saul Bellow's *The Bellarosa Connection*," *Saul Bellow Journal*, 23.1–2 (Fall 2007/ Winter 2008): 75–76.
6. Gustavo Sánchez Canales, "'The Benevolent Self Was a Disgrace Beyond Measure for Every Argentine Jew': Between the Need to Remember and the Desire to Forget in Nathan Englander's *The Ministry of Special Causes*," *Partial Answers*, 13.1 (2015): 57.
7. Alan L. Berger, "Remembering and Forgetting: The Holocaust and Jewish-American Culture in Saul Bellow's *The Bellarosa Connection*," in *Small Planets: Saul Bellow and the Art of Short Fiction*, eds. Gloria Cronin and Gerhard Bach (East Lansing: Michigan State University Press, 2000), p. 315.
8. S. Lillian Kremer, "Saul Bellow," in *Holocaust Literature: An Encyclopedia of Writers and Their Work*, Volume I, ed. S. Lillian Kremer (New York: Routledge, 2003), p. 130.

6

S. LILLIAN KREMER

Humboldt's Gift and Bellow's Intellectual Protagonists

Throughout his prolific career, Saul Bellow privileged memorable cerebral protagonists, intellectuals and writers searching for deep meaning or transcendent exaltation, who he dramatized in mental combat with each other in *The Dean's December* or in conflict with lesser thinkers in *Dangling Man*, *The Adventures of Augie March*, and *Herzog*. Joseph, angst-filled dangling man, asks existential questions in his quest for personal spiritual freedom. Augie March, part-time book thief, seeks money to attend university yet is incapable of parting with the books he has stolen. Herzog, obsessive letter-writer, intellectual, demystifies suffering and refutes Nietzsche, Spangler, and T. S. Eliot, "the commonplaces of the Wasteland outlook."[1] Sammler, preHolocaust Polish-Jewish Anglophile attached to the Bloomsbury intellectuals, becomes a postHolocaust seeker of enlightenment in the mystical writings of Meister Eckhart. Charlie Citrine, biographer and playwright, and Humboldt Fleisher, poet and master storyteller, in Bellow's Pulitzer Prize winning eighth novel, *Humboldt's Gift*, wrestle with vital questions about the human condition and art. Against the dramatic backdrop of Citrine's growing cultural reputation and Humboldt's decline into poverty and obscurity, leading to his dissipation and wretched death, Citrine memorializes his friend and meditates on the "disjunction between the writer and the public figure of the writer,"[2] on the role and status of the American artist, the demise of the poetic imagination, the struggle between material and spiritual yearning, the meaning of love, death, and immortality.

Biographers concur that Citrine's character registers much of Bellow, and Bellow confirmed that Humboldt is modeled on writers whose work and friendship he valued highly who met untimely deaths: Delmore Schwartz, Isaac Rosenfeld, and John Berryman.[3] Ruth Miller writes "Citrine comes as close to Bellow can to telling the truth about himself," that he "lent his failures to Charlie Citrine," that "the accusations brought against Charlie by his ex-wife, Denise, reads like an overview of Bellow's career," a man of many insights; author respected by scholars and intellectuals, recipient of numerous grants, fellowships, and honors.[4] She reads many of the novel's characters as a "pastiche of recognizable counterparts in reality, as well as characters familiar from Bellow's fiction."[5] In a 1983 article predating the Miller biography by eight years, James Atlas, biographer of Delmore Schwartz and forthcoming Bellow biographer, recognized Schwartz in "eloquent monologues on success and its perils."[6] Among repeated acknowledgments of his relationship with Schwartz, Bellow cites their first meeting in Greenwich Village: "That was where the cultural action was in those days, and Delmore was the man to know."[7] But it was when Bellow and Schwartz were teaching at Princeton that they "really got to be friends."[8] Although Miller attributes "the long and troubled friendship" between Bellow and Schwartz as the primary model for the novel, she notes the Isaac Rosenfeld influence based on the marked discrepancies between Bellow's and Rosenfeld's career recognitions. Similarly, she contends that John Berryman, who had been at Princeton the year Bellow and Schwartz held temporary appointments, was also much on Bellow's mind while writing the novel. That the connection to Schwartz was explicit in early drafts of the novel appears in Bellow's 1966 statement "'My friend the poet Delmore Schwartz died last week in New York, presumably of heart failure, in a derelict's hotel in the Broadway area,'" and in his letter to Richard Stern a few months later, describing "'a memoir of D. Schwartz which metamorphosed into the 'D.S. novel.'"[9] Atlas chronicles the relationships of Bellow and Schwartz as well as that of Bellow and Isaac Rosenfeld as models for *Humboldt's Gift*'s delineation of literary success, rivalry, and guilt. Schwartz's flamboyant self-destruction, concluding with his tragic death, served Bellow, Atlas contends, "as a convenient vehicle for [his] high-flown meditations on art and success in America."[10]

Among Bellow's numerous references to literary friendships and associates are recollections of heady 1950s days at Princeton and in New York, of brilliant conversation among intellectual heavyweights and artists: Edmund Wilson, Ralph Ellison, Delmore Schwartz, John Berryman, Sidney Hook, Princeton, and *Partisan Review* people.[11] The novel conveys the intellectual and artistic excitement of New York as a place of passionate interest in literature, politics, and ideas, a place where Humboldt could devote himself to "his mind, and his spirit, and his sense of the importance of art and ideas."[12] Here Humboldt and Charlie "listened to the finest talkers" and "Humboldt was one of the best of them all.... the Mozart of conversation."[13] Charlie thrills to Humboldt's mentorship and lectures on Modernism, Symbolism, Yeats, Rilke, and Eliot, to Humboldt's view of "what it meant to knock the Village flat with your poems and then follow up with critical essays in the *Partisan* and the *Southern Review*" (12).

Reflecting the author's anxieties, the novel's exhilarating Greenwich Village and Princeton literary life contrasts with antisemitic hostility in the academy and the publishing industry. In a 1965 *Paris Review* interview, Bellow expressed concerns about the literary establishment's perceptions of Jewish writers as threatening foreigners, incapable of the proper feeling for English, and again during a 1988 talk, a portion of which appeared in "The Jewish Writer in America," published in 2011/2012. The problem for Bellow was "how to combine being a Jew with being an American and a writer,"[14] the dual pressures of presenting his credentials to hostile representatives of the Protestant majority while anticipating Jews assessing whether his work is too Jewish or not Jewish enough. The fictional Princeton scene provides the backdrop for fear experienced by Jewish American contemporary writers. Citrine, descended from Russian Jews, and Humboldt, descended from Hungarian-Jewish immigrants, jocularly described by his friend and protégé as "Orpheus, the son of Greenhorn" (119), anticipate a response by literary authorities who regard their Jewish perspective as alien. Acknowledging that Jewish writers are perceived as interlopers on the American cultural scene, Charlie worries that Humboldt's "syntax would be unacceptable to fastidious goy critics on guard for the Protestant establishment and the Genteel Tradition.... it expected Anti-Christ to burst out of the slums" (10–11).

The essayist's tone is somber, defiant, even mournful, as he charts early to mid-century enmity designating the Jew as "outsider" or "resident alien."[15] In contrast, the novelist adopts a satiric tone. During a brief teaching stint similar to one Bellow and Delmore Schwartz shared in 1952, Humboldt understands that his position as poet-in-residence can be countenanced only on a temporary basis. Confident that a Jew, no matter how competent, will be no threat, Professor Sewell has arranged for Humboldt to substitute for him while he is on leave to lecture on *The Spoils of Poynton* in Damascus, much as Sewell's model, R. P. Blackmur, recommended Schwartz to cover the creative writing program while he lectured in the Middle East, and Schwartz arranged a position for Bellow.[16] Humboldt, crudely but astutely, counsels Citrine about their precarious Princeton positions: "We're Jews, shonikers, kikes ... Try thinking of yourself as Sheeny Solomon Levi ... In Princeton you and I are Moe and Joe, a Yid vaudeville act.... Unthinkable as members of the Princeton community" (124). Reminiscent of Bellow – who consciously defied critical cultural guardians Henry Adams, Henry James, T. S. Eliot, and Ezra Pound by asserting "If the WASP aristocrats wanted to think of me as a Jewish poacher on their precious cultural estates then let them,"[17] and creating a much celebrated body of writing – Humboldt pursues his campaign against cultural anti-Semitism by staging a delightful mock battle of the books. He ceremoniously deposes Sewell's Toynbee collection and installs volumes by Rilke and Kafka, displacing an historian of pronounced supersessionist Christian bias with an apostate poet who rejected his early Christian upbringing, repudiating Christian other-worldliness and asceticism in *Visions of Christ*, and Kafka, a Jewish novelist who rejected his father's assimilation and embarked upon a period of Hebraic study and Yiddish theater attendance, eventually strengthening his connections with Jewish culture and introducing Jewish matter into his writing. Humboldt's dispatch of Toynbee echoes the pain Bellow felt as a high school student reading Oswald Spengler's *The Decline of the West*, with its depiction of Jews as "fossils, spiritually archaic" thereby, Bellow thought at the time, disqualifying him by heredity.[18] He suffered similar discomfort in college, as he explains in "Distractions of a Fiction Writer," when he "brooded over Spengler: "As a Jew, I was in his vocabulary, a magian and therefore obsolete." As Zachary Leader (Bellow's most recent biographer) notes, Bellow connects Spengler's theory of Jewish obsolescence with Toynbee's pronouncement that the Jew is "a sort of fossil."[19]

Prompted by guilt for his neglect of Humboldt during his severe physical and psychological decline, Citrine meditates on the disjunction between the artist and society and situates culpability in each entity. According to Peter Hyland, "The idea of the writer embraced both by Humboldt and by Citrine is essentially a romantic one: the poet is dedicated to the pursuit of beauty and spiritual ideals, to some sort of higher truth, which he has to communicate to the world at large."[20] As he analyzes Humboldt's ephemeral success and protracted decline, Citrine conjures a picture of the romantic artist weighed down and finally crushed by a culture that no longer values the poet's vision or "passionate speech" (232). Humboldt succumbs to manic-depressive paranoia, drug and alcohol addiction, badly abusing his friends' generosity, acting out the stereotypical behaviors of the romantic artist – "alienation, poverty, turbulent mental activity"[21] – until his untimely heart attack and death. Commenting on his characters, Bellow explains that Citrine is critical of Humboldt taking the conventional pattern of "the doomed poet, he's doing what the middle class expects him to do."[22]

Although Citrine castigates American society for its complicity in the destructive process, for its "satisfaction in the poets' testimony that the USA is too tough, too big, too much, too rugged, that American reality is overpowering" (118), his major focus is on the wounded poet. Artists and intellectuals suffer in a soulless, materialistic, technocratic society having no use for intellect, art, and the imagination. In Citrine's judgment "Humboldt did what poets in crass America are supposed to do. . . . He blew his talent and his health and reached home, the grave, in a dusty slide" (117). As he

reads Humboldt's obituary in the *New York Times* and continues to mourn
his loss, Citrine locates Humboldt's fall in the self-destructive pattern of
"Edgar Allan Poe ... Hart Crane ... Jarrell ... And poor John Berryman"
(118).[23] Further, Citrine attributes Humboldt's decline to his detour from
devotion to writing. "Instead of being a poet," Citrine says, "he was merely
the figure of a poet. He was enacting 'The Agony of the American Artist'"
(156). Obsessed with the materialistic American definition of success,
Humboldt rationalized "What kind of American would I be if I were
innocent about money ... With a million bucks, I'll be free to think of
nothing but poetry" (159). Charlie's critique of intrusive societal obstacles
to the poet's imagination and his assessment of Humboldt's decline is
founded on behavior borrowed from literary models as well as by
Wordsworth's enduring influence on Bellow's thinking about the poet
and the poetic imagination. Bellow considers it likely that "The World
Is Too Much With Us" "may have been my introduction to the subject of
distraction, for Wordsworth's warning not to lay waste our powers by
getting and spending was not lost on me. ... Nor did I miss ... his emphasis
on the supreme importance of a state of attention or aesthetic concentration
that would put the world of profit and loss in its place."[24] Asked about the
critical differences between Humboldt and Citrine, Bellow opines,
"Humboldt accepts the principles of modernism. ... Charlie does not,
and Charlie is making an end run, a comic end run ... He's circumventing,
he's getting around a lot of things of which he disapproves. He thinks that
modernism has become a mass of worn-out ideas, and he rejects them. He
thinks of Humboldt as their victim."[25]

Beyond falling victim to the desire for fame and the torment of literary
rivalry, Charlie understands Humboldt's decline occurred because "He con-
sented to the monopoly of power and interest held by money, politics, law,
rationality, technology" (155). That worldly distractions could impede the
writer's imagination was much on Bellow's mind, appearing also in "Starting
Out in Chicago," published the same year as *Humboldt's Gift*, "Distractions
of a Fiction Writer," "Machines and Storybooks: Literature in the Age of
Technology," and "A World Too Much with Us." The 1975 essay clearly
identifies the distractions, the obstructive "Great Noise" that interferes with
the requisite contemplation the writer requires:

> By noise I mean not simply the noise of technology, the noise of money or
> advertising and promotion, the noise of the media, the noise of miseducation,
> but the terrible excitement and distraction generated by the crises of modern
> life. ... the sounds of the public sphere, the din of politics, the turbulence and
> agitation that set in about 1914 and have now reached an intolerable volume.[26]

Humboldt's transformation from "avant-garde writer, the first of a new generation, " (1), praised by T. S. Eliot, Conrad Aiken, and Yvor Winters (11), to impoverished neglected poet is the catalyst for Citrine's self-scrutiny. When Charlie sees Humboldt in New York, and recognizes his wasted physical health, notes that his poems are absent from recent anthologies and that interest in his work seems limited to graduate students looking for a dissertation topic, he fears for his own downfall, understanding that his failures resemble those of his friend. Rudolf Steiner enters Citrine's thinking at a time when the popular biographer and successful playwright has reached an impasse in his life and career, when he is on the verge of decline. Charlie is divorced and believes his ex-wife is trying to ruin him financially. His mistress is pressuring him to marry her and then betrays him when she concludes he is no longer a good financial prospect. His work is suffering, and he dreads the finality of death. In the course of exploring his angst motivated by Humboldt's demise, Charlie is forced to confront his mortality in a manner reflecting Bellow's interest in Steiner's anthroposophy.

Although we must acknowledge that Citrine is not Bellow, Bellow's study of Rudolf Steiner's anthroposophy enters the novel as a major consideration for Charlie's spiritual health. Psychotherapist Greg Bellow attributes his father's multiyear study and practice of Steiner's meditative techniques on "the possibility of an expanded consciousness that continued after physical death [to his] lifelong preoccupation with death."[27] He contends that as his father's interest in Steiner "deepened, the phrase *inner life* came to be replaced by the *human soul* [italics added] ... and he infused the term with a spiritual component that convinced me he had come to believe in the soul's immortality."[28] In the essay "A World Too Much with Us," published the same year as *Humboldt's Gift*, Bellow uses the word *soul* for the immortal spirit in man, referring to "something we all hesitate to mention though we all know it intimately – the soul."[29] And Citrine insists that despite the prevailing scientific view, most people are aware that the soul exists: "The existence of a soul is beyond proof under the ruling premises, but people go on behaving as though they had souls, nevertheless" (479).

According to James Atlas, Bellow's "Introduction" for Steiner's lecture collection *The Boundaries of Natural Science*, was sympathetic to Steiner's effort to bridge the gulf that "existed between the private, inward-dwelling experience of human consciousness and the primacy of science in the modern world, Steiner's ambition ... to transcend the limit of empirical human knowledge and attain another, higher form of con-sciousness, a higher 'spiritual reality.'"[30] Ellen Pifer interprets Citrine's study of Steiner as an element of "Citrine's internal dilemma ... between the mind's knowledge and the soul's understanding."[31] Citrine thinks that philosophical treatises, political ideologies, and scientific theories no longer provide viable answers to the growing spiritual concerns of contemporary man. His growing interest in Steiner's spiritual philosophy is evident in his belief "that man must recover his imaginative powers, cultivate "living thought and real being" and reject "insults to the soul" (250). He is attuned to the idea that "The old philosophy distinguished between knowledge achieved by effort (*ratio*) and knowledge received (*intellectus*) by the listening soul that can hear the essence of things" (306). He consults with Dr. Scheldt, who functions as the voice of Steiner, discussing matters ranging from the "Consciousness Soul" to an exploration of transmigration and reincarnation, the primary reality of the soul, and the essential unity of subject and object, inner and outer reality in *The Philosophy of Spiritual Activity*.[32] Citrine asks, "Let me see if I understand these things at all – thought in my head is also thought in the external world. Consciousness in the self creates a false distinction between object and subject. Am I getting it right?" Dr. Scheldt answers, "Yes, I think so, sir" (261–262). After his conversation with Scheldt, Charlie becomes less materialistic, undertakes meditative exercises to achieve a higher level of consciousness, and writes articles on anthroposophy. He introduces a journalist friend, Pierre Thaxter, to Steiner's work, contemplates a pilgrimage to the Swiss Steiner center at Dornach, and tries to communicate with the dead Humboldt.

Citrine's reflections on his artistic purpose, his efforts to live a life of the spirit, his belief in the soul, and his testimonial of the value to him of Steiner's principles of anthroposophy parallel Bellow's study of Steinerian thought. Citrine is fascinated with Steiner's doctrine of transcendence and the immortality of the soul, yet remains aloof from its theosophical components. Under Steiner's influence Citrine realizes he "seldom thought of death in the horrendous old way. I wasn't experiencing the suffocating grave or dreading an eternity of boredom" (220–221). He now ponders "reincarnation of the soul"[33] and reasons that since he does "not believe [his] birth began [his] first existence.... therefore, [he is] obliged to deny that so extraordinary a thing as a human soul can be wiped out forever. No, the dead are about us, shut out by our metaphysical denial of them" (141). He wants to believe in an alternative to the finality of death, insisting on "the soul's journey past the gates of death" (176). Not unlike Bellow, who praised Steiner as a man of "great vision... a powerful poet as well as philosopher and scientist," yet resisted identifying himself as "a Steinerian,"[34] Citrine, "As an intellectual suspicious of the occult ... mocks himself for swallowing [Steiner's philosophy] ... [although] it seems to quench his spiritual thirst."[35] Although Citrine does not embrace the totality of Steiner's teachings, he

74

adopts a philosophical view that becomes less skeptical and more affirmative.

Throughout the Bellow oeuvre there are recurring character relationships and interactions between thoughtful protagonists searching for a meaningful life despite the spiritual barrenness of society who are tutored by "reality instructors." Through aggressive humorous antics, the "reality instructor" – frequently an ambiguous character such as the sinner–saint Tamkin in *Seize the Day*, Einhorn and Robey of *The Adventures of Augie March*, and Valentine Gersbach in *Herzog* – helps his charge examine his life and transform his beliefs. Much comedy in *Humboldt's Gift* springs from Citrine's exposure to his "reality instructor," Rinaldo Cantabile, the clownish scion of an underworld family celebrated for its ineptitude. Cantabile functions as a parallel to Humboldt, forcing Citrine "to undergo symbolic shock treatments that make him realize the truth about himself."[36] In comic hyperbole Cantabile punishes and humiliates Charlie for defaulting on his gambling debts but serves him, as a literary subject and more importantly, "as a catalyst for certain fundamental revelations."[37] Charlie perceives that Cantabile "seemed to have a spiritual office to perform. He had appeared in order to move me from dead center" (287–288). Although the Cantabile passages border on comic hyperbole, Charlie's ironic assessment of his day with Cantabile as "a whole day of atonement" (103) registers significantly as a ritualistic prelude to his spiritual restoration.

The mentor–protégé pattern gains heightened significance in this novel with Humboldt's role as the "imagination-instructor" whose posthumously delivered letter and manuscript warn Citrine of the hazards of success and the loss of imaginative vision, urging him to reinvigorate and honor his creative powers. As Mark Weinstein contends, "the role of the imagination-instructor is "to awaken the protagonist, to break the spirit's sleep, to make him see. He speaks of things that matter, addressing the heart's deepest needs. He asserts the nobility of the individual, the possibility of change."[38] Charlie remains skeptical of Humboldt, who "wanted to drape the world in radiance, but ... didn't have enough material" (107), overwhelmed by American reality and inclined to desert his art for fame and other trappings of success, yet he is attracted to the poet's imaginative vision. Attracted to the idea that "there's something in human beings beyond the body and brain and that we have ways of knowing that go beyond the organism and its senses" (227–228), Citrine "wants to understand why the divine imagination of man has become deadened"[39] He speaks of "the concealed divinity of other human beings ... [able] to cross by means of thought the abyss that separates him from Spirit" (294). To achieve such imaginative freedom one "cancels the world's distraction, activity, noise, and become[s] fit to hear the essence of things" (312). Charlie recognizes that "Mankind must recover its imaginative powers, recover living thought and real being" (250). Thus, he is elated by Humboldt's posthumous confirmation, especially his quotation from Blake, "This World Is a World of Imagination and Vision," and Humboldt's own loving reminder, "we are not natural beings but super-natural beings" (347). Charlie is now certain that he "had business on behalf of the entire human race" (396). Thus, the poet who inspired the young idealistic Charlie by showing him what modern literature could be influences him spiritually by demonstrating with his posthumous gift "that the dead are alive in us if we choose to keep them alive" (311).

Although textual emphasis is on Steinerian anthroposophy, the voices of English romantic poets and American transcendentalists intermittently reverberate through the novel to chart the protagonist's spiritual quest. He is moved by Keats' cautionary commentary explaining "how a luxurious imagination deadens its delicacy in vulgarity and in things attainable" (341). He is elated by Humboldt's posthumous quotation from Blake, and his own memory of Wordsworth's "Ode: Intimations of Immortality from Recollections of Early Childhood," which further enhances his spiritual regeneration in its reassuring possibility of immortality and the restorative power of the imagination.[40] The development of the higher consciousness Citrine seeks is initiated with the Wordsworthian recognition that he must "perceive the world with a child's sense of awe and enchantment as well as with the inner light that illuminates a dark world."[41]

Citrine's interest in American Transcendental writers predates (and may even prepare the way for) his receptiveness to Steinerian thought. Like Emerson, Citrine realizes that "the essential self is spirit, but a spirit organically related to the external world, Emerson's 'other me' and to the life force animating it."[42] Similarly, Citrine is Emersonian in his explanation of nature's emblematic function, claiming he "had the strange hunch that nature itself was not *out there*, an object world externally separated from subjects, but that everything external corresponded vividly with something internal, that the two realms were identical and interchangeable, and that nature was my own unconscious being.... Each thing in nature was an emblem for something in my own soul" (356–357). Similarly, he describes the nature of selfhood in Emersonian terms: "I had decided to listen to the voice of my own mind speaking from within, from my own depths, and this voice said that there was my body, in nature, and that there was also me. I was related to nature through my body, but all of me was not contained in it" (186).[43] Emersonian transcendental concepts and images, as transmitted by Whitman, appear sporadically but significantly in the celebration of non-conformity, support of the poetic imagination, and recognition of the need of action to evolve from thought. Charlie's realization and commitment to an awakening of the self evoke Whitman's description of his progression as "simmering, simmering, simmering; Emerson brought me to a boil." Charlie echoes Whitman's diction *to* acknowledge his evolution toward a higher consciousness: "Now I was only simmering still, and it would be necessary at last to come to a full boil. I had ... responsibility not only to fulfill my own destiny but to carry on for certain failed friends like Von Humboldt Fleisher who had never been able to struggle through into higher wakefulness" (396).

Citrine's response to Humboldt's gift provides a powerful illustration of affirmation of life through development of the moral imagination, a recurrent Bellovian theme. The novel not only parallels closely Bellow's literary friendships, but also reflects Bellow's admissions of failings toward friends, his confession of avoiding Delmore Schwartz shortly before his death and shortcomings in his relationship with Isaac Rosenfeld. In the forward to a posthumous collection of Rosenfeld's essays, Bellow acknowledges "I love [Isaac] but we were rivals, and I was peculiarly touchy, vulnerable, hard to deal with – at times, as I can see now, insufferable, and not always a constant friend."[44] Humboldt's gift, according to Sarah Blacher Cohen, absolves Citrine of his guilt "so that he no longer has to berate himself for injuring or neglecting the dying. Citrine can now transform his destructive self-blame into a constructive concern for others. ... Like Bellow's other keepers of the covenant, Citrine meets his obligations."[45] Charlie, whose Hebrew name (Chaim) means life and whose last name suggests the citron, a life giving fruit used in Jewish religious ceremonies,[46] tries to retrieve the body of his lover killed in a South-American plane crash; helps his brother cope with pre-surgery anxiety; moves a friend from an old-age home into a comfortable apartment; and, most significantly, disinters Humboldt and his mother to rebury them in ample graves in an appropriate cemetery. Another of Bellow's "higher thought clowns" (391), he finally resolves to be an autonomous individual who listens to the voice of his own soul, vowing to "listen in secret to the sound of the truth that God puts into us" (477).

Like Bellow's earlier protagonists, Citrine is "altered but not transformed."[47] Although he is impressed by Steiner's philosophy of "the immanence of spirit and thought in the material world and the active participation, by means of thinking, of the individual in so-called objective or 'external' reality"[48] he regards himself as "a beginner in theosophical kindergarten" (356), retains a measure of skepticism from his rational and scientific training, and recognizes that he is not a completely believing Steinerian. The novel concludes not with a pilgrimage to Dornach, but suggestively, as many of Bellow's novels do, with Humboldt's reburial at Valhalla Cemetery and a symbolic statement of hope and renewal in the emergence of a spring crocus adjacent to

Humboldt's grave and echo of American Transcendental thought. Having engaged "The main question, as Walt Whitman had pointed out ... the death question," (332) Citrine's concluding vision reiterates Bellow's characteristically affirmative view of human possibility evoking the optimistic vision of "Song of Myself": "The smallest sprout shows there is really no death." Death's finality is offset by an image of the regenerative capacity of spring, of the continual cycle of life and Citrine's declaration that he plans "to take up a different kind of life" (482–483). Charlie Citrine thus joins the pantheon of Bellow's protagonists who have struggled and found their metaphysical place. Augie rejects Machiavellian powers and announces his belief, derived from Emerson, Whitman, and Wordsworth, in "a feeling about the axial lines of life, with respect to which you must be straight or else your existence is merely clownery, hiding tragedy."[49] Tommy Wilhelm, in *Seize the Day*, expresses his faith in human brotherhood. Herzog rejects Hobbes, Locke, Bacon, Heidegger, and the German existentialists and opts for Blake's vision of love and brotherhood. And Arthur Sammler seeks solace in the Bible and religious writers, especially Meister Eckhart, and prays for his deceased benefactor who did "what was required of him ... aware that he must meet, and he did meet ... the terms of his contract. The terms that, in his inmost heart, each man knows."[50]

Notes

1. Saul Bellow, *Herzog* (New York: Viking, 1964), p. 75.
2. Peter Hyland, *Saul Bellow* (New York: St. Martin's Press, 1992), p. 79.
3. See Ruth Miller, *Saul Bellow: A Biography of the Imagination* (New York: St. Martin's Press, 1991), p. 204, and James Atlas, *Bellow: A Biography* (New York: Random House, 2000), pp. 430–431.
4. Miller, *Saul Bellow*, p. 203.
5. Ibid., p. 204.
6. James Atlas, "Unsentimental Education," *The Atlantic Monthly* (June 1983): 82.
7. Ibid., p. 83.
8. Ibid.
9. Atlas, *Bellow: A Biography*, p. 430.
10. Ibid., p. 429.
11. Saul Bellow, Interview "A Second Half Life: An Autobiography in Ideas," *Bostonia* (January–February, 1991), Part Two, p. 47.
12. Saul Bellow, Interview with Melvyn Bragg, "'Off the Couch by Christmas' Saul Bellow on His New Novel," *The Listener* (November 20, 1975), p. 675.
13. Saul Bellow, *Humboldt's Gift* (New York: Viking Press, 1975), p. 13. Further citations from this book are placed in parentheses in the text.
14. Saul Bellow, "A Jewish Writer in America," *The New York Review of Books* LVIII.16 (October 27, 2011): 26.
15. Ibid.

16. Miller, *Saul Bellow*, p. 204 and Zachary Leader, *The Life of Saul Bellow: To Fame and Fortune, 1915–1964* (New York: Alfred A. Knopf, 2015), p. 403.

17. Bellow, *The New York Review of Books*, p. 26.

18. Ibid.

19. Leader, *The Life of Saul Bellow*, p. 533 quoting from "Distractions of a Fiction Writer," p. 19.

20. Hyland, *Saul Bellow*, p. 83.

21. Alvin Kernan, "*Humboldt's Gift*," *Saul Bellow*, ed. Harold Bloom (New York: Chelsea House, 1988), p. 182.

22. Bellow, *The Listener*, p. 675.

23. See Bellow's views on the subject of the poet's self-destruction and the societal view that it is incumbent upon the poet to be a martyr in "Literature and Culture: An Interview with Saul Bellow," *Salmagundi*, 30 (1975): 20.

24. Saul Bellow, "The Distracted Public," originally delivered as the Romanes Lecture, Oxford University, May 10, 1990, reprinted in *Saul Bellow, It All Adds Up: From the Dim Past to the Uncertain Future* (New York: Viking Press, 1994), p. 153.

25. Bellow, *The Listener*, p. 675.

26. Saul Bellow, "Prologue: Starting Out in Chicago," in Bellow, *There Is Simply Too Much to Think About: Collected Non-fiction*, ed. Benjamin Taylor (New York: Viking, 2015), p. 7.

27. Greg Bellow, *Saul Bellow's Heart: A Son's Memoir* (New York: Bloomsbury, 2013), p. 145.

28. Ibid., p. 146.

29. Saul Bellow, "A World Too Much with Us," *Critical Inquiry*, 2.1 (Autumn 1975): 8.

30. Atlas, *Bellow A Biography*, p. 436.

31. Ellen Pifer, *Saul Bellow Against the Grain* (Philadelphia: University of Pennsylvania Press, 1990), p. 135.

32. For a thorough discussion of the Steinerian principles paralleled in *Humboldt's Gift*, see Herbert J. Smith, "*Humboldt's Gift* and Rudolf Steiner," *Centennial Review*, 22:4 (Fall 1978): 479–489.

33. Ibid., p. 482.

34. Saul Bellow, Interview with Joseph Epstein, "A Talk with Saul Bellow," *New York Times Book Review* (December 5, 1976): 93.

35. Sarah Blacher Cohen, "Comedy and Guilt in *Humboldt's Gift*," *Modern Fiction Studies*, 25.1 (Spring 1979): 53.

36. For analysis of the Humboldt/Cantabile parallels see Eusebio L. Rodriques, "Beyond All Philosophies: The Dynamic Vision of Saul Bellow," *Studies in the Literary Imagination* XVII.2 (Fall 1984): 108–109.

37. Pifer, *Saul Bellow: Against the Grain*, p. 132.

38. Mark Weinstein, "Bellow's Imagination-Instructors," *Saul Bellow Journal*, 2.1 (Fall/Winter 1982): 21.

39. Mark Weinstein, "Charles Citrine: Bellow's Holy Fool," *Saul Bellow Journal*, 3.1(Fall/Winter 1983): 33.

40. Allan Chavkin, "Bellow and English Romanticism," *Studies in the Literary Imagination*, XVII.2 (Fall 1984): 15.

41. Ibid., p. 17.

42. M. Gilbert Porter, "Is the Going Up Worth the Coming Down? Transcendental Dualism in Bellow's Fiction," *Studies in the Literary Imagination*, XVII.2(Fall 1984): 32.

43. For a full discussion of parallels to American transcendentalist thought in *Humboldt's Gift*, see Sanford E. Marovitz, "The Emersonian Lesson of *Humboldt's Gift*," *Saul Bellow Journal*, 14.1 (Winter 1996): 84–95.

44. Saul Bellow, "Forward" to *Isaac Rosenfeld, An Age of Enormity*, ed. Theodore Solotaroff (Cleveland: World Publishing 1962), p. 12.

45. Cohen, "Comedy and Guilt," p. 55.

46. Ben Siegel, "Artists and Opportunists in Saul Bellow's *Humboldt's Gift*," *Contemporary Literature*, 19.2 (Spring 1978): 151.

47. Smith, "*Humboldt's Gift* and Rudolf Steiner," p. 488.

48. Pifer, *Saul Bellow Against the Grain*, p. 137.

49. Saul Bellow, *The Adventures of Augie March* (New York: Fawcett Publications 1953), p. 472.

50. Saul Bellow, *Mr. Sammler's Planet* (London: Penguin Books, 1970), p. 313.

7

ALAN L. BERGER

On Being a Jewish Writer: Bellow's Post-War America and the American Jewish Diaspora

The characters in Saul Bellow's novels all seem to be saying, with a mixture of horror and fascination: "What's the world coming to?" Familiar landmarks are missing in Bellow's works, but his books make clear how important those landmarks are to us, how they help to keep us human.[1]

Although Saul Bellow early in his career expressed disdain for the label "Jewish Writer," it is well known that he subsequently came to embrace this designation. This move parallels Bellow's transition from what his oldest son Gregory terms the "young Saul" to the "old Saul." The writer David Mikies helpfully observes that the Nobel Laureate was one "for whom Jewishness was simply a fact of life, not an identity."[2] Bellow himself addresses the "identity problem" in a manner that simultaneously reveals his immigrant perspective and the modern fascination with identity politics. The identity issue, he opines, "has vexed and plagued the modern intellect, sponsored by highly influential existentialist, deconstructionist, and nihilist designers."[3] In order to comprehend Bellow's critique of post-War America, it is necessary to briefly review three key concepts: changes in the Jewish situation in modernity; the existential meaning of living in diaspora; and the meaning of culture in America. Although theoretically separable, these three phenomena frequently merge and become three dimensions of the same issue. Bellow viewed the world though a Jewish lens. He was a Jew, a child of Jewish immigrants who spoke Russian to each other: "We children," he notes,

spoke Yiddish with our parents and English with each other. At age four we began to read the Old Testament in Hebrew. We observed Jewish customs ... we recited prayers and blessings all day long. Because I had to memorize most of *Genesis*, my first consciousness was that of a cosmos, and in that cosmos I was a Jew ... To turn away from those origins ... has always seemed to me an utter impossibility. It would be a treason to my first consciousness to un-Jew myself.[4]

This discussion focuses first on what may broadly be termed the Jewish Question and is divided into three parts: Bellow's Jewish identity – what it was and what it was not; the issue of what it means to mentally live in diaspora – an attitude that colors one's perception of his or her surroundings and of human interaction; and Bellow's understanding – and indictment – of American culture, noting the distinction between celebrity and culture. I then address Bellow's transition from the Young Saul to the Old Saul,[5] noting the momentous upheavals in American culture accompanying this transition: culture wars, student protests, dissent over Vietnam, and the political correctness movement, as portrayed in selected novels, short stories, interviews, and letters. The chapter then briefly analyzes Bellow's self-castigation for not having written sufficiently about the Holocaust. Underlining all of this is Bellow's transition from a liberal to a conservative perspective on his craft and on America at large. This chapter concludes with an assessment of Bellow's contribution to Jewish storytelling in America.

The Jewish Question

1. Bellow's Jewish Identity

Bellow distinguishes between Jewish identity and the currently fashionable politics of identity. Responding to a query by Nina Steers on why he decided to become a writer, he attests:

> I was born into a medieval ghetto in French Canada (Lachine, Quebec). My childhood was in ancient times which was true of all orthodox Jews. Every child was immersed in the Old Testament as soon as he could understand anything, so that you began life by knowing Genesis in Hebrew by heart at the age of four. You never got to distinguish between that and the outer world. Later on there were translations: I grew up with four languages, English, Hebrew, Yiddish and French ... It was a verbal environment. Writing was really just a continuation of something I had always done.[6]

Bellow did, however, believe that being described as a "Jewish Writer" was tantamount to being "shunted to a siding." "This taxonomy business," he continued, "I saw as an exclusionary device."[7] Moreover, he was ill-disposed to do "public relations work" for the Jewish community. Bellow's concern was, rather, with his art. He viewed the nurture of the human soul, modernity's corruption of high culture, and the loss of transcendence, which has been "kicked out of modern literature on all sorts of grounds," as primary themes.[8]

As previously noted, Bellow was quintessentially a Jew. In contrast to Morris, his assimilationist older brother, the novelist – who was already in his forties when his father died – wept at the funeral. Morris, said to him "Don't carry on like an immigrant." He had business friends there and was ashamed of such open emotionalism.[9] Furthermore, Bellow felt keenly that Judaism offered a set of values which were in stark contrast to the hedonism of contemporary culture. Mr. Sammler, reflecting on the sexually licentious Angela Gruner, "[d]oubted the fitness of these Jews for this erotic Roman voodoo primitivism. He questioned whether release from long Jewish mental discipline, hereditary training in lawful control, was obtainable upon individual application."[10] Bellow frequently employed biblical allusions, Hebrew language, and rabbinic wisdom to critique both misguided contemporary Jews and the American Jewish diaspora, which he found very far from being "a kingdom of priests and a holy nation" (Ex. 19:6). Loss of ancestral memory in many of Bellow's works leads inevitably to loss of Jewish identity, which is rooted in emotion.

Although not religious in the formal sense of the word, Bellow utilizes the trope of religion in advocating for a sense of transcendence and the faith of the soul in modernity where it plays little or no role. One critic goes so far as to say that Bellow and Isaac Bashevis Singer are the only American writers who address the problem of the modern soul.[11] In a 2002 interview, Bellow observed that "there has been much talk about God, about religion, about spirituality, about the soul. In the last century these ideas seemed destined to disappear. Do you recall everyone saying 'God is Dead'? Well, the only thing that is dead is those ideas."[12] The issue, like most things connected with religion, is complex. Moses Herzog exclaims that "History is the history of cruelty, not love, as soft men think … If the old God exists he must be a murderer."[13] Responding to this observation, Bellow continues, "Herzog reflects on mankind's constant abominations, but that never interrupts his own relations with God."[14] Concerning his relationship to the deity, Bellow notes: "I consider prayer above all an act of gratitude for existence." Personally, he concludes, "I see prayer as an intimate checkup with the headquarters of the universe."[15]

The Enlightenment ushered in vast changes in Jewish identity, yielding what the historian Harriet Murav terms the type of Jew who wishes to be both Jewish and non-Jewish and, consequently, has the "personality structure of the impostor."[16] The "previously unrecognized modern Jewish type: the impostor, chameleon, the man (typically) who has no fixed identity and lives, as one of the type put it, 'without a label.'"[17] The author Marc Cohen views Bellow's Dr. Tamkin (*Seize the Day*) and Valentine Gersbach (*Herzog*) as representative of this new type of Jew. Their "impostor personalities," writes Cohen, "drive them to take on the coloring of their surroundings and this signals their difference and arouses suspicion. Normative Jews in these two novels distrust Tamkin and Gersbach." Bellow sees Tamkin and Gersbach as possessing a "pretender soul."[18] In other words, they are the antithesis of the Jewishness with which Bellow was infused as a youth. They scheme, betray, and lie while merely putting on a Jewish mask, so to speak. Of the many illustrations of the falling away from Jewishness one could cite in the Bellow oeuvre, the example of Professor Shapiro in *Herzog* comes to mind. Shapiro was a linguist and a learned man. Unimpressed, Herzog remembers Shapiro's penniless father who "peddled rotten apples ... in a wagon. There was more of the truth of life in those spotted, spoiled apples, and in old Shapiro, who smelled of the horse and of produce, than in all of [his son's] learned references" (70).

2. *Existentially Living in Diaspora*

Exile and return are two basic motifs of Jewish history. The challenge of living in diaspora is articulated by the Psalmist who enquires on behalf of the exiles in Babylon, "How Shall we sing the Lord's song in a Foreign Land?" (Ps. 137.4). In a fundamental way, many of Bellow's works offer at least a partial response to this ancient query, not so much on a national as on an individual level. This is not to suggest that his protagonists achieve this goal, but their efforts reveal the growing estrangement between diaspora culture and the normative Jewish tradition. Moreover, this observation excludes certain Bellow protagonists who are either not Jewish-Henderson or whose ethnic identity is ambivalent-Dean Albert Corde. Interviewed by Norman Manea, Bellow articulates his special understanding of the impact of living in diaspora. Asked to respond to Philip Roth's furious contention that he (Roth) was not in diaspora, but rather lived in his "country and I'm here and free and I can be whatever I want to be,"[19] Bellow observed:

> I'm older than Philip and my parents were older than Philip's parents and they were Europeans through and through. They came here in 1913 as grown, mature people and for them the problem could not be disposed of so easily. I grew up under this influence myself. Philip, I think, did not. So he did have that alternative of being an American. I had it too, but in my case it would need to have been announced with a certain bravado because the alternatives are altogether too clear for me. They're not so clear for Philip and the simple reason is that he grew up as a different Jew in a different America.[20]

Bellow's statement underscores the impact of the reality of the notions of exile and diaspora on Jewish European families who – unlike their American counterparts – bore the brunt of Jewish history on their bodies and in their souls.

Yet Bellow was also clearly American – "I am an American, Chicago born," observes Augie March, the protagonist of Bellow's first commercially successful novel, which catapulted him to fame. But it was a path strewn with obstacles for the Canadian immigrant who eventually became the Nobel Laureate in Literature. His parents, he observed, sent him to *heder* (religious school): "They didn't want me out in the sandlots or playing pool in the poolroom. All these matters were discussed or disputed by us in Yiddish ... The only life I can love, or hate, is the life that I – that we – have found here, this American life of the twentieth century, the life of Americans who are also Jews."[21] Bellow writes of the choice he had, between "the Hebrew school and the pool room and the playground, and the pool room and the playground won out. Together with the public library."[22]

In addition, there was also a vast amount of anti-Semitism in the contemporary literary world in which Saul Bellow found himself. Jews by definition were not WASPS. Therefore, they lacked sufficient language to write an "acceptable" novel. "It was made clear to me," Bellow notes, "when I studied literature in the university that as a Jew and the son of Russian Jews I would probably never have the right *feeling* for Anglo-Saxon traditions, for English words."[23] This was at a cultural moment in America when T. S. Elliott and the deranged Ezra Pound – two troubadours of modern anti-Semitism – held cultural sway. Bellow adds as a type of mitigating factor that he was fortunate to have grown up in the Middle West rather than on the East Coast where such pernicious influences were much stronger.

3. Bellow's Understanding – and Indictment – of American Culture

There is, of course, a third component to Bellow's identity. He was an award winning novelist with a keen sense of the comic, of dialogue and of detail. His prizes include three National Book Awards, the 1976 Nobel Prize in Literature, a Pulitzer Prize, a National Medal of Arts, A National Book Foundation Lifetime medal for distinguished contribution to American Letters, and a Guggenheim award. Bellow himself abandoned his early Trotskyite position and became increasingly conservative culturally and politically. Yet he told an interviewer in 1994: "I consider myself some sort of liberal, but I don't like where liberalism has gone in this country in the last twenty years. It's become mindless – medallion-wearing and placard-bearing."[24]

"My father's major objections to liberalism," attests Greg Bellow, "were to the attacks on culture, literary tradition, and the Western core of intellectual thought in the name of mindless political correctness."[25] In this sense, Bellow's comment brings to mind Irving Krystal's observation: "I was a liberal who got mugged by reality."[26] Bellow was, in a manner of speaking, both a triple insider and a triple outsider. He was, nevertheless, unafraid of utilizing the norms and mores of Jewish storytelling and Jewish values to judge and evaluate post-War America and its Jewish diaspora, which he witnessed as being both an obsession with the materialism of American culture and a radical abandonment of Jewish tradition. Culture has become confused with celebrity. Bellow confides that he sought to "combine being a Jew with being an American and a writer." He was fond of telling the anecdote about Professor Morris S. Cohen and his student. The student enquires "How do I know that I exist?" Professor Cohen responds: "So? And who is esking?"[27]

The Meaning of Culture in America: Young Saul/Old Saul

"Bellow's books," observes Keith Botsford, in a 1990 interview, "are probably the best paradigm we have of America from the Thirties to the present."[28] Yet it was during that same period that Bellow's political, artistic, and cultural values underwent a sea change. Gregory Bellow notes that:

> there were three distinct phases in how palpably my father identified himself as a Jew: childhood, in which the Bellow family's Jewish immigrant status predominated; adolescence and adulthood, where his Jewish connections were attenuated by his development as a writer and by his attraction to the radical political views prevalent in the 1930s; and after age fifty, when his Jewish identity was reaffirmed by his coverage of the 1967 War and was accompanied by a dramatic shift in his political worldview that is most directly expressed in *Mr. Sammler's Planet*.[29]

The political distance traversed from Bellow's high school fascination with Trotsky, to the University of Chicago where he co-organized (with Isaac Rosenfeld) "Cell Number Five" of the Trotskyite Youth Group, to his later embrace of neoconservative positions is clear not only in his post 1963 novels, essays, letters, and interviews. His three sons – Gregory, Adam, and Daniel – also bear witness to their father's changed cultural/political stance. Gregory, his oldest son, chronicles this movement in his 2013 volume *Saul Bellow's Heart: A Son's Memoir*, where he distinguishes the "young Saul" from the "old Saul." Greg's childhood was under the tutelage of the young – liberal – writer seemingly indifferent to his Jewish identity; neither Greg nor his own son had a Bar Mitzvah, although Saul became angry when his grandson followed the same path. Greg's two younger brothers, Adam and

Daniel, experienced a father whose politics and philosophy were decidedly different, increasingly conservative, increasingly patriarchal, and revealed a willing embrace of his Jewish identity. Bellow himself opined in 1968, "Our own movement ... was often foolish, even comically absurd. During the Spanish civil war, the issue of material aid for the Spanish Republic was furiously debated by comrades who didn't have a dime to contribute."[30]

The novelist recalls that, as a young teen, he and his friends "were passing Freud from hand to hand [at Tulley high school]. And Marx and Lenin."[31] Bellow adhered to his Trotskyist left-wing political ideology while at Northwestern University, where he studied Anthropology and where he was a regular contributor to the radical student newspaper, the *Daily Northwestern*. His subsequent involvement with the *Partisan Review* group during the journal's Trotskyist phase seems – in retrospect – inevitable, although as Judie Newman points out, "he appears to have been recruited ... because of his established political reputation rather than for his as yet unproven literary talent."[32] Like Irving Howe – a senior colleague at the *Partisan Review* – Bellow believed that the looming war was a conflict between two imperialist powers. Newman argues that the Trotskyist position on war is expressed in Bellow's *Dangling Man*.[33] In that early novel, Joseph observes that by the time he left the party, he had become disillusioned by abstractions that prioritized ideology over flesh and blood people: "I realized that any hospital nurse did more with one bedpan for *le genre humain* than they did with their entire organization" (22).

Greg Bellow contends that there was a reason for his father's move away from Trotskyist to political conservative, if not neoconservative:

> I think at a certain point he came to believe that the idealism of his early years and of the *Partisan Review* crowd and its socialist utopian beliefs were in error, and that they even turned out to be destructive. This was partly because their idealism blinded them to the horrors of the Holocaust and to Stalin's atrocities. He thought the world view of the *Partisan Review* crowd did not take into account either evil.[34]

Turning to his father's novels, Greg singles out *Mr. Sammler's Planet* as signifying Saul's "turning from the rebellious son into a patriarchal father."[35] Greg and his father argued bitterly over America's involvement in Vietnam.

Adam, thirteen years younger than Greg, and Daniel, seven years younger than Adam, recall their father as a political conservative. Adam observes that Saul was nearly sixty "by the time I was old enough to have an adult conversation with him about politics or anything else" (199). By then he referred to his youthful radicalism "by dismissing it as a far-off folly."[36] At that time, in addition to *Herzog, Mr. Sammler's Planet* and *Humboldt's*

Gift had appeared; both novels expressed grave concern about contemporary culture; *Sammler* notes that "great cities are whores" while *Humboldt's Gift* castigates culture for its indifference to poets. Daniel recalls that his father "didn't give a damn about politics *per se*. All he cared about was literature and the truth of human relations."[37] Moreover, he regarded the first Mayor Daley as "the ringmaster of the great circus of corruption." This bears out the truth of Andrew Gordon's observation that for Saul Bellow there was "a feeling that the proper subject matter of the writer was not politics but the soul."[38]

Bellow's post-war American literary protagonists offer a trenchant critique of humanity in the shadow of what Dean Albert Corde in *The Dean's December* termed "the big-scale insanities of the twentieth century" (73). Unlike his contemporaries Earnest Hemingway and Norman Mailer, Bellow's works eschew a fascination with violence. Instead, he bemoans what he sees as the collapse of contemporary culture, which, rather than embracing the Deuteronomist's command to "choose life," lusts after false gods while embracing an all too facile nihilism. In one of his numerous mental letters, Herzog observes: "how quickly the visions of genius become the canned goods of the intellectuals. The canned sauerkraut of Spengler's 'Prussian socialism,' the commonplaces of the Wasteland outlook, the cheap mental stimulants of Alienation, the cant and rant of pipsqueaks about Inauthenticity and Forlornness. I can't accept this foolish dreariness" (74–75). Herzog, like Bellow, still sees the possibility of redemption for those individuals brave enough to be in touch with their soul.

Post-war America and the American Jewish Diaspora have, attests Bellow's protagonists, become enmeshed in a miasma of violence and a loss of purchase on Jewish identity. Losing sight of the soul, they have lost sight of everything important. While Bellow is of course not the first writer to critique the Jewish diaspora, his was an insistent voice comparing the values of "The Old System," whose European-born protagonist Isaac Braun, a successful realtor, reads from the Book of Psalms while waiting in his car for freight trains to pass. Isaac also travels to New York City from Upstate New York to consult with the Lubavitcher Rebbe – whom he knows – about a deeply personal family matter. Tina, Isaac's sister, had falsely accused him of cheating the family in a real estate venture which required the payment of a bribe. "The Old System" consciously contrasts a biblical, Hebrew set of values with the emergence of an American ethos. Braun's American-born family has taken to the ways of America and abandoned the deep family feeling of classical Judaism. The story is recalled by Dr. Samuel Braun, Isaac's cousin, on a late December Shabbat. Dr. Braun, a scientist specializing in genetic transmission, could not understand the emotionalism of his deceased cousins. Ijah, the protagonist of Bellow's short story "Cousins" also comments on this breakdown. Citing Hegel, Ijah notes, "the seams of history opening, the bonds in dissolution," the constraints of centuries "removed" (286–287). Adrift on a foreign sea, Jews in modernity have lost sight of the fact that they are even lost.

Bellow: A Self-Critique

The Adventures of Augie March (discussed in Chapter 3), was different in tone, substance, and outlook from Bellow's earlier novels. Gone were the mentally and emotionally claustrophobic protagonists. In their place stood Augie March, proud to be an American and convinced of the possibilities of making it in the world. Moreover, the novel marked Bellow as a major novelist and went a long way toward establishing the legitimacy of Jewish writing in America. The critic Christopher Hitchens notes, "This was the first time in American literature that an immigrant would act and think like a rightful Discoverer, or a pioneer."[39] Furthermore, Bellow "normalized" Jewish culture; his novel took "Yiddishkeit out of the 'torture rooms' and out of the ghetto, and help[ed] make it an indissoluble and inseparable element in the great American tongue."[40] Bellow's portrait of America in this novel is the most clearly drawn and optimistic among his works.

Chapter 5 discusses Bellow's writing on the Holocaust. Here, I intend a summary statement that aims to shed light on Bellow the person as well as the novelist. He refers to a je m'accuse when it comes to his failure to have written about the Holocaust. However, hints of this earlier attitude appear throughout his literary work as well as his letters. He describes himself in referring to Artur Sammler by contending that until age forty he had been a man of culture, "relatively useless." Describing Dr. Willis Mosby in "Mosby's Memoirs," Bellow attests that he made some of the most interesting mistakes a man could make in the twentieth century" (157). The concentration camps were deplorable, argues Mosby, but nevertheless they "showed at least the rationality of German political ideas" (160).

Herzog: The Crisis of Modernity

Herzog is Bellow's comedy of survival. The author told an interviewer that he "got very tired of the solemnity of complaint ... Obliged to choose between complaint and comedy, I choose comedy, as more energetic, wiser, and manlier."[41] He dislikes his own early novels, which he finds "plaintive, sometimes querulous."[42] Bellow's meditation on Moses E. Herzog's existential crisis reveals several of the novelist's major concerns facing the Jewish writer in the diaspora. He writes:

> But there is one point at which, assisted by his comic sense, he is able to hold fast. In the greatest confusion there is still an open channel to the soul. It may be difficult to find because by midlife it is overgrown, and some of the wildest thickets that surround it grow out of what we describe as our education. But the channel is always there, and it is our business to keep it open, to have access to the deepest part of ourselves – to that part of us which is conscious of a higher consciousness, by means of which we make final judgments and put everything together. The independence of this consciousness, which has the strength to be immune to the noise of history and the distractions of our immediate surroundings, is what the life struggle is all about. The soul has to find and hold its ground against hostile forces, sometimes embodied in ideas which frequently deny its very existence, and which indeed often seem to be trying to annul it altogether.[43]

Here, in an encapsulated fashion, are Bellow's concerns about diasporic Jewish life: the distractions of history; the failings of education; the loss of awareness of a higher consciousness; and, chief among them, the fate of the soul in the modern and postmodern world. Civilization itself is collapsing. The novel appeared at a time of violent protest against America's involvement in Vietnam, and there were raucous and even violent generational upheavals. Yet Herzog, PhD in Humanities, does not fully yield to despair. He is a cuckold, divorced, and has failed to pursue his major scholarly writing. He nonetheless composes un-mailed letters to the dead and the living, famous people and the not so famous. Herzog refuses to give in or to give up. Even in the midst of his misery, he nonetheless composes inspirational aphorisms: "On the knees of your soul?" he muses, "Might as well be useful. Scrub the floor" (3).

Frequently readers enquire about the relationship between an author and his or her protagonist. The question typically assumes the form "Is this novel autobiographical?" Greg Bellow, in his memoir, comments on the similarities between Saul Bellow the novelist and Artur Sammler the literary creation. "Like Artur and many Jews," writes Greg, "my father kept his eyes closed to the full horror of the Holocaust for two decades."[44] Moreover, the two shared a *pre-Holocaust* blindness in three important areas: "the prewar excess of optimism fed by a utopian ideology about the betterment of mankind; the excess vanity of talented young men lauded by their peers and friends; and the disavowal of their Jewish origins as [each] sought to widen their cultural horizons and gain acceptance."[45] "My father," Greg continues, "rarely mentioned the Holocaust before the 1967 Arab-Israeli war broke out." Yet when the war did break out, Saul Bellow – without telling Gregg – flew to Israel as a correspondent for *Newsday*. Responding to his son's anger that Saul had not told him of his journey to Israel, and concern that he had exposed himself to great danger, Saul responded, "I had to go."[46]

This sense of mission or duty to respond to historical events both as an American writer and as a Jew informs Bellow's final novel *Ravelstein*, written when the novelist was eighty-five. The work is a tribute to his late friend, the philosopher Allan Bloom, called Abe Ravelstein in the novel. *Ravelstein* addresses both the life of the mind, a coming to grips with death and sensuality, and the contemporary meaning of Jewish identity. Ravelstein, the novel's protagonist, is a reality instructor, a term Bellow frequently used, for Chick (a thinly disguised Bellow). He admonishes Chick to stop fawning over Professor and Madam Grielescu. Radu Grielescu (a fictionalized, likely allusion to Mircea Eliade), a Rumanian Historian of Religion and University of Chicago colleague, had – during the war – sympathized with the anti-Semitic Iron Guard. His patron had been the Rumanian fascist Ionescu. Ravelstein warns Chick that Grielescu was a "Hitlerite," and chides him for becoming "chummy with those Jew-haters" (125). The fact that Grielescu was a multi-lingual man of culture only serves to illustrate that culture is no barrier to murder. Disconnected from one's soul, Bellow suggests, one loses one's stability. Ravelstein, dying of AIDS, persuasively concludes that "a Jew should take a deep interest in the history of the Jews – in their principles of justice, for instance" (179).

Over thirty years prior to writing his self-castigating letter to Cynthia Ozick about coming late to the Holocaust (see Chapter 5), Bellow wrote an earlier letter that revealed the depth of his Jewish consciousness. He had been appointed to participate in "People to People," a committee of writers and publishers established to counter Soviet propaganda and to promote American values abroad concerning the signing of a petition. Bellow's 1956 letter was to William Faulkner, who had suggested the committee ask for the release of Ezra Pound. Bellow wrote, in part:

> Pound is not in prison but in an insane asylum. If sane he should be tried again as a traitor; if insane he ought not to be released merely because he is a poet. Pound advocated in his poems and in his broadcasts enmity to the Jews and preached hatred and murder. Do you mean to ask me to join you in honoring a man who called for the destruction of my kinsmen? Free him because he is a poet? Why, better poets than he were exterminated per- haps. Shall we say nothing in their behalf? What staggers me is that you and Mr. Steinbeck who have dealt for so many years in words should fail to understand the import of Ezra Pound's plain and brutal statements

about the "kikes" leading the "goy" to slaughter. Is this – from *The Pisan Cantos* – the stuff of poetry? It is a call to murder. If it were spoken by a farmer or a shoemaker we would call him mad. The whole world conspires to ignore what has happened, the giant wars, the colossal hatreds. The unimaginable murders, the destruction of the very image of man.[47]

Bellow here raises the fundamental moral, existential, and ethical issues of what it means to be a human being after the Holocaust.

Conclusion

Bellow viewed with grave concern both the future of art and the teaching of literature. Art needs, he said, "a certain degree of tranquility or spiritual poise." Unfortunately, he opined, "one of the specialties of modern life is to abolish this quiet."[48] Concerning the teaching of literature, Bellow is even more uneasy: "What has been substituted for the novel itself is what can be said about the novel by the 'educated.'"[49] Some professors prioritize educated discourse over the novel itself. For Bellow, this approach is wide of the mark. His perspective on art is radically different. It has to do "with the achievement of stillness in the midst of chaos. A stillness," he continues, "which characterizes prayer, too, and the eye of the storm."[50] Bellow's works challenge their readers to transcend civilizational "noise," seeking instead access to their souls by way of literature.

Based on his childhood reading of the Gospels when confined to a hospital, Bellow's Mr. Sammler believed that Christianity had betrayed Judaism by espousing anti-Semitism. Because of this betrayal, Christianity had failed. Bellow was far more persuaded by what theologians had to say about humanity than the observations of sociologists. As Edward Mendelson writes, "Bellow was driven throughout his life by his search for some ultimate and invisible spiritual reality," which might elevate humanity spiritually and morally.[51] But this goal was being constantly thwarted by a countervailing force in modernity which, as Gooley McDowell notes in his address to the Has Beens Club of Chicago, leaves the individual not with a desire for transcendence, but with being "bowel glutted by ideas." Finally, part of Bellow's predicament is neatly summarized by the critic Michiko Kakutani: "European Jews," Kakutani observes, "burdened with a tragic sense of history, meet their American brethren, who have ardently embraced their country's ethos of instant gratification."[52]

Bellow once wrote that "The record will show what the twentieth century has made of me and what I have made of the twentieth century."[53] Several preliminary findings come to mind. Bellow's use of Hebrew and Yiddish legitimated this vocabulary in mainstream writing, both Jewish and non-Jewish. His translation of Isaac Bashevis Singer's "Gimple the Fool" made accessible to a widespread audience the world of Yiddish storytelling. Moreover, Cynthia Ozick once asserted that English was the New Yiddish – i.e., the language read and spoken by most Jews. Although she has since retreated from this position, it is noteworthy that she pointed to the works of Saul Bellow as exemplifying this hybrid language. Concerning himself, Philip Roth, and Bernard Malamud – the trio he termed the "Hart, Schaffner, and Marx" of Jewish American Literature – Bellow contended that Roth's works, frequently seen as outrageous by the Jewish community, made his own work seem tame by comparison. Compared to Malamud's work, Bellow's oeuvre tends to portray Jews in the complexity of their reality rather than in symbolic terms. Bellow's impact on Jewish writing and storytelling in America is considerable and will doubtless continue to be debated and discussed for the foreseeable future. Writing in his Introduction to *Great Jewish Short Stories*, Bellow observes: "And in the stories of the Jewish tradition the world, and even the universe have a human meaning."[54] Seeking to restore at least a scintilla of human worth in a world relentlessly pursuing the superficial, Bellow's literary legacy provides the hope for transcendence and possibly even redemption.

Notes

1. Michael Ignatieff, "Our Valuation of Human Life Has Become Thinner," in *Conversations with Saul Bellow*, eds. Gloria L. Cronin and Ben Siegel (Jackson: University Press of Mississippi, 1994), p. 223. Hereafter this work will be cited as *Conversations*.
2. David Mikies, "Saul Bellow Is Having a Very Quiet Birthday," *Tablet Magazine* (June 10, 2015): 3.
3. Saul Bellow, "A Jewish Writer in America," Part One, *The New York Review of Books* (October 27, 2011): 26. This source will be cited as "A Jewish Writer."
4. Ibid.
5. I am grateful for discussions on this essay with Greg Bellow although he bears no responsibility for any error in content.
6. Nina Steers, "Successor to Faulkner?" *Conversations*, p. 29.
7. Saul Bellow, *There Is Simply Too Much to Think About: Collected Nonfiction*, edited by Benjamin Taylor (New York: Viking, 2015), p. 417. Hereafter cited as *TM*.
8. Saul Bellow, "Our Valuation of Human Life Has Become Thinner," in Michael Ignatieff, *Conversations*, p. 227.
9. Bellow, *TM*, p. 452.
10. Saul Bellow, *Mr. Sammler's Planet* (New York, Penguin Books, 1978), p. 69.

11. Frederick Glaysher, cited by Antonio Monda, *Do You Believe: Conversations On God and Religion*, trans. Ann Goldstein (New York: Vintage Books, 2007), p. 30. Glaysher, while seeking to make a point, has overstated the case. What he contends about Bellow and I. B. Singer as writers interested in the soul is true. However, other names come to mind, such as Hugh Nissenson, Robert Kotlowitz, and Cynthia Ozick.

12. Monda, *Do You Believe*, p. 29.

13. Saul Bellow, *Herzog* (New York, Penguin Books, 1976), p. 290.

14. Ibid., p. 31

15. Ibid., p. 32.

16. The term belongs to the historian Harriet Murav. Her work is cited by Mark Cohen, in "'A Recognizable Jewish Type': Saul Bellow's Dr. Tamkin and Valentine Gersbach as Jewish Social History," in *Modern Judaism*, 27.3 (October, 2007): 356.

17. Cohen, ibid.

18. Cohen, ibid., p. 361.

19. Bellow, *TM*, p. 462.

20. Bellow, *TM*, pp. 462–463.

21. Bellow, *TM*, p. 302.

22. Cathleen Medwick, "A Cry of Strength: The Unfashionably Uncynical Saul Bellow," *Conversations*, p. 192.

23. Gordon Lloyd Harper, "The Art of Fiction: Saul Bellow," *Conversations*, p. 63.

24. David Remnick, "Mr. Bellow's Planet," *Conversations*, p. 294.

25. I am pleased to acknowledge discussions on this essay with Greg Bellow, although he bears no responsibility for any interpretive error. (Greg Bellow email to Alan Berger).

26. Cited in *The New York Times Magazine* (December 6, 1981).

27. "A Jewish Writer," ibid.

28. Keith Botsford," Saul Bellow: Made in America," *Conversations*, p. 242

29. Gregory Bellow and Alan L. Berger, "Blinded by Ideology: Saul Bellow, the *Partisan Review*, and the Impact of the Holocaust," in *Saul Bellow Journal*, 23. 1–2 (Fall 2007/Winter 2008): 7.

30. Saul Bellow, *It All Adds Up: From a Dim Past to an Uncertain Future: A Nonfiction Collection* (New York: Penguin Books, 1994), pp. 100–101.

31. Saul Bellow, "A Half Life: An Autobiography in Ideas," *Conversations*, p. 259.

32. Judie Newman, "Trotskyism in the Early Work of Saul Bellow," in *A Political Companion to Saul Bellow*, eds. Gloria L. Cronin and Lee Trepanier (Lexington: University of Kentucky Press, 2013), pp. 9–10. This work will henceforth be cited as *Political Companion*.

33. Ibid., p. 15.

34. Gregory Bellow, "Our Father's Politics: Gregory, Adam, and Daniel Bellow," in *Political Companion*, p. 197.

35. Ibid., p. 198.

36. Adam Bellow, *Political Companion*, p. 199.

37. Ibid.

38. Daniel Bellow, *Political Companion*, p. 212.

39. Andrew Gordon, "*Mr. Sammler's Planet*: Saul Bellow's 1968 Speech at San Francisco State University," in *Political Companion*, p. 153.

40. Christopher Hitchens, "Introduction," *The Adventures of Augie March* (New York: Penguin Books, 2001), p. viii.
41. Harper, *Conversations*, p. 68.
42. Ibid.
43. Saul Bellow, "Introduction," in Allan Bloom, *The Closing of the American Mind* (New York: Simon and Schuster, 1988), pp. 16–17.
44. Greg Bellow, *Saul Bellow's Heart: A Son's Memoir* (New York: Bloomsbury, 2013), p. 131.
45. Ibid.
46. Ibid., p. 132.
47. Saul Bellow, *Letters*, ed. Benjamin Taylor (New York: Viking, 2010), pp. 144–145.
48. Bellow, *TM*, p. 247.
49. Bellow, *TM*, p. 283.
50. Harper, *Conversations*, p. 70.
51. Edward Mendelson, *Eight Twentieth-Century American Writers* (New York: New York Review Book, 2015), p. 113.
52. Michiko Kakutani, "Heartbreak and Humor," *The New York Times* (April 7, 2005): B7.
53. "A Jewish Writer," Part Two, p. 29.
54. Saul Bellow, *Great Jewish Short Stories* (New York: Dell, 1963), p. 10.

8

TIMOTHY PARRISH

Bellow and His Literary Contemporaries

It is difficult to speak of Saul Bellow's contemporaries. He published his first story in 1942; his first novel, *Dangling Man*, in 1944; and his last novel, *Ravelstein*, one of his best, in 2000. Few writers can claim such a span. In the 1930s he was, he says, "the only full time romancier in Chicago (apart from Nelson Algren)" and by 2000 he was speculating to Martin Amis that he had lost the habit of writing letters, though not quite novels, because of "the death of so many pals" with "a first generation and then a second and even a third dying."[1] A generous colleague who wrote more than fifty letters of recommendation for Guggenheim awards, Bellow was just as likely to speak of dead writers as if they were near contemporaries or perhaps older siblings: Tolstoy, Dostoevsky, Goethe, and Emerson are present in his writings from the beginning to the end. Late in life he wrote Amis of a dream wherein Tolstoy "in a beat-up white van on the expressway" drives up to him with a "flapping door" that keeps banging against the finish of Bellow's car (*Letters* 477).[2] The Russian writer, alive as ever, leads Bellow from the highway to a tavern where he confides, "I just wanted you to have this jar of pickled herring" before adding, "I knew your brother" (477). Bellow then bursts into tears.

At the heart of the dream is a myth of familial piety. When Bellow wrote to Amis of this dream, his brothers were dead. Tolstoy might well be an uncle, certainly a family friend, bringing food to comfort a nephew bereaved from his loss. The loss at the heart of this dream cannot be compensated, not even with food from the homeland brought by its greatest writer. Perhaps because he was the child of immigrants and an immigrant himself, Bellow seemed to feel always a sense of permanent loss. His protagonists were always trying to square themselves with a world that belittled their existence, seemed made to press out humans until they became machines, but occasionally yielded glimpses of something better. "Three thousand million human beings exist," Herzog thinks, "each a microcosmos, each infinitely precious, each with a peculiar treasure."[3] And in a distant garden, illuminated by lovely dusk light, "the heart of Moses E. Herzog hangs like a peach" (175). Bellow's novels consume the hearts of their heroes, and at the end they are left suffering for a loss they cannot quite name. Tommy Wilhelm sobbing for a dead man he does not know at the end of *Seize the Day* (1956), Sammler offering a prayer for his dead nephew at the end of *Sammler's Planet* (1970), or Herzog asking for silence at the end of *Herzog* (1964) all compose the same gesture. Each wants to know what act is required of him to justify the mysterious fact that he has been given life and has been required to die. No parents, no brother or sister, and no representative from G-d is nearby to provide the answer. They must make it up themselves – or look for it in the pages of Tolstoy, Dostoevsky, or perhaps the Bible. Bellow did both, and hence we have his remarkable (and I would say still unappreciated) oeuvre.

Bellow's parents were Russian immigrants and from them he learned to love the nineteenth-century Russian masters. Indeed, loving Russian writers is possibly a way for Bellow to commune with his dead parents and their relatives whom he never knew. So often the Bellow protagonist's purpose is to keep in touch with the dead. Moreover, as a writer, Bellow understood himself not only to be giving voice to what it means to have been born into this moment, but also to be conversing about the same concerns that writers before him portrayed. For this reason, to speak of Bellow's contemporaries strictly means to name the dead since he imagined them as his own peers and often spoke of them as if they were alive. In *Herzog*, a novel that is often a family reminiscence, Emerson's words are as much in his mind as are his recollections from childhood, his fights with his father, or his mother's death. As Moses' mind drifts back and forth across the traumas of his life, he keeps recalling his high school graduation commencement address because the speaker had read from Emerson's "American Scholar." In *The Victim*, Allbee quotes to Levanthal from Emerson's "Transcendentalist," as Bellow does in a letter to Lionel Trilling concerning his guardedly positive review of *The Adventures of Augie March* (1953). In both instances, the one quoting Emerson is trying to stimulate his interlocutor to a better version of himself. When in "Distractions of a Fiction Writer" he sought to justify himself as a novelist, a gesture Bellow never left off feeling that he had to make, he reaches for Goethe. "That undisturbed, innocent, somnambulatory production by which anything great can thrive," Goethe told Eckermann, "is no longer possible."[4] Such a dream-like trance the best moments in Bellow's fiction also seek. Here Goethe is like an older brother who has left behind in the family trunk words with which Bellow may use to justify himself when others doubt his vocation.

Bellow's mother, like Herzog's mother, had hoped her son would be a rabbi. Instead, he became a writer with the concerns of a rabbi.

The Jewish tradition does not precisely imagine a specific heaven as the Christian one does, but it does speak of *Olam Ha-Ba*, a place where the righteous gather. It marks a higher state of being, a perfected world, created in part by the works of the righteous on this earth. Bellow's protagonists concern themselves with the workings of the world and the fate of their own souls. They suffer, albeit comically. His heroes suffer alone, but they do not want to leave the others suffering behind. I would not say they are ruptured, but they often seem to try to heal an existing situation through their memory of their loved one, usually dead or distant. This love for family that animates their recollections is a way for them to create the perfected place that is a version of *Olam Ha-Ba*.

Consequently, Bellow's heroes often dwell in childhood memories to resituate the pain of their parents that they did not understand as children. In *Seize the Day*, Tommy Wilhelm visits his mother's grave to ask for understanding he does not receive from his living father. In *Herzog*, Moses remembers when he was a small child his mother rubbed her hand until a small speck of dirt came from it. She says it's "what Adam was made of" (232). A few years later, Herzog, still not grown, sees the hair falling from his mother's head and her fingernails turning blue. "That's right, Moses, I am dying now," her body seems to say to him. In her fingernails he sees "the blue loam of graves. She had begun to change into earth!" (234). Elsewhere, Herzog recalls a letter from his grandfather, still in Russia, in which he asks his immigrant son, Herzog's father, "And who will bury me?" (138). Herzog is the answer, through the agency of his memories. Surely, the ball of dirt his mother taught him to roll in his hands is the not the only legacy he has from her or that she has to give. Herzog, like Bellow, rages against such knowledge and seeks a higher truth through the love his healing memory restores to his mind.

Writing is a form of memory, and Bellow often felt the need to justify his calling to be a writer. Late in life he told Philip Roth "somewhere in my Jewish immigrant blood there were conspicuous traces of a doubt as to whether I had the right to practice this trade." It was not Henry Fielding or Herman Melville who prohibited him from writing, he added, but "our own WASP establishment, represented by Harvard-trained professors" (*Letters* 469). Neither did Bellow's own family quite understand his quest to be a writer. He loved them, but he felt he was not encouraged by them.

The Torah speaks of the illustrious dead who are gathered to their people. The concept seems to describe an event separate from dying or burial. Abraham, Isaac, Ishmael, Jacob, Aaron, and Moses are all accorded this mysterious privilege. As we shall see, Bellow accorded this same privilege to his family through his writing, and his novels are the place they are gathered, renamed, and transfigured by this novelist who also wrote as a son and brother. According to Bellow, the novelist has "called himself out and anointed himself" and "no prophet [has] picked him" to become a writer (*There* 81). Since no prophet picked Bellow to be a writer, and neither did anyone in his family, Bellow picked writers to guide him as if they had been prophets chosen to anoint him. Hence, Tolstoy may bring him peace concerning his dead brother. Perhaps no one else could since Bellow's characters' deepest motivations are to return to the family hearth. Thus, to speak meaningfully of Bellow's writer contemporaries, those who shared his life span, is a tricky matter. Who could give him what Tolstoy did?

Bellow's range of acquaintance was great and he mixed with most of the highly regarded writers of the 1950s and 1960s. Robert Penn Warren and John Cheever were friends from the 1950s on. He knew and thought highly of poets Robert Lowell, John Berryman, and Karl Shapiro. His closest writer friend he knew from childhood: Isaac Rosenfeld, whom we remember mostly because Bellow knew him and whose death at thirty-eight devastated Bellow. Warren and Cheever, though, were from the Protestant majority and upheld by those "fastidious goy critics on guard for the Protestant Establishment and the Genteel Tradition," as Citrine writes in *Humboldt's Gift*.[5] Neither their relationship to their profession nor their subject matter caused Bellow to identify with their work as he did the dead writers whose consanguinity he had chosen.

Generationally and culturally, the writer closest to Bellow arguably was Bernard Malamud, about whom Bellow joked of being grouped, along with Philip Roth, simply because they were American writers who were Jews. Malamud was born a year before Bellow and was also the child of Russian immigrant Jews. When Malamud died in 1986 Bellow wrote a moving and perceptive eulogy. "Well, we were here, first-generation Americans, our language was English and a language is a spiritual mansion from which no one can evict us" (*Letters* 436). Bellow's words betray his sense that American Jews of his generation were outcasts to American culture. Malamud, Bellow says, "discovered a sort of communicative genius in the impoverished, harsh jargon of immigrant New York" (436). His tribute tacitly calls attention to their differences as writers since Bellow's language is characteristically rich, at once intensely descriptive and philosophical. It more recalls Emerson or De Quincey than broken Yiddish. Neither writer's relationship to the English language, or American culture, could ever have anything in common with Cheever's *the Wapshot Chronicle* (1957), a family story whose origins go back centuries to the first English settlers in New England. Cheever, whose father-in-law was Malcolm Cowley, never doubted his right to the English language or that a place in American cultural life was available for one with his talents.

When Bellow began publishing his work in the *Partisan Review*, Delmore Schwarz was already an established writer and potential role model for the younger writer. His 1930s stories about Jewish immigrants put into the English language an experience close to Bellow's. Later, Schwarz and Bellow taught together at Princeton and Bellow tried to look after the older writer when his madness caused him to destroy himself and those near him. In his way, Bellow was at the heart of a Jewish family of American writers. Schwarz is an uncle, Malamud a distant cousin, Karl Shapiro a first cousin who writes poetry, and Roth and Cynthia Ozick, whom he also befriended in the later part of his life, his gifted and doting nephew and niece. Martin Amis would be an adopted son. There is no brother or sister or mama or papa. Even among Jewish-American writers, there was no true contemporary. Bellow insisted on making his own way. For this reason the dead were necessary as faithful company. They asked nothing of him he did not ask himself.

If Bellow does have a contemporary, perhaps an unacknowledged half-brother, it is the one with whom he shared a house for two years: Ralph Ellison. "We did not form a great friendship," Bellow writes, but "he had a great deal to teach me; I did my best to learn." Theirs was a "warm attachment" in which Ellison "respected" Bellow and Bellow "admired" Ellison (*There* 420). What did Ellison have to teach Bellow? First, their quests as American writers were almost identical. "I was a Jew and an American and a writer," Bellow says, who felt that being described as "a Jewish writer" meant he was being "shunted to a siding" (*There* 417). Ellison felt the same way when he was referred to as "a Negro writer." "Unlike the majority of his Negro contemporaries," Bellow observes, "he was not limited in his interests to the race problem. He was an artist."[6] In describing Ellison here he is describing himself. Bellow too wanted to be known first as an artist.

To Bellow, any taxonomy based on race and ethnicity was "an exclusionary device" not dissimilar from keeping Jews out of clubs or jobs. In the eulogy for Malamud he says that "in religion the Christians had lived with us, the Bible of the Jews, but when the Jews wished to live Western history with them they refused" (*Letters* 435–436). Bellow never stopped feeling that way. Among their neighbors in Tivoli, New York, were the critic Fred Dupee and the novelist Gore Vidal. Due to their genealogies, wealth, or literary interests (he mentions Dupee's affinities with Henry James and Proust), they represented the cultural elite reluctant to accept Bellow and Ellison. Vidal "viewed us with a certain ironic pity; socially we didn't exist for him" ("Preface" x). Though Ellison and Bellow were frequent dinner guests of these gentlemen, "the presence of a Jew or a Negro is apt to produce a sense of superiority," Bellow notes, "in those who are neither Jews nor Negroes" (x).

Bellow identified with Ellison as an outsider to white Protestant American culture who insisted that his perspective as a Negro artist neither limited him to speaking as a minority nor prevented him from speaking as an American. Ellison, like Bellow, identified with a so-called minority group but refused, *as an artist*, to be limited by how either the dominant majority group or the minority in-group defined their positions as artists because they were black, Jewish, etc. For Ellison, this meant that he was often fighting both the Jim-Crow-oriented white perspective that refused to see the full humanity of black writers and the militant black political perspective that insisted that white readers could never fully understand or appreciate the perspective of black artists. "It took great courage in a time when racial solidarity was demanded, or extracted," Bellow testifies, "to insist as Ralph did on the priority of art and the independence of the artist" (xii).

Bellow admired Ellison's courage, but the relationship between them is deeper than one of simple admiration. When Bellow felt attacked by critical or cultural prejudice, he fought back in his essays to assert his right to be an artist regardless of others' cultural assumptions. If anyone can be an artist, then any artist can speak to anyone. For this reason, Bellow often suggested that art and politics did not mix well. So did Ellison. "The universal in the novel," he told the *Paris Review* in 1955, "is reached through the specific man in a specific circumstance."[7] Yet, as an American who had been denied basic human rights (where to eat, sleep, sit) never denied to Bellow as an American, he understood the irony of his assertion. Consequently, his work had a political edge that Bellow's lacked and even self-consciously avoided. Augie March steals books and read them. Charlie Citrine and Von Humboldt Fleisher rage against the philistinism of American society. They do not feel physically at risk. Their souls are at stake, not their bodies or their livelihoods.

By contrast, Ellison's most well-known work, *Invisible Man* (1952), concerns a character whose life is at stake on practically every page. Curiously, the fact that Ellison's protagonist is a victim of racism and thus must make his way in a world where millions of people have a license to harm or kill him does not compel or drive the story. His historical condition as a post-Civil War black person in the era before the civil rights movement is simply a fact of existence. It's the given of his story. What interests Ellison is the aesthetic challenge of creating a world in which the protagonist's historical situation is acknowledged but does not condition the meaning of his every act, which includes telling his own story. Art here is opposed to life, but not because they are opposed worlds. The narrator-hero does not wish to create art to transcend the world through its creation. He does not want to abstract himself from the concerns of the world – to be a modernist god paring his fingernails – though he does not want the world to tell him how to make his art. He wants to make the world, or his audience, subject to his art as a condition of transforming the world he and they have inherited. He is not writing propaganda. He is making an aesthetic gesture that changes the world it confronts by binding that world to his aesthetic conception of that world through his engagement with the audience of his narrative act. In other words, he writes for everyone, not just his racial group.

Consequently, *Invisible Man* requires the artist to develop an aesthetic that does justice to the narrator's obscene historical situation in such a way that makes evident to the reader that what he or she assumes to be true, or just, is in fact not. It takes as its aesthetic premise that neither the narrator-protagonist nor the reader can see (imagine, envision) the hero of the novel, despite knowing his story through its narration. Each is limited by the social and historical prejudices that have brought them together. To tell his hero's story, Ellison must create the aesthetic conditions that would make his hero visible to the reader. More than that, he must create a hero not subject to the historical conditions that have rendered him invisible. If he succeeds in creating a hero of sufficient self-consciousness, then the hero may survive the reader's blindness of him – aesthetically, if not socially. For if one person, white or black, wants to hurt another person, black or white, based on his or her own social blindness, and the society tolerates that act taking place, there is little the black narrator can do to stop it.

Ellison's narrator addresses this outrageous situation at the novel's outset when he tells the story of "the tall blond man" with blue eyes who is "mugged by an invisible man" (4–5).[8] The "invisible man" is the narrator who has just beaten up, though not robbed, a white man who has called him "an insulting name" (4). The narrative does not specify what that name is – the reader, ironically, may fill in the blank. The point is that the repressed word designates both the ignorance and the condescension with which the white man views the black man. The white man need not acknowledge the other's humanity because each has inherited a history in which white people need not treat black people as equals. This situation has endured so long that neither party, white nor black, can imagine otherwise. The black man wants to react against this situation. Against the man's hostile, though unthinking, dismissal of his identity, he wants to strike out and stand up for himself. Verbal response in this context seems less gratifying than a physical one. So he grabs the man and beats him to the point where he considers finishing him with his knife. He stops there, though not because he is afraid of killing him or the consequences of killing him. In the society in which he lives, could go to jail just as easily for a crime he did not commit as for one he did. He stops because his act of violence would give him limited relief from his historical situation. To the one murdered, he would remain merely the blank name who had killed him. Only when the history behind that name is changed, which means only when the society in which they both live is transformed, could the meaning of his anger be understood. And in that situation, the two would be visible to each other as equals. The inherent violence of their situation would no longer exist.

Invisible Man put into art the story of racism and its effects on black Americans. As the historian Leon Litwack observes, Ellison's novel is the paradigm for understanding what happened to African Americans between the Civil War and *Brown v. Board of Education* (1954).[9] However, Ellison, like Bellow, accepted the challenge of writing as American, and thus his novel refuses to accept what it calls "the biochemical accident to his epidermis" as the necessary premise to his aesthetic achievement. He is not simply a black man telling a black story (*Invisible* 3). In the novel's famous opening chapter, which Bellow read as a story before it was published with the novel, the narrator is invited to give a speech to a gathering of white men. He thinks he is being afforded an honor because he is an outstanding student, but actually he is being reminded of his place in a segregated society. Before the speech he is made to fight blindfolded among a gaggle of other blindfolded young black men. When it comes time to give his speech, his mouth is filled with blood. His speech is a version of a Booker T. Washington one in which he pleads accommodation with white power. The blood foaming in the narrator's mouth is the manifest history of that awful accommodation bubbling forth. At one point, though, he makes a mistake. Accidentally, almost against his will, he announces the need for "social equality" rather than "social responsibility," the code words for business as usual. His audience is outraged and he quickly apologizes.

In a 1955 interview, Ellison said that his hero is imperfect. The hero's invisibility is not simply a matter of not being seen, "but a refusal to run the risk of his own humanity, which involves guilt" (*Collected Essays* 221). In the opening chapter the narrator retracts his demand for equality. In other chapters, a similar pattern unfolds. He puts himself, or is put into, a situation where he could demand recognition. He could insist upon being seen. The terrible conundrum is that such insistence can cost him his place in school, his job, or even his life. Yet, he persists and is moved from station to station in American society, always encountering a different version of the same situation. Almost unconsciously, with a degree of innocence that would be implausible outside the novel, he seeks a situation in which he will have the courage to demand that he be seen. On almost every occasion he becomes a martyr – but one who lives to tell the tale. He is sacrificed, as he was after the Battle Royal, so that the status quo could at once be questioned and maintained. By the end of the novel, he has lived his story again through its telling and he is at last willing to run the risk of his own humanity. He speaks to the reader not as a person with a skin color but as a human confronting a world he dares to embrace. He asks only that he be met in kind.

In his review of *Invisible Man*, Bellow singled Ellison out for being "willing to make [himself] morally and intellectually responsible" for "this enormously complex and difficult American experience of ours" (*There* 61). Shortly thereafter, they were roommates with intertwining lives and intellectual interests. After Bellow left his position at Bard College, Ellison took up teaching duties there. In 1957 they each contributed an essay to a book Granville Hicks edited, meant to redefine the importance of the novel in the contemporary world. During this time Bellow began his literary journal, the *Noble Savage*, a version of his ideal of "getting writers into the world again" (*Letters* 174). Though an admirer of Joyce, Hemingway, and the other modernists, he felt they had restricted the compass of literature to form and technique. Ellison, too, had learned from the modernists and, like Bellow, strove to bring the world into his art and vice versa. "The invisible victim is responsible for the fate of all," Ellison's hero insists (*Invisible* 14). Ellison's narrator takes responsibility not only for the victims of racism, but for its perpetrators too. He accepts and names the historical situation for everyone and then dares the reader to recognize his or her place in it. I would say this is precisely what Bellow aimed for in his novels too.

Bellow's heroes look to align themselves with the world, and vice versa, through the acceptance of their own suffering. *The Victim*, published five years before *Invisible Man*, is perhaps the best example, not least because it has a similar logic to Ellison's novel. Asa Levanthal suffers two afflictions to which he is asked to respond. His brother's son is ill, and a man he barely knows, Albee, blames him for his unemployment and the death of his wife. Reluctantly, Asa takes responsibility in each case. In his brother's absence, Asa supervises the care of the child. He arranges for a doctor who removes the child to a hospital where he dies. It is not Asa's fault – but he worries that it is. His connection to Albee is more tenuous, but the crux of it is that Albee thinks Asa hurt him because of anti-Semitic remarks he made at a party. Albee's casual anti-Semitism has nothing to do with Asa's actions, but Asa comes to feel responsible and does what he can to alleviate Albee's pain. In the novel's crucial exchange, Albee accuses Levanthal of refusing to help him because "you people" – meaning the Jews – "take care of yourselves before anything." Levanthal responds, "Millions of us have been killed? What about that?"[10] (131).

These words refer to the Holocaust, which is at the margins of Bellow's fiction but never at the center. Even *Mr. Sammler's Planet*, concerning a Holocaust survivor, is not exactly a confrontation of the Holocaust. For Bellow, the Holocaust is part of the twentieth-century devaluation of human life not dependent exclusively on anti-Semitism. In *The Victim*, however, Levanthal takes responsibility for Albee's situation despite the man's racism, as Ellison does when speaking to readers potentially hostile to his narrator's race. Insofar as Levanthal unconsciously did Albee a bad turn, they are both victims of the same situation. He recognizes Albee not as a WASP, but as a suffering human like himself. Levanthal's sense of sacrifice is not as great or as profound as that of Ellison's narrator, but it enacts a similar logic in that he takes responsibility for the history, larger than their personal destinies, that has brought them together.

Invisible Man ends with a question: "Who knows, but on the lower frequencies, I speak for you?" (572). The hero dares the reader to interact with his story. If the reader accepts the narrator's story, if the reader can see him, then that is the first step to changing the society in which they live. It would change history. A work of art, not a work of propaganda, would be the mechanism by which this change was effected. Bellow's novels take the rupturing of the world as a given and are less likely to envision widespread change. Consequently, his narrators are more modest concerning whom they speak for. Unsympathetic readers of his work have sometimes accused Bellow of treating his "personal problems" as "indications of the state of the world."[11] Actually, his work is an example of *tikkun olam*, which is a Hebrew phrase that means "repairing the world." The Rabbi Jesus Christ practiced it, and so does each one of Bellow's protagonists since Levanthal. Citrine speaks for Humbolt, Chick speaks for Ravelstein, Herzog speaks for himself, though Artur Sammler does not speak for the Holocaust dead. He is a Survivor who tries to repair the damage his American family suffers since the Holocaust blotted out neither suffering nor the Jews.

After *The Victim*, Bellow's manner of writing changed – it became more like Ellison's. With *The Adventures of Augie March* he let go of tight narrative forms to embrace, he hoped, a richer sense of modern reality in longer narrative forms. In the essay included in the Hicks volume, Ellison praises *Augie* for "its conception of human possibility" and "a knowledge of chaos which would have left the novelists of the twenties discouraged" (*Collected Essays* 710). In Bellow's subsequent novels, Bellow subjected his protagonists to the sense that the chaos of modern life threatened the souls, or the human individuality, of everyone implicated in it – which is to say everyone alive. In this respect, Herzog does not simply speak for himself. As we have seen, he speaks for his family, which happens to be the Jewish dead. Can Herzog's effort to repair in his mind the hurts from his childhood family speak for the world beyond them – the world that Bellow and his readers share?

In a key passage, Herzog thinks of the past, of Napoleon Street in Montreal where he lived as a child, and asks, "What was wrong with Napolean Street?" (Herzog 140). Nothing. His family surrounded him and, despite their suffering, he was safe. He knew their love then and if he did not, he recreates it through his act of memory, of witness. Is this story too narrow? Reflecting upon his "old personal histories, old tales from old times that may not be worth remembering," Herzog cannot leave them. He chooses to "remember. I must," he insists (149). This is also the role Bellow assigned himself as novelist. "The primary social function of the novel," Ellison notes, "is that of seizing from the flux and flow of our daily lives those abiding patterns of experience which, through their repetition and consequences in our affairs, help to form our sense of reality, and from which emerge our sense of humanity and our conception of human value" (Collected Essays 698). Who does not have a father or a mother who has died and felt the world torn by their death?

Did Ellison make it possible for Bellow to write as he did? No. Bellow read Tolstoy, Dostoevsky, Emerson, Goethe, Dreiser, and so many others and chose to follow them. Ellison was the contemporary whose origins, expectations, and quest as an artist most resembled his own. Ellison too practiced a tikkun olam, and in this sense Invisible Man is a novel as Jewish as Bellow's were. Bellow insisted that he was a Jew who was also an American writer. Starting out in Chicago, Bellow was aware that no one expected him to write – neither his family nor the genteel Christian literary establishment. Arguably, a trajectory exists in Bellow's work that moves from the defiant Americanism of Augie March, his declaration of artistic independence, to an increased sense of his obligations as a Jewish writer in Mr. Sammler's Planet, The Bellarosa Connection (1989), and Ravelstein. Regardless of his hero's cultural origins, though, Bellow's work insists on the writer's responsibility to heal and transform the world he encounters.

For his part, Ellison insisted on connecting his narrator's story as a black American to that of everything else American. After publishing his first novel, he did not publish another, though Bellow coaxed him to contribute a chapter from his never completed second novel for the Noble Savage. In his eulogy for Ellison, Bellow recalls Georges Simenon asking Ellison how many novels he had published. When Ellison responded one, Simenon said Ellison was not a novelist. To Simenon's remark, Bellow retorts with what Albert Einstein said when he asked about his quantum theory: "but isn't one enough, Madame?" (*Letters* 505). Here Bellow defends the achievement of a dead contemporary whose conception of the novelist's relationship to the world was the same as his own. Bellow survives to thank the other writer for affirming what he too needed to know as a writer. In his eulogy for Ellison, Bellow recalls, "All day long I heard the humming of his electric typewriter" and "its long rhythms made me feel that we were on a cruise ship moving through the woods" (*There* 418). As writers, they sailed together through the era they each helped to make.

Notes

1. Saul Bellow, *Letters*, ed. Benjamin Taylor (New York: Viking, 2010), p. 547. Hereafter cited in the text as *Letters*.
2. Zachary Leader, *The Life of Saul Bellow: To Fame and Fortune, 1915–1964* (New York: Knopf, 2015), p. 529.
3. Saul Bellow, *Herzog* (New York: Penguin, 1984), p. 175. Hereafter cited in the text as *Herzog*.
4. Saul Bellow, *There Is Simply Too Much to Think About*, ed. Benjamin Taylor (New York: Viking, 2015), p. 87. Hereafter cited in the text as *There*.
5. Saul Bellow, *Humboldt's Gift* (New York: Viking, 1984), p. 10
6. Saul Bellow, "Preface," in *The Collected Essays of Ralph Ellison*, ed. John Callahan (New York: Modern Library, 1995), p. xi. Hereafter cited in text as "Preface."
7. Ralph Ellison, *The Collected Essays of Ralph Ellison*, ed. John Callahan (New York: Modern Library, 1995), p. 212.
8. Ralph Ellison, *Invisible Man* (New York: Modern Library, 1992), pp. 4–5. Hereafter after cited in the text as *Invisible*.
9. Leon Litwack, *Trouble in Mind: Black Southerners in the Age of Jim Crow* (New York: Knopf, 1998), p. xi.
10. Saul Bellow, *The Victim* (New York: Penguin, 1988), p. 131.
11. Leader, *The Life of Saul Bellow*, p. 457.

9

PAULE LÉVY

Women and Gender in Bellow's Fiction: *Herzog*

In *More Die of Heartbreak*, Saul Bellow proposes a perplexed, pessimistic, albeit highly amused vision of gender relations:

> Every life has its basic, characteristic difficulty ... One theme developed in thousands of variations. Variations, variations, until you wish you were dead. I don't think obsession is the right word you want. I don't like repetition, compulsion either, with all my respect for Freud ... Towards the end of your life, you have something like a pain schedule to fill out – a long schedule like a federal document, only it's your pain schedule ... Endless categories. First physical causes – like arthritis, gallstones, menstrual cramps. Next category, injured vanity, betrayal, swindle, injustice. But the hardest items of all have to do with love. The question is: So why does everybody persists? If love cuts them up so much and you see the ravages everywhere, why not be sensible and sign off early? *(More Die of Heartbreak*, 3–4)[1]

In its rhetorical extravagance, anguished hyperbolic tone, and incongruous metaphors, this statement places the battle between the sexes at the very heart of the human predicament. Bellow in fact makes it a central issue in his entire production ("one theme developed in thousands of variations," *More Die of Hearbreak*, 3). More often than not, however, his novels come up with a biased and distorted perspective: that of a male (anti)hero, in deep existential conflict about his gendered cultural identity and prone to self-pity or downright misogyny as he reassesses his sentimental failures. While the focus is on masculine interiority, women characters, by contrast, tend to appear somewhat stereotypical, two-dimensional, as if the author – perhaps compensatorily – had been content to place them in stable culturally accepted roles highlighting the male protagonist's inner turmoil, rather than grant them the full autonomy of personhood. In most cases, Bellow's women appear as foils to his angst-ridden, wise-cracking, ruminating male heroes.[2]

Numerous critics have expressed indignation or dismay at Bellow's alleged inability to delineate vivid and fully convincing women characters: "There is not a single woman in all of Saul Bellow's work whose active search for identity is viewed compassionately, while every vice of his male introspectives is given some genuine imperative."[3] More perceptive and balanced judgments have been made, however,[4] and some later critics have even attempted to reread his oeuvre from a feminist perspective.[5]

This chapter will discuss masculine and feminine identities in Bellow's fiction in the context of the author's historically situated distance from contemporary attitudes about gender ("that prefeminist era"[6]), while laying the stress on his capacity to cast a sardonic eye both on his characters and on himself. I will devote special attention to the clusters of metaphors in Bellow's prose. For the author's peculiar depiction of the battle between the sexes, which in fact opens onto a wide realm of ontological and epistemological speculation, is above all a comedy of language:

> His ... books comprise a hectic and at times ghastly bazaar of contemporary experience, they ring with the noise of struggle, characters dash in and out, glistening with bravura; adventures pile up merrily as if the Decline of the West had not been definitely proclaimed; the male characters plunge and rise, mad for transcendence; the women (a little tiresomely) are all very beautiful and mostly very damaging. And the language spins.[7]

The novel *Herzog* (1964), recipient of the National Book Award and the *Prix Littéraire International*, will be taken as a case in point for it occupies a central position in Bellow's life and oeuvre. This book, which re-orchestrates the themes hitherto developed by the author while following them out "to their extremist reaches,"[8] is also by far his most personal book "and the most immediate in self-reference."[9] To borrow an expression from Philip Roth, "[i]t is the transformation, through elaborate impersonation of a personal emergency into a public act."[10] According to Bellow's biographer, James Atlas, the novel in its early versions consisted mostly of raw transcriptions of the pain and furor experienced by Bellow upon realizing that his second wife, Sondra, was having an affair with one of his best friends, Jack Ludwig.[11] Initially, the book also incorporated a project about Bellow's childhood in Montreal ("Memoirs of a Bootlegger's Son"), a work which he had abandoned in the '50s.[12] It took the author a long time to unify such heterogeneous and emotional autobiographical material and to keep at a safe distance from it: "I hoped that comic effects might protect me. Nevertheless I crossed the border many times," he admitted in a letter to Philip Roth (*Letters*, 340).[13] As he kept revising his manuscript,[14] however, Bellow realized that this novel, yet another experiment in form and perception, would be a breakthrough: "I am well into a book which makes *Henderson* look like the Scoutmasters Handbook," he stated as early as 1961.[15] At that point, he just hoped to sell about eight thousand copies and did not anticipate the novel's success: "beyond anything I ever projected or wanted."[16] Though it received somewhat contrasted reviews, this intensely cerebral piece became an instant best-seller.[17] It propelled Bellow to center stage and turned the anguished Jewish male intellectual into a literary archetype ("a new cultural hero"), the very emblem of man's alienation in the modern world.[18]

Herzog proposes a portrait of the discoursing masculine ego in the self-defeating process of trying to retain its dignity. The novel depicts the crisis experienced by Moses Herzog, a respected scholar of intellectual history, in the aftermath of his second divorce. As he feels his sanity is failing him, the hero, another "Dangling Man," has withdrawn to Ludeyville, an isolated country house in the Berkshires, in order to recover his grip on himself and the world. This goes together with a sort of epistolary mania. A former lady-killer, already "aging" (18), losing his hair, and doubting his sexual potency (11, 46), Herzog first addresses all the women in his life ("Dear Mama ... Dear Rinka, Dear Libbie, Dear Ramona, Dear Sono, I need help in the worst way"), trying to sort out his quarrels with them (17). Yet he soon finds himself writing to "everyone under the sun" (to friends, relatives, famous figures, whether dead or alive, to himself, to God), each of these epistles a narrative of masculine consciousness in the process of revealing, amending, or justifying itself. Little happens in terms of action. Letters and reminiscences flow into one another. Summoned up in love or anger, characters and events teem through the narrator's densely populated memory, drifting in and out of his distracted mind.

The protagonist's eager attempt at self-reconstruction is undermined, however, by his comic inability to overcome his obsession with his ex-wife, Madeleine, whom he has come to see as the very embodiment of the false values of his time. His state of alienation is illustrated by the circular structure of the novel, by the constant oscillation between present and past, between the first- and third-person-singular narration, as well as by the comic gap between action and the letters. From a stylistic point of view his alienated condition is suggested by the recurrent and interrelated motifs of windows, mirrors, and masks, which epitomize the protagonist's difficulty in breaking through the walls of his masculine egotism, fixations, and anxieties.

Through a Glass, Darkly

In his frustration and isolation, Herzog often envisions himself as a man behind a barrier: "My behavior implies that there is a barrier against which I have been pressing from the first, pressing all my life ... Perhaps ... I can eventually pass through" (238). Thus, we see him pressing his face against apartment windows (18, 191), shop windows (25), plane windows (248), and train windows ("tinted, immovable, sealed," 74). In Chicago he hides behind a window to spy upon his wife's lover. In New York, he feels spied upon by his mistress's former companion: "And perhaps in the whirling fumes of the street, his rival watched him" (187). Blocked by blinds (18, 131), covered with cobwebs (8), or made opaque by the rays of the sun (25), these windows symbolize the filter through which Herzog is allowed only a fragmentary, distorted vision of the world. They also represent the screen upon which he keeps projecting his own version of things. Like Bellow's protagonist Henderson, in the novel *Henderson the Rain King*, Herzog might reflect: "Owing to the peculiarity of my mental condition the world was not itself" (*Henderson the Rain King*, 146).[19] Realism verges on the eerie and the grotesque as he sees nothing but a gallery of monsters in all those around him: Gersbach, his wife's red-headed lover, has a wooden leg; Himmelstein, her lawyer, is a hunchbacked dwarf; while the city crowds are just as incongruous – "On faces, on heads the strong marks of decay, the big legs of women and blotted eyes of men, sunken mouths and inky nostrils" (186).

Like Augie March, Herzog feels assailed by the fierce "Machiavelli" eager to engulf and enslave him so as to fulfill a mad thrust for power. Among those who beset him, the women are the worst. Herzog perceives women to be murderers or vampires: "*Will never understand what women want. What do they want? They eat green salad and drink human blood*" (48; emphasis original). Even his devoted mistress, Renata, a businesswoman in her thirties, slightly foreign, well-educated, an experienced lover and a fine cook, seems a potential devourer to him ("*la devoradora de los hombres*," 321), or at least an opportunist ("she was looking for a husband," 23), eager to use him to her own advantage: "She would lead him like a tame bear in Easthampton, from cocktail party to cocktail party" (29). Of course, it is on Madeleine, his ex-wife, that the paranoid litany of his grudges tends to crystallize. A caricature of the ruthless phallic woman with her frigid beauty ("pale bitch eyes" [40], "medallion profile," 27) and sharp sense of repartee, Madeleine triggers constant fears of castration in Herzog.[20] Always perched on high heels (69, 118, 82, 124), she cuts her bangs "as if discharging a gun" (117), "and [t]o put on lipstick, after dinner in a restaurant, she would look at her reflection in a knife blade" (325). Even during love-making (70), Herzog reads in her eyes "a total will that he should die" (308). Oblivious of the wrongs he has done to her (though aware of her intelligence, he has never shown any interest in her intellectual pursuits),[21] Herzog complains that Madeleine divested him of his social prestige: "[she] lured me out of the learned world, got in herself, slammed the door and is still in there, gossiping about me" (83). Then she urged him to resign from his post at the university and to settle down with her in a country village where he was unable to continue his research. Last but not least, she hurt his manly dignity by cheating on him with his best friend. In his jealousy and humiliation Herzog views the two lovers as cannibals, each of whom absorbed a vital part of him: "Yes, they divided me up. Valentine took my elegant ways and Mady's going to be the Professor" (275); Gersbach imitates me – my walk, my expressions. He is a second Herzog" (197).

Herzog feels surrounded by impostors eager to steal both his identity and his place, even while proposing a sinister reflection of his own person. In Hoberly, his mistress Ramona's former lover, he sees a mirror image of his own suffering (187). Criminals encountered in a courthouse arouse a sense of shame in him, while the trial of an infanticide couple reminds him of the guilt he feels toward his own daughter, June, and of his anxieties regarding the way Madeleine and Gersbach have treated her. The window isolating Herzog from the world is also the mirror in which, like a perplexed Narcissus, he contemplates preposterous doubles of himself and vainly searches for an identity that keeps eluding him. Herzog contemplates in dismay his image in the looking-glass: "That mouth – heavy with desire and irreconcilable anger, the straight nose, sometimes grim, the dark eyes! And his figure! . . . Barelegged he looked like a Hindu" (28). Another mirror of his psychic disintegration is the dilapidated country house which he has failed to repair, or the entropic city streets where he keeps roaming like a distracted zombie: "*his* Chicago: massive, clumsy, amorphous, smelling of mud and decay, dog turds; sooty facades, slabs of structural nothing" (206).

The World as a Stage

The hall of mirrors is also a gallery of masks. To Herzog, everyone is wearing a disguise or playing a role. Ramona is amusing with her Castilian outfits, her "erotic monkeyshines" (22, 23) and elaborate poses. As for Madeleine, she is just terrifying. The daughter of an impresario, she is a make-up artist and a born actress (14). Everything is "a theatrical event" for her: her conversion to Catholicism (118), her marriage to Herzog ("To her he was a fatherly, greying, patient seducer . . . the parts had been distributed. She had her white convert's face and Herzog could not refuse to play opposite," 118) – even the scene of rupture she has carefully "rehearsed" (14–15). Gersbach, an expert double-dealer, is a fit partner for her. Together the lovers have manipulated Herzog into playing his role as cuckold in a vaudeville show: "I sometimes see all three of us as a comedy team" (297). They have also turned his relatives and friends away from him. With their hypocrisy and absurd sentimentalism ("potato love," 275), the lawyers Himmelstein and Simkin, for example, now arouse Herzog's disgust. As does the entire city: "Moses took a keen interest in the uptown public, its theatrical spirit, its performers" (186). To him the world is a stage, a Vanity Fair, and all relationships are based on pretense.

This perception is all the sharper since Herzog has built his own life on masquerading and lies. A son of Jewish immigrants, he has done his best to erase all traces of his origins and to emulate the WASPS. The obsession with imitation and masks he ascribes to the "Machiavelli" is but a projection of the guilt engendered by his own cultural denial, by his betrayal of her, who was the first woman in his life and whom he may be trying to recapture in all his big-breasted mistresses:[22]

> Herzog's mother ... wanted Moses to become a rabbi and he seemed to himself gruesomely unlike a rabbi, now ... his face charged with heavy sadness, foolish utter longing of which a religious life might have purged him.   (28)

Turning away from the "worn black gabardines" of his Old Country ancestors, Herzog, the lady-killer, first chose to disguise himself as a dandy (26). Then he turned into a renegade by marrying Madeleine, the Catholic convert. To please her, he even attempted to play the gentleman farmer on his property in Ludeyville: "And there was I, myself in Ludeyville, as Squire Herzog, The Graf Pototski of the Berkshires ... trying to take stock of my position" (82).

The repressed Jewish self, however, has made its return under the guise of a mysterious *dybbuk* persecuting him: "There is something inside me. I am in his grip. When I speak of him, I feel him in my head pounding for orders" (17). Is it this evil spirit in him that leads Herzog to reject all the intellectual constructions proposed to him?

The Tyranny of "Ideologies"

The pressures exerted by the "Machiavelli" are in fact paralleled by those of the cultural models they seem to embody. Herzog views them as indefatigable lecturers, self-appointed "Reality Instructors" eager to impose their own vision of the world. Each of them advocates a specific ideology. Daisy, Herzog's first wife, has dedicated her life to petit bourgeois respectability. Ramona, an avid reader of such neo-Freudians as Herbert Marcus and Norman O. Brown, poses as great priestess of the cult of Eros. Professing humility, Himmelstein, the lawyer, urges Herzog to abdicate all moral scruples in the name of "historical necessity" (99). As for Madeleine: "She brought ideology into my life. Something to do with catastrophe. After all it's an ideological age" (341). As Herzog, harassed and confused, comically seeks refuge in abstraction, his fierce indictment of his "persecutors" opens onto a reflection on the intellectual systems they subscribe to – or believe they subscribe to, for their creeds have degenerated into grotesque cultural clichés, pale reflections of the original idea: "But we mustn't forget how quickly the visions of genius become the canned goods of the intellectuals" (81).

Though a welcome reprieve from solitary cerebration, sex and the hedonism professed by Ramona provide no lasting solace to the suffering soul. For all the elaborate preambles or rituals (which involve Shrimp Arnaud, Pouilly Fuissé, and classical music), a night spent in Ramona's arms leaves Herzog ("a petit bourgeois Dyonisian," as he humorously calls himself) with "with a lip made sore by biting and kissing," yet with his problems unsolved (23, 214). As for his tender Oriental interludes with his Japanese mistress, Sono (the only woman who never made any demand on him), they are short-lived and inconsequential.

Herzog has little more esteem for Madeleine's high-brow interests, which he views, in his patronizing ways, as "learned badinage" (82) – or worse, as a cover for crude considerations. A jealous husband, he perceives dubious innuendoes in his wife's learned exchange with one of his academic friends:

[H]e was enjoying Madeleine's company. She excited him ... Stirred by Madeleine, Shapiro was particularly lively, almost shrieking when he laughed, and his laughter becoming more frequent, wilder, uncaused ... Madeleine was greatly stirred by him too ... They found each other exceedingly stimulating. ... As she bent ... Shapiro couldn't keep his eyes from the shape of her behind in the tight cotton-knit fabric. (76)

At other times, Herzog views Madeleine's culture as the very token of her frigidity: "She's built a wall of Russian books around herself. Vladimir of Kiev, Tikhon, Zakonsky. In my bed! It's not enough they persecuted my ancestors!" (180)

In the opportunism or cynicism of those around him, Herzog sees an expression of what he intends to denounce in an upcoming book as two avatars of romanticism: on the one hand, fierce individualism, which corresponds to an absurdly magnified vision of human kind; on the other, complacent nihilism, which proposes an unjustly devalued vision. In his opinion both conceptions proceed from a refusal to accept the limits of our human condition.

For all their theorizing, the women in Herzog's life (just like the great men he addresses in his delirious letters: "Dear Eisenhower," "Dear Marx," "Dear Martin Buber," "Dear Kierkegaard," "Dear Martin Luther King") provide no answer to the fundamental question: "What it means to be a man.

In a city. In transition. In a mass. Transformed by science. Under organized power. Subject to tremendous controls. In a condition caused by mechanization. After the late failures of radical hopes. In a society that was no community and devalued the person" (208).

But isn't Herzog as much of a pretentious snob as the "Machiavelli" as he intellectualizes his personal misery into universal problems? What a *schlemiehl* and grotesquely self-absorbed husband he must have been, he, who, "in a Faustian spirit of discontent and universal reform" (74), intended a huge Hegelian cultural synthesis, a revolutionary and prophetic piece of work, yet kept in his closet eight hundred pages of chaotic notes (10). Intellection proves no means to assert or restore his masculine pride, no panacea to the complexity of human relations. Herzog remains caught in the circle of his obsessions, as shown by the repetition of the opening sentence at the end of the narrative: "If I'm out of my mind, it's alright with me" (*Herzog*, 7, 322).

Toward Reconciliation

The circle is broken; Herzog walks through the looking-glass when, instead of moving from place to place, seeking the company of whoever he can discuss Madeleine with, he undertakes a purely mental journey, which leads him through layers of time and memory to the blessed world of his childhood: "My ancient time, remoter than Egypt" (146). In search of the fundamentals from which he has wandered, blundering into personal chaos, he reminisces about his youth in the slums of Montreal. To soothe his pain and humiliation, he recalls his mother's unconditional love for him, his closeness to his siblings, and their respect for his father – "a sacred being, a king" – though he had failed in the New World (154). Through ludicrous and touching anecdotes he resurrects the family dead, their virtues as well as their petty quarrels. He also resurrects the tight Jewish community of long ago: destitute people, united, however, by very strong ties of solidarity and "a biblical sense of personal experience and destiny" (155).

Evoked in elegiac and lyrical terms, the world of childhood turns into a Paradise Lost, a sphere of heart and feelings, synonymous with psychological integrity and social cohesion, as well as with possibilities of transcendence. Herzog remembers his sense of plenitude as a child during the morning prayer:

> "*Ma tovu ohaleha Yaakov* … "
> "How goodly are thy tents, o Israel."

Napoleon Street, rotten, toylike, crazy and filthy, riddled, flogged with harsh weather – the bootlegger's boys reciting ancient prayers … Here was a wider range of human feelings than he had ever again been able to find . . . All he ever wanted was there. (146)

The magic is short-lived, however, for Madeleine derides her husband's vain nostalgia and escapism with sharp lucidity: "Always crying for the old home and the kitchen table with the oilcloth on it . . . Oh, what balls!" (130).

Though they provide no viable alternative, Herzog's prolonged incursions into the past do allow a partial rebirth. After he has returned to the family house and retrieved his father's old gun (Bellow likes playing on Freudian stereotypes) Herzog feels ready to confront the Reality Instructors. He flies to Chicago with the intention of murdering Madeleine and Gersbach so as to reassert his manhood and deliver his daughter from what he believes to be their evil influence. Yet, when hidden behind a window, he sees Gersbach tenderly giving a bath to the little girl: "his intended violence turned into theatre, into something ludicrous. He was not going to make such a fool of himself" (265).

Now confronted with a reality irreducible to abstractions, Herzog is forced to acknowledge the ambiguities and "tensions without which a human being can no longer be called human" (279). He realizes that good and evil are inextricably linked and that human life, "far subtler than any of its models" (279), eludes all definitions or explanations. No longer oscillating between self-pity and self-derision, he feels there is only one possible answer to the questions torturing him: "I am a human being, more or less" (324). At this point, ironic approximations have replaced the compulsion to explain, "to justify, to put in perspective, to clarify" (8). The novel ends in pure contemplation. The spell has been broken. The world is accepted as it is: "Madeleine refused to be married to him and people's wishes have to be respected" (13). Herzog has learned humility and reacquainted himself with the ordinary.

The centrifugal pull of the narrative is replaced by a centripetal drive as, like most Bellovian heroes (Mr. Sammler or Charlie Citrine, for instance), Herzog rediscovers solidarity and compassion: these virtues he associates with his Jewish heritage. He realizes that full manhood implies commitment to others and an acknowledgment of one's moral responsibilities. Now perceiving himself as part and parcel of a larger community of beings (including both the living and the dead), he declares himself "a child of this mass and a brother to all the rest" (209). Quite symbolically, he renews contact with his brother, Will. He comforts an old friend suffering from depression. Alone in Ludeyville, he sends the "Machiavelli" letters devoid of resentment. He repaints an old piano for his daughter, June. Now gladly expecting Ramona's visit, he tidies up the house and picks up flowers for her – something which he has never done for a woman before.

"Perhaps he'd stop writing letters"[23]

The novel ends in a moment of equilibrium and serenity. The epistolary mania has ebbed: "Yes, that was what was coming, in fact. The knowledge that he was done with these letters ... At this time he had no messages for anyone. Not a single word" (348). Quite ironically, the novel remains unresolved, suspended, as it were, in silent contemplation. Herzog finds himself alone at the very moment when he reaffirms his faith in human engagement. Has writing, in the long run, proven ineffective? The gap that opens at the end of the narrative casts doubt on the validity of all attempts to capture reality through words: "I go after reality with language. Perhaps I'd like to change it all into language ... I conjure up a whole environment ... I put my heart into these constructions but they are constructions" (280).

Yet, of course, other letters, other writings will come, formulating the same obsessions. "One theme developed in thousands of variations" (*More Die of Heartbreak*, 3). Herzog, the failed husband and father, the helplessly soliloquizing intellectual, "*bellowing* in pain and anger" (emphasis mine), can be viewed as an ironic double of the artist himself: at grips with painful autobiographical material, as we have already seen, but above all at grips with the complexity of human relationships and the refractory nature of language (*Herzog*, 227).

His delirious letters – rancorous, desperate, incisive, pontificating, inventive – allow him to reaffirm his hold on the world, to give vent to his resentment, to formulate his tentative faith and inchoate beliefs, and to preserve his sanity. His reliance on wisecracks, distorted quotations, twisted proverbs, or ludicrous aphorisms – however outrageous and misogynous they may seem to contemporary readers – permit him to acknowledge the burlesque implications of his predicament: "Hitch your agony to a star" (22), he declares with Emersonian accents when aroused by his voluptuous mistress, Ramona. Or, parodying Shelley: "I fall upon the thorns of life. I bleed. And what next? I get laid, I take a short holiday, but very soon after I fall upon those same thorns with gratification in pain or suffering in joy" (214). He may even sound more sardonically "philosophical" in his eagerness to deride common places and cultural clichés:

> The bitches come and the bitches go. (86)
> *A bitch in time breeds contempt.* (27)
> One thought murder a day keeps the psychiatrist away. (102)

The letters do allow catharsis, albeit precarious and short-lived. Like Plato's *Pharmakon*,[24] however, they are both antidote and poison, they point to a dimension of solitude and absence, to the gap that opens between the world and words, between emotion and transcription, reality and fiction: "If absence does not allow itself to be reduced by the letter, this is so because it is the letter's ether and respiration."[25] Quite significantly, Herzog's letters remain unsent, they remain dead letters: "The desire for emission existed but reception was lacking for my passionate speech," as Charlie Citrine, another disoriented artist, humorously declares (*Humboldt's Gift*, 413).[26]

After the publication of *Herzog*, Bellow himself received thousands of enthusiastic letters, "from people pouring out their souls to me, saying 'This is my life, this is what it's been like for me.'" Yet he also received most puzzling messages from some women readers, "writing to ask me how they should behave with intellectuals, or the recipes of dishes mentioned in the book ... They make me feel like an editor of Vogue."[27]

Beyond the depiction of human passions and that of the failure of the intellect, *Herzog* may be viewed as an ironic reflection on literature itself as presence/absence, as uncertain reception of a message always "lost in translation," and as an epistle to the missing Other: "About essentials almost nothing could be said. Still signs could be made, should be made, must be made," declares Mr. Sammler (209).[28] With *Herzog*, Bellow "signs" his most remarkable novel.

Notes

1. Saul Bellow, *More Die of Heartbreak* (New York: Dell, 1987).
2. There are notable exceptions, however, such as Valeria, and Minna Corde in *The Dean's December* (New York: Harper & Row, 1982), or Sorella in *The Bellarosa Connection* (New York: Viking, 1989).
3. Charles Newton, in Allan Chavkin, "The Feminism of *The Dean's December*," *Studies in American Jewish Literature*, 3, *Jewish Women Writers and Women in Jewish Literature* (1983), p. 114. See also Leslie Fiedler, *Love and Death in the American Novel* (New York: Stein and Day, 1967), p. 363, and Robert Boyers, "Attitudes Toward Sex in American 'High Culture,'" *The Annals of the American Academy of Political Science*, 376, *Sex and the Contemporary American Scene* (March 1968), p. 42, for example.
4. See Ada Aharoni, *Women in Saul Bellow's Novels*, eds. Gloria Cronin and L. H. Goldman, in *Saul Bellow in the Eighties: A Collection of Critical Essays* (East Lansing: Michigan University Press, 1989): "He has built a world of women as seen by men and it illuminates a whole region of the relationship between men and women," p. 119; see also Sarah Blacher Cohen's nuanced discussion of "Saul Bellow's Hedonistic Joke," *Studies in American Fiction*, 2.2 (Autumn 74): 223–239.
5. Thus, Allan Chavkin examines "The Feminism of *The Dean's December*," for example, while Gloria Cronin proposes a feminist reading of Bellow's entire production in *A Room of His Own: In Search of the Feminine in the Novels of Saul Bellow* (Syracuse: Syracuse University Press, 2001).

6. James Atlas, *Bellow: A Biography* (New York: Modern Library, 2002), p. 258.
7. Irving Howe, "Odysseus, Flat on His Back," in *Modern Critical Views: Saul Bellow*, ed. Harold Bloom (New York: Chelsea House Publishers), p. 46.
8. Tony Tanner, "The Prisoner of Perception," in Bloom, *Modern Critical Views*, p. 53.
9. Philip Rahv, "Bellow the Brain King," in *New York Herald Tribune Book Week* (September 20, 1964): 540. Rosette Lamont went as far as to view it as "a parallel to Rousseau's *Confessions*" (quoted in Atlas, 20).
10. Philip Roth, *Reading Myself and Others* [1967] (New York: Vintage, 2001), p. 126.
11. Atlas, 255–259.
12. Ibid., 335.
13. *Letters*, ed. Benjamin Taylor (New York: Viking, 2010).
14. Which, he did until the very last minute, "practically following it to the bindery" (Atlas, 329).
15. Ibid., 313.
16. Ibid., 338, 341.
17. For a panorama of the critical responses, see Atlas (329–330) or Robert Kiernan, in *Saul Bellow* (New York: Continuum, 1989), p. 94, for example.
18. Rachel Ertel, *Le Roman juif américain: Une écriture minoritaire* (Paris: Payot, 1980), p. 167.
19. *Henderson the Rain King* [1969] (New York: Penguin, 1966).
20. Madeleine is in fact the very embodiment of these "nympholeptic fantasies" which Leslie Fiedler had in mind when he deplored Bellow's poor treatment of his women characters (*Love and Death in the American Novel*, 363). As for Robert Boyers, he viewed her as "in the tradition of the all-American Bitch-Goddess, a figure we need never consider too closely, for we know she is a mere creature of those dire fantasies which we maintain to justify our inexplicable terrors" (42).
21. See Aharoni (96–101).
22. Herzog recalls the motherly kindness of Wanda, his Polish mistress ("a full, soft-bosom woman," 31) when he was troubled and sick ("and what made her kindness even more significant was the radiant buxom beauty of the woman," 31). Likewise he feels deeply moved by Ramona's firm breasts ("he might think himself a moralist but the shape of a woman's breast matter greatly," 22), a clear case of fixation on the mother figure.
23. Ibid., 348.
24. See Jacques Derrida's discussion of Plato's Pharmakon in "Plato's Pharmacy," *Dissemination*, trans. Barbara Johnson [1972] (New York: Continuum, 2004), pp. 67–119.
25. Jacques Derrida, *Writing and Difference* [1967] (New York: Routledge, 2005), p. 86.
26. *Humboldt's Gift* [1975] (New York: Penguin, 1982).
27. Atlas, 334.
28. *Mr. Sammler's Planet* [1970] (New York: Penguin, 1977).

10

MARTÍN URDIALES-SHAW

Race and Cultural Politics in Bellow's Fiction

The representation of race and ethnicity in Saul Bellow's fiction is, necessarily, a contentious arena, one that stubbornly resists uncomplicated, definitive readings, and one that is variously conditioned by his changing stylistic modes, his ideological moods in cultural contexts, and Bellow's political evolution. This chapter will discuss certain key texts, spanning thirty years, where issues of race and cultural politics, within or beyond the American scene, become paramount: the short story "Looking for Mr. Green" (1951), and the novels *Henderson the Rain King* (1959), *Mr. Sammler's Planet* (1969), and *The Dean's December* (1982).

Early Bellow: Reserving Judgment

Collected in *Mosby's Memoirs* (1968, pp. 85–109), "Looking for Mr. Green" was published much earlier (1951) and marks a turning point from the early existentialism of *Dangling Man* (1944) to the lighter quest narratives of the fifties.[1] In Depression times, George Grebe, a college graduate who has been instructor in classical languages, is temporarily employed delivering relief checks in Chicago's Negro district: "although ... a native Chicagoan, this was not a part of the city he knew much about."[2] Grebe's physical search for Mr. Green serves to reveal the dismal living conditions of the "blight-bitten portion of the city between Cottage Grove and Ashland" (93), as he paces apartment houses with "hall toilets" and unlit, graffiti-covered corridors with falling plaster (90). Among this invisible, anonymous working-class black multitude, where tenants sublet to other tenants and crowd into apartments, Grebe must also confront the muteness of the inhabitants, instinctively distrustful of any white on public business. Diverging greatly from the discursive modes of Bellow's later work, this social reality is presented through Grebe's taut dialogues and the "active reception" of his experiences, unmediated by his own judgment. In this urban ghetto, blacks are generally reticent

and withdrawn, but the white working classes easily voice racist prejudices: a disturbed immigrant Polish mother publicly complains about
blacks swindling the relief agency (97–98) and an Italian grocer describes
blacks as degenerate criminals and beasts (100). The one exception to the
silence of blacks is Winston Field, a patriot and ex-marine. A believer in
American capitalism despite the Depression and his own circumstances,
Field advocates before Grebe the creation of Negro millionaires by
subscription to set up businesses employing Negroes, "a capitalist
reworking of ... Du Bois's notion of the 'talented tenth.' "[3] Ironically
enough, and despite his surname, Field's American heritage is representative not only of slavery, but also of disinheritance: "Field was a Negro of
mixed blood, perhaps Cherokee, or Natchez; his skin was reddish" (102).

The story's ambivalent ending is powerfully unsettling. Grebe's discovery
of a bungalow with a mailbox labeled "Green" brings forth "a heavy
woman, naked and drunk" (107), who stumbles down a staircase and
collides with him, mumbling "furious with insult, "So I cain't fuck, huh?
I'll show that son of a bitch kin I, cain't I." (108). Grebe, always formal,
repeatedly queries if she is "Mrs Green," to no avail: "Maybe I is, maybe
I ain't" (108). Eventually mindful of her nakedness in the freezing night, and
her abusive language at his inapt formalities, he hesitantly gives her the relief
check, thinking "Whoever she was, the woman stood for Green" (109).
The story ends with Grebe's oddly smug articulation of inconclusive success
("after all, he *could* be found," 109), but what underlies his Kafkaesque
quest for Green is the unbridgeable gap between his rational, "Platonic"
world view (and its related discourse) and the unfathomable realities of the
"black slum, standing for a world not so much of matter, as of flux,
instability."[4]

Doubtlessly, this story has disturbing racial implications, which will
resurface in *Mr. Sammler's Planet*, summed up in Grebe's ambivalent
"stood for Green." African Americans are represented as unvoiced,
assimilative to mainstream American values (Field) or sexually objectified
in abject terms: Green's partner may be a prostitute. In this context, critic
Carol Smith notes that the invoking of negative stereotypes and his
persistent *othering* of African Americans "allows Bellow and his characters to so securely represent Americanness,[5] just so long as Blackness is
otherwise deployed" ("The Jewish Atlantic," 106). Smith's argument
notwithstanding, the story's ambivalent ending also stresses the inexperi-
ence of its central character, one of the first teachers in Bellow's fiction,
who has little to teach and much to learn from his present occupation: his
name, Grebe, recalls in English the diving water bird, while it also evokes
Yiddish *greber*, meaning "minor."

Late 1950s: Parodic Interlude

In several important respects, *Henderson the Rain King* (1959) is Saul Bellow's most atypical work, departing from the American city, featuring an explicit (but arguable) WASP central protagonist, and a strangely anachronistic African setting. This novel is structured as a mock palimpsest of styles and genres as diverse as British colonial travel writing (and modernist rewritings like *Heart of Darkness*), the picaresque and *Quixotic* traditions, the American quest narrative in the grain of Twain's *Huckleberry Finn*, and even Hemingway's tales, invoked in the choice of the white, rich, and dissatisfied Henderson, looking for a soul-baring authenticity in the African "wilderness." Weeks before the novel's release, the always provocative Bellow published "Deep Readers of the World, Beware!,"[6] where he cautions literary critics about reading only for symbols. Bellow's critics generally read this piece as a caveat against "too serious" academic approaches to his then imminent novel.

The hyper-energetic, self-centered, protean Henderson, declared by Bellow to be his closest fictional alter ego,[7] leaves his complicated American family life behind, including tensions with his wife Lily and their daughter, to travel inside Africa. The trip initially involves an old school friend, now a photographer, and his wife, but Henderson, deriding their touristic approach, willingly parts from them: "I didn't come to take pictures of [Africa]."[8] His break with all the trappings of American civilization has been read by Jonathan Wilson, in the wake of earlier criticism, as signaling Bellow's response to the materialism and conformism of the fifties: "in America, Henderson feels himself trapped in a society that can sustain him materially but not spiritually."[9]

Henderson is led into Africa by a "faithful" Christianized native guide-translator, Romilayu. The Henderson/Romilayu relationship has well-known eighteenth- and nineteenth-century literary precedents (Crusoe/Friday in Defoe's *Robinson Crusoe* or Huck/Jim in Mark Twain's novel) and, as such, is clearly open to charges of cultural imperialism from a postcolonial perspective, if not read as a parodic intertext to such writings. Romilayu is sketchily portrayed, his actions limited to praying and fretting over Henderson, whom he calls "sah." Although a competent translator with two African tribes, Romilayu says little on his own initiative and speaks, according to Henderson, a "limited English," (45) in fact, one that is totally contrived and alien to the novel's background: "the language of American 'Negroes' in minstrel shows, described by Bellow's friend Ralph Ellison [in a 1958 essay] ... as 'pseudo-Negro dialect,' ... 'This blackfaced figure of white fun,' Ellison writes of the blackface minstrel, 'is for Negroes a symbol of everything they rejected in the white man's thinking about race' (p. 23)" (*The Life*, 519).

Romilayu guides Henderson to two tribes: first the Arnewi (chapters 5–10) and later the Wariri (chapters 10–21), both fictional names. Although Henderson observes topographical details, time is deliberately vague and no actual geography informs either trek (45, 113). Bellow was never in Africa, and the detailed descriptions regarding the dress, customs, and rites of the two tribes are solely based on his readings of African anthropology and ethnography, thoroughly catalogued in a classic article by Eusebio Rodrigues.[10] The sacredness of cattle for the Arnewi derives from Melville Herskovits' *The Cattle Complex in East Africa* (1926), and some of their traits from Rev. John Roscoe's missionary accounts *The Soul of Central Africa* (1922) and *The Banyankole* (1923). The "militaristic" Wariri tribe is drawn from accounts of the historical West African Dahomey kingdom (present-day Benin), namely Herskovits' *Dahomey: An Ancient West African Kingdom* (1938), Frederick Forbes' *Dahomey and the Dahomans* (1851), Sir Richard Burton's *First Footsteps in East Africa* (1856), and *A Mission to Gelele, King of Dahomey* (1864), among others.[11]

The use of British Empire colonial travel writing (Burton, Forbes) or missionary accounts (Roscoe) as sources for the tribal characterization in *Henderson the Rain King* has led a number of scholars, as Eric Strand remarks, to "postcolonial readings of *Henderson* ... [following] a tendency to read Bellow as reproducing nineteenth-century discourse about the supposed dark continent" ("Lighting Out," 289). Yet this critic persuasively challenges such readings, arguing that the rendering of the Arnewi and Wariri actually serves the primary purpose of foregrounding a parody of the "civilized" American white Henderson, in his blunders with and misapprehensions among them. Strand highlights Bellow's discipleship to his professor, Herskovits, himself a disciple of the great anthropologist Franz Boas in the 1920s:

> Bellow was influenced by anthropologists who promulgated a new approach to cultural difference ... [Anticipating Edward] Said's critique, Boas and his protégé Herskovits saw nineteenth-century anthropological knowledge as a direct reflection of the spatial power relations inhering in [European] colonialism. Boas ... emphasiz[ed] "different ultimate and coexisting types of civilization," [and] Herskovits ... helped to codify the doctrine of cultural pluralism, which he labeled cultural relativism. ("Lighting Out," 289–290)

In an often reviewed episode, Henderson is informed, by Prince Itelo of the Arnewi, of the tribe's tragedy: cattle die of thirst because their only water tank is polluted by frogs, which tradition forbids disturbing (59). Under the spell of the Arnewi queen's devotion for him and his own narcissism, Henderson casts himself into the role of messiah, conjuring up his (all-American) technical army know-how to make an underwater bomb to kill the frogs. Predictably, the charge is too powerful and bursts the tank wall, wasting all their drinkable water, and Henderson and Romilayu are forced to flee. Despite Bellow's warning, some critics read the episode as symbolic of American intervention abroad: "all those high intentions, cross-cultural misunderstandings, and outright debacles which littered our international record in the fifties and beyond ... Henderson ... is a one-man foreign policy, part Peace Corps, part Expeditionary Force."[12]

The comedy turns macabre in the Wariri chapters, as Henderson is initially tested by the appearance of a corpse in his hut. Courageously disposing of it, he believes this to be a secret trial for his successful lifting of the statue of a mountain goddess, a feat that makes Henderson *Sungo* (rain king). But the trials are elsewhere. This section prominently features Henderson's apprenticeship to Dahfu, the Wariri king. Culturally hybrid, a "combination of Western learning and tribal wisdom" (*On Bellow's Planet*, 125), Dahfu is largely a "reality instructor," a stock character of Bellow's fiction, here modeled on the eccentric Wilhelm Reich.[13] Dahfu keenly fosters Henderson's animal nature by training him with a lion, a kind of soul-baring therapy that actually screens his preparation of Henderson-Sungo as a successor at his death: "Bellow play[s] upon anthropological conventions ... the plot turn in which a stranger is substituted for a king as sacrificial victim is 'amply recorded' in Sir James Frazer's *The Golden Bough*" ("Lighting Out," 306). It finally dawns on the naïve and self-centered Henderson that nobody wants to be king of the Wariri, whose initiation rituals involve capturing a wild lion and end with sacrificial death when the king's wives decree his impotence. Earlier, the faithful Romilayu had warned: "Dem chillen dahkness" (115).

The general portrayal of Henderson as a well-intentioned bungler likens him to the *schlemiehl* archetype. While Bellow, perhaps to emphasize a symbolic "American innocen[ce] abroad" ("The Idea of *Henderson*," 319), finally wrote his central character as a wealthy WASP from a prominent genteel family involved in American politics (7), his physical features (bushy hair and a great nose, 4) are Jewish, and this self-parody hints at his latent identity: "An elegant establishment, they accept no Jews, and they get me, E.H. Henderson" (7). Several early critics noted the Jewish traits in Henderson: Norman Podhoretz underscored his implausibility "as a Hudson Valley aristocrat"[14] and Daniel Fuchs later verified "early drafts of the novel [with] Henderson exclaiming "oyoyoy!" during tense moments."[15]

Late Bellow: "embattled spokesmen"

A significant inflection point in Bellow's career is *Mr. Sammler's Planet* (1970). Today largely dated, this novel is usually described as epitomizing Bellow's about-face toward conservatism and his bitter reaction to the late 1960s, with its militant student movements, the emergence of civil rights and Black Power movements, and the liberation of the new youth culture, signalled by the advent of May 1968.

On its initial reception,[16] readers and critics of Bellow's preceding works, particularly the 1950s novels featuring "life-affirming" protagonists such as Augie or Henderson, were taken aback at the bitterness and bigotry of Artur Sammler, a Jewish Polish Holocaust survivor with an elite British cultural background, having lived in the London Bloomsbury district before the war. Rescued from a DP camp in the aftermath of World War Two by his successful nephew, Elya Gruner, who arranged his exile to the US and still financially sustains him and his daughter, Sammler lives out – in a sense, survives – his last days in New York, with no occupation but reading Meister Eckhart, a thirteenth-century German theologian and philosopher.

The novel's sparse and rather contrived plot relies on the eccentric behaviors of Sammler's relatives and acquaintances, including his own daughter Shula-Slawa, her ex-husband Eisen, his widowed niece Margotte Arkin, his nephew's son Wallace, and his ex-student Feffer, among others. These characters, aptly labeled by Peter Hyland as "grotesque" and "childishly self-absorbed,"[17] act in ways that lead the highbrow and morally authoritative Sammler into lengthy intellectual reflections on the decadence of American civilization, symbolized by New York life.[18]

Sammler is notably older than Bellow (then aged 55), and the "device of the septuagenarian alien" who is the novelist's first "post-sexual creation" (*Vision and Revision*, 89, 85) is essential in a novel underscoring the generational gap and dealing insistently with Sammler's perception of the damaging implications of sexual freedom and sexual discourse in the sixties. Shula-Slawa has become an erratic bohemian after fleeing her violent husband Eisen, Margotte is depicted as a sexually unrestrained woman, and Sammler's university lecture is interrupted by a student who shouts "Why do you listen to this effete old shit? ... His balls are dry. He's dead. He can't come."[19] Central to the distressful power of sex in this era is Bellow's inclusion of the black pickpocket, an anonymous and voiceless character who frames the novel. In chapter one, Sammler reflects on an elegantly dressed black pickpocket, in his thirties, he observes on one bus route. After reporting him to an indifferent and overworked New York police force, Sammler continues to take that bus as he perversely enjoys watching the man act. In one ride, he is "seen seeing" (47), and the scene that follows is "no deflected Freudian symbol of aggressive virility"[20] but the reversal of phallic symbolism into actuality. The black pickpocket follows Sammler back into his own deserted lobby, corners him, and, never speaking, slowly and deliberately forces Sammler to view his penis: "The man's expression was not directly menacing, but oddly, serenely masterful. The thing was shown with mystifying certitude. Lordliness ... *Quod erat demonstrandum*" (49–50).

In the reduction of this character to silence, criminality, and sexual hegemony, as opposed to the discursive intellectual, morally authoritative, and "post-sexual" elderly Jew, the young pickpocket has been read as Sammler's *doppelganger*,[21] an interpretation that is suggested within Sammler's thoughts (66), and which finds a precedent in the Allbee/Leventhal relationship in *The Victim*. But problematically for a double, the black pickpocket in *Mr. Sammler's Planet* remains a sexually objectified figure who is empowered and silent, a reversal of the naked woman in "Looking for Mr. Green" that is equally controversial (see Carol Smith, quoted above). Further, the pickpocket's act is provokingly reinscribed in Sammler's mental discourse within a racialist paradigm where blackness/"non-whiteness," epitomizing sexual unrestraint, dominates this American era: "Then suddenly [Shula] too was like the Negro pickpocket. From the black side, strong currents were sweeping over everyone. Child, black, redskin – the unspoiled Seminole against the horrible Whiteman. Millions of civilized people wanted oceanic, boundless, primitive, neckfree mobility, experienced a strange release of galloping impulses, and acquired the peculiar aim of sexual niggerhood for everyone" (162).

Much of Sammler's discourse, read today or in 1970, is characterized by racism and cultural imperialism, especially in his observations of a dilapidated New York. As he walks across Stuyvesant Park obsessing over dog excrements, "Mr Sammler was testy with White Protestant America for not keeping better order. Cowardly surrender. Not a strong ruling class. Eager in a secret humiliating way to come down and mingle with all the minority mobs" (105–106). Disparaging comparisons between New York and southern cities across the Atlantic, reminiscent of the essentialist outlook of what Edward Said terms "*latent* Orientalism" serving a male world view and perspective,[22] are frequent in Sammler's interior monologues: "outdoor phones were smashed, crippled. They were urinals, also. New York was getting worse than Naples or Salonika. It was like an Asian, an African town" (7); "the boys like Bombay beggars" (106).

Critics have been at pains to minimize or disestablish the identification between Sammler[23] and Bellow. Malcolm Bradbury argues that while

Sammler is a surrogate for Bellow, "he is a clearly angled [one] ... not to be read ... as the author direct" (81), and suggests this is "a satirical novel" also at Sammler's expense.[24] David Galloway underlines Bellow's comic portrayal of Sammler's obsessive nature and also cautions "about accepting [Sammler's] judgement at face value" (*Absurd Hero*, 179). Invoking Kierkegaardian categories of knowledge, Ellen Pifer sees the duality *within* Sammler, whose voice runs a "dialectic" between "two different speeches" of a divided psyche, in a novel that involves Sammler's quest from detached observer to partaker of reality (*Against the Grain*, 22–25).

Pifer's argument is illuminating in view of late developments in the novel. In an odd plot turn gathering several characters, Sammler must prevail upon the brutal Eisen, now a militant Zionist sculptor, to stop beating the black pickpocket, after Eisen comes in defense of Feffer, surprised by the pickpocket with a camera (290–292). Thus, Sammler's evolution from "observer" to "participant" implies a correction of viewpoints and attitudes. In this line, Peter Hyland persuasively argues that "the novel itself insists on the limitations of perspectives" (Hyland *Bellow*, 72–73). The fact that Sammler has only one "seeing" eye, having lost the other in the war, suggests his partial unreliability as a narrator. At one point, he self-evaluates: "being deficient in contemporary American information, Sammler was tentative here ... the way he saw things could not be right. His experiences had been too peculiar, and he feared that he projected peculiarities onto life" (110). He finally learns the truth about the ethical Elya Gruner, the prestigious gynecologist – "Wallace, then, had been right about his father. [Elya] had done favors for the Mafia. Performed some operations. The money did exist" (311) – a discovery that necessarily challenges Sammler's moral certainties, as it becomes evident that the "sexual madness" he decries has contributed to support him and his daughter through Elya's financing.

Bellow's first novel after the Nobel Prize in 1976, *The Dean's December* (1982), shares the introspective modes and ideological stances of *Mr. Sammler's Planet*, but is generally agreed to evidence a sharp decline in Bellow's fictional powers: "I wasn't thinking 'novel' when I wrote the book," Bellow admitted in an interview.[25] Tellingly, he called it "the Chicago book," and wrote it in an exhausting rush, as he admits in letters to Philip Roth and William Kennedy over the winter of 1981/82.[26]

The Dean's December is a hybrid narrative[27] whose action is set in Bucharest during the most repressive and deprived period of Communist Romania, but with a discursive focus on Chicago, derived from an unfinished personal account (Hyland *Bellow*, 89) that is narrativized through Dean Corde's cogitations, dialogues, and self-reflexive reassessments. The "Chicago story" basically concerns Corde's interest in criminal cases involving black murderers and white victims, and his authoring two polemical articles in *Harper's* magazine describing the sordid conditions of the "black underclass" in the city's South Side, rampant with drug-abuse, sexual assaults, and crime. By casting his protagonist as Dean Corde of a well-known Chicago university, Bellow aims to explore the consequences of such exposure, within the thorny topic of race relations in the US, for the American public intellectual-as-humanist: Corde evokes Latin *cor(-dis)*, simultaneously signifying heart, soul, and intellect. On an interconnected plane, this novel, like *Mr. Sammler's Planet*, also foregrounds generational/familial conflict, since Corde's nephew Mason and his cousin, the lawyer Detillion, side against Corde in his public engagements.

A controversial aspect of this work is Bellow's use of facts within the "Chicago narrative." The racially sensitive murder cases of a white student by blacks that Dean Corde wants to clarify by promoting a reward for witnesses, or that of the housewife repeatedly raped and finally murdered that Corde debates with the Public Defendant Varennes,[28] are factually based on murder cases that occurred in Chicago in the late seventies. As Bellow's biographer James Atlas notes, the writer reinscribed these cases not unproblematically:

> Curiously, the two victims in the book ... are submitted to ethical cross examinations [by Corde] that manage to turn them both into subtle accomplices ... There was something grotesque in the way Bellow appropriated Mark Gromer's story for his own literary purposes ... in [the unpublished memoir by Gromer's wife] the event ... achieves a primal terror absent from Bellow's fictional narrative. (*A Biography*, 498)

The real, horrifying murder accounts are actually subservient to Corde's speculative discourse, basically "the author's unmediated opinion" (Hyland *Bellow*, 89), as a basis for Corde's/Bellow's explorations into Chicago's social and urban degeneration: "the true subject ... is obscured by Corde's shrill complaints that he is misunderstood. For Bellow, the really compelling drama [here] is the controversy surrounding Corde's articles – a preemptive strike against Bellow's own critics" (*A Biography*, 496).

As a novel, this work examines, always from the Corde/Bellow evaluating consciousness, the inadequacies and limitations of language and discourse in *re*-presenting reality. In Bucharest Corde cannot, literally, communicate with his wife's Roumanian relatives, because he doesn't speak the language. This is paralleled, figuratively, by his inability to "get across" in his *Harper's* articles, where his raw descriptions of Chicago's destitute ethnic ghettoes (a Housing Project, 132; black gangs dealing drugs, 149; County Hospital, 166–168; the South Side streets, 187), recalled fragmentarily through different narrative modes, have generated letters of protest and even "hate mail" (145, 186). Corde's discourse can be perceived as moralistic, culturally elite, and highbrow, disconnected from the "hard realities" of Chicago: his nephew, Mason, who supports the black youth responsible for the white student's death and whose "true voice of Chicago … blends with the voices of Zaehner and Detillion"[29] reproaches: "you don't know a damn about what goes on" (52). But, paradoxically, it is Corde's forthright descriptions of "rapes, robberies and sexual acts in public places" (162) that motivate a formal complaint by a student group of "revolutionary Marxists" demanding "a public apology 'to Black, Puerto Rican and Mexican toilers' for making them look 'like animals and savages.'" (163): "[Corde] has found himself in a peculiarly ironic position where, having accused Chicago of racism, he is himself the target of the same accusation" (Hyland *Bellow*, 91). And, indeed, there are hints suggesting Corde's ingrained racism: he is unsettled to meet a black US Ambassador in Bucharest, revealingly remarking upon his ethnicity after their appointment: "the black Ambassador from first to last was very sympathetic" (74). Yet, in his articles Corde also writes admiringly about African Americans, when he vindicates "moral men" like Ridpath, a supervisor who fights corruption in the County Jail (151–156) or the redeemed Winthrop, an ex-hit man who starts a detox center (188–191), but these are unpopular figures with the Chicago policy-makers.

Roughly mid-novel, Corde considers how he has been perceived as a public intellectual, in the wake of his *Harper's* articles: "Liberals found him reactionary. Conservatives called him crazy" (186). His cultural politics are trapped in an ideological no-man's land by what critic Robert Kiernan aptly calls "dividedness" (*"The Dean's December,"* 261–265). As such, they are illustrative of what is perhaps the most appealing aspect of this novel: the dialogic opposition of discourses – the 'hard' sciences versus the humanities; the academic versus the journalistic; the social-philosophical versus the political – all of which partly account for the state of the world, but do not necessarily cohere into a unified worldview.

Conclusions

In evaluating Bellow's cultural politics and his outlooks on ethnicity as represented in his fiction, it should be noted that such issues achieve their greatest significance in long fiction which is far from Bellow's best, and in a parodic quest novel, *Henderson the Rain King*, where racial representations are essentially artificial, derived from an interplay with social and literary archetypes or ethnographic sources, which include even the masking of the title character as a WASP. Thus, *Henderson* is not really suited to critical scrutiny from angles that overlook such intertextuality.

Readers of *Mr. Sammler's Planet* should note that this is essentially a highly symbolic "period novel," with Sammler partly voicing Bellow's late-sixties conservative outlook, but whose identity as an intellectual "world citizen" (Bradbury *Bellow*, 79) and as a survivor of the *Shoah*, thus familiar with absolute evil, initially entitles him as a legitimate judge of lesser ills: "the Holocaust remains the point of origin, that against which everything must be measured and observed."[30] If the black pickpocket scene is offensive for African American readers, no less disturbing for certain Jewish readers is Eisen's brutal aggression of the pickpocket, using as weapons the brass medallions representing Judaism, in what emerges as a (heavy-handed) symbolic critique of Israel's role in the June 1967 Six-Day War, again a period reference. On the other hand, the novel's closing ultimately proposes, as noted earlier, that Sammler's intellectualism and worldliness does not exempt him from misjudging the American scene, although this may remain unconvincing in a work where "the imaginative structure fails to provide adequate support for the intellectual structure" (*Absurd Hero*, 184–185).

The racial question receives its most deeply felt treatment in the two Chicago fictions, which are disparate in scope, style, and quality. "Looking for Mr. Green" is a superb story, with its Kafkaesque quest for the untraceable Green which actually serves to illuminate the "parallel universe" of the Chicago slums surrounding him. Although set in the Depression, this is an urban dystopia represented in a timeless way that speaks for the social conditions in ethnic ghettoes within the "inner cities" of the great twentieth-century American metropoles, among which Los Angeles is also paradigmatic.

As noted often, the "Chicago story" in *The Dean's December* is essentially dreary, not only in its fragmented discursiveness, but also in its self-reflexive evaluation of Corde's discourse. Bellow is more convincing in the brief nonfiction piece "Chicago: The City That Was, the City That Is" (1983) than he is masking as Corde inside *The Dean's December*. Since Bellow clearly felt strongly about the fate of Chicago's ethnic neighborhoods, one wonders why the "Chicago book" did not become a report or a memoir in the mode of *To Jerusalem and Back* (1976), particularly as he could cope well with controversy.

Bellow's outlooks on race and cultural politics should always be contextualized by the intensity and weight of cultural ethnography and social history in his fiction, an atypical mode in modern American literature. His formative (progressive) years were shaped by his studies in anthropology, while his adult (conservative) years were marked by his affiliation (1962 to

1993) with the University of Chicago's *Committee on Social Thought*, an interdisciplinary academic body fostering a holistic approach to the humanities, where literature is put on a par with philosophy, religion, history, politics, and sociology. A characteristically Bellovian approach is to construct characters from cultural, ethnic, or historical paradigms, or have them act in ways that they fulfill these. In *Mr. Sammler's Planet*, Sammler relates the loquacious Margotte Arkin to "full German pedantry" and soon identifies her as German-Jewish (14, 17). Sammler's own entitlement derives, a priori, from European cultural backgrounds and his identity as a Holocaust survivor. In *The Dean's December*, Albert Corde's polite formality and belligerent mindset might be explained through his hybrid Huguenot/Irish roots (131). The list goes on, beyond the scope of Bellow's fiction discussed here.

Bellow's engagement with ethnography has, perhaps, never been fully grasped, partly because it has not always succeeded in fictions that also blend in autobiography, via his "embattled spokesmen"[31] with professorial attitudes. Such engagement has failed him also in his projection as a public intellectual. Fulfilling Dean Corde's vision of the distorting power of public opinion and the press, certain media took Bellow to task in the late eighties for declaring "Show Me the Zulu Tolstoy" in a seemingly dismissive tone. This was a partial, decontextualized misquote, which, in today's terms "went viral," of two rhetorical questions – "Who is the Tolstoy of the Zulus? The Proust of the Papuans? – spoken in an interview to drive home the distinction "between literate and preliterate societies."[32] Saul Bellow could often be acerbic, and at a sensitive "time of heightened debates over literary canons and curricula in North America,"[33] this distorted phrase was crudely taken as showing contempt for multiculturalism and discrimination of non-Western cultures. Indeed, this is an absurd allegation to pin on a writer who read Hebrew in childhood, translated from Yiddish, was fluent in French and Spanish – a writer whose academic interests included a Senior Thesis on the role of France in the African slave trade and extensive research into the pre-colonial West African Dahomey kingdom.

Notes

1. Eusebio Rodrigues, "Koheleth in Chicago: The Quest for the Real in 'Looking for Mr. Green,'" in *Critical Insights: Saul Bellow*, ed. Allan Chavkin (Pasadena: Salem Press, 2012), p. 312.
2. Saul Bellow, *Mosby's Memoirs and Other Stories* (Harmondsworth: Penguin, 1971), p. 85.

3. Carol Smith, "The Jewish Atlantic: The Deployment of Blackness in Saul Bellow" in *A Political Companion to Saul Bellow*, eds. Gloria Cronin and Lee Trepanier (Lexington: University Press of Kentucky, 2013), p. 108. In his essay "The Talented Tenth" (1903), W. E. B. Dubois advocated access of this proportion of African Americans to higher education as a way to forward intellectual leadership in the interests of the Negro community.

4. Zachary Leader, *The Life of Saul Bellow: To Fame and Fortune, 1915–1964* (New York: Knopf, 2015), p. 444.

5. Significantly, Smith's contention on Bellow's upholding of "Americanness" is also manifest in the contemporary "The Gonzaga Manuscripts" (1954), set in late 1940s Spain. In his romantic quest for the unpublished poems of the late Gonzaga (echoes of García Lorca) the American student Clarence Feiler encounters clichéd assumptions of US militarism and cultural barrenness in all the Spaniards he meets.

6. "Deep Readers of the World, Beware!," *New York Times* (February 15, 1959): BR1.

7. Nian Steers, "Successor to Faulkner?" in *Conversations with Saul Bellow*, eds. Gloria Cronin and Ben Siegel (Jackson: University Press of Mississippi, 1994), p. 34.

8. Saul Bellow, *Henderson the Rain King* (New York: Viking Press, 1966), p. 43.

9. Jonathan Wilson, *On Bellow's Planet: Readings from the Dark Side* (Rutherford: Farleigh Dickinson University Press, 1985), p. 118.

10. Eusebio Rodrigues, "Bellow's Africa," *American Literature*, 43.2 (May 1971): 242–256.

11. For comprehensive information on Bellow's anthropological sources in this novel, see Zachary Leader's *The Life of Saul Bellow*, p. 204 and Eric Strand's essay "Lighting Out for the Global Territory: Postwar Revisions of Cultural Anthropology and Jewish American Identity in Bellow's *Henderson the Rain King*" in *ELH*, 80 (2013): 290.

12. Bruce Michelson, "The Idea of *Henderson*," *Twentieth Century Literature*, 27.4 (Winter 1981): 318.

13. Wilhelm Reich (1897–1957) was a controversial Austrian psychoanalyst, whose radical practices in psychiatry (such as vegetotherapy) were scorned by the profession as inappropriate.

14. Quoted in Steven Axelrod, "The Jewishness of Bellow's Henderson," *American Literature*, 47.3 (November 1975): 442.

15. Daniel Fuchs, *Saul Bellow: Vision and Revision* (Durham: Duke University Press, 1984), p. 117.

16. See Ruth Miller, *Saul Bellow: A Biography of the Imagination* (New York: St. Martin's Press, 1991), pp. 198–200 and *On Bellow's Planet*, pp. 143–144.

17. Peter Hyland, *Saul Bellow* (New York: St. Martin's Press, 1992), p. 69.

18. Bellow's brief essay "New York: World Famous Impossibility" (1970), on the symbolic quality of people's behavior in New York, can be productively read as a companion piece to this novel. See Saul Bellow, *It All Adds Up* (New York: Viking, 1994), pp. 217–220.

19. Saul Bellow, *Mr. Sammler's Planet* (New York: Crest Books, 1971), p. 42. On the oversimplification of this real-life incident, see Andrew Gordon's essay "Saul Bellow's 1968 Speech at San Francisco State University" in Gloria Cronin and

Lee Trepanier, *A Political Companion to Saul Bellow* (Lexington: University Press of Kentucky, 2013), pp. 153–166.

20. David Galloway, *The Absurd Hero in American Fiction: Updike, Styron, Bellow, Salinger* (Austin: University of Texas Press, 1981), p. 181.

21. See Ellen Pifer, *Saul Bellow Against the Grain* (Philadelphia: University of Pennsylvania Press, 1990), pp. 20–21 and *On Bellow's Planet*, pp. 148–149.

22. Edward Said, *Orientalism* (Harmondsworth: Penguin, 1995), pp. 206–207.

23. The sociologist Edward Shils, Bellow's patron at the University of Chicago's *Committee on Social Thought*, helped the writer edit Sammler's discourse in the manuscript. Bellow's biographers James Atlas and Zachary Leader have noted that Sammler's psychology and language owes much to Shils' contribution. See James Atlas, *Bellow: A Biography* (New York: Random House, 2000), pp. 390–391 and Leader's *The Life*, pp. 617–619.

24. Malcolm Bradbury, *Saul Bellow* (London: Methuen, 1982), pp. 81–82. Bradbury avoids discussion of the pickpocket episode, and his proposed reading of *Mr. Sammler's Planet* as a satire of the title character is problematic, given the pervasiveness of Sammler's consciousness.

25. Matthew Roudané, "An Interview with Saul Bellow," *Contemporary Literature*, 25.3 (Autumn 1984): 274.

26. Saul Bellow, *Letters*, ed. Benjamin Taylor (New York: Viking, 2010), p. 389.

27. Structurally, Bellow creates an interplay between Corde's scrutiny of two early eighties urban dystopias, Chicago and Bucharest, metonymically embodying capitalist America and the Eastern bloc.

28. Saul Bellow, *The Dean's December* (Harmondsworth: Penguin, 1983), pp. 197–205.

29. Robert F. Kiernan, "*The Dean's December*," in *Critical Insights: Saul Bellow*, ed. Allan Chavkin (Pasadena/Hackensack: Salem Press, 2012), p. 254.

30. Victoria Aarons, "'Washed Up on the Shores of Truth': Saul Bellow's Post-Holocaust America," in *A Political Companion to Saul Bellow*, eds. Gloria Cronin and Lee Trepanier (Lexington: University Press of Kentucky, 2013), p. 143.

31. Sanford Pinsker, *The Schlemiel as Metaphor* (Carbondale: Southern Illinois University Press, 1991), p. 133.

32. Saul Bellow, "Papuans and Zulus," in *There Is Simply Too Much to Think About*, ed. Benjamin Taylor (New York: Viking, 2015), p. 408.

33. John B. Foster, "'Show Me the Zulu Tolstoy': A Russian Classic Between 'First' and 'Third' Worlds," *The Slavic and East European Journal*, 45.2 (Summer 2001): 261.

II

LEONA TOKER

Bellow on Israel: *To Jerusalem and Back*

Written following Bellow's trip to Israel in 1975, *To Jerusalem and Back* (1976) is a travel memoir whose declared aim is not to "make a scoop," or offer solutions to the Arab–Israeli problem, but to record the author's attempts "to observe, to sense a condition or absorb qualities" (111). It is a crafted work in which the desire to understand the complexities of life and thought in Israel encounters its own limitations. The narrative is characterized by rhythmically recurrent motifs, a sequence of ideas and reflections coming from many voices (including the author's own), and Escher-like shaded drawings of extraordinary people (as well as ordinary ones), interlocutors in whom the author senses the depths that, in contrast with the agenda of his fictional works,[1] remain respectfully unprobed.

Bellow had already been in Israel, as a reporter for *Newsday*, during the Six-Day War of 1967. He recalls the criticism he received for running up Telex bills to describe what still continues to haunt him in 1976 – the battlefield with bloated corpses of Egyptian soldiers (58–59). His current visit is that of a celebrated writer rather than of a journalist who could not stop being an artist. In the meantime, the country has undergone significant changes. By 1975, following the Yom Kippur War of 1973, the Israelis have lost the euphoria of the victory of 1967. There is, practically, a consensus about the formerly divided Jerusalem as the capital of the country, but the movement of the settlement on the Left Bank is only incipient – Bellow sides with those who diagnose it as a source of trouble. The dramatic future events are still not foreseen. The Egyptian President Anwar Sadat, whose erstwhile admiration of Hitler is still not forgiven or forgotten, has already visited the United States, but no one yet expects him to make peace with Israel and be killed by militant extremists shortly afterwards. Nor is the first Palestinian uprising (the first *intifada*) anticipated. Lebanon is riven by the civil war. The Soviet Union (referred to, in shorthand, as Russia), still exists, is still buying American grain, has not yet re-established diplomatic relations with Israel. The labor party is still ruling in Israel; it is the following year, 1977, that the Likud Party led by Menahem Begin will win the elections. And yet a great deal in Bellow's representation of the political complexities is as relevant to the present day as it was then, even after several pendulum swings in collective hopes and dominant public opinions. Nor is this true only of Israel: Bellow's cousin Nota Gordon, "two years out of the Soviet Union," comments on the Russian–American relationships in a way that may pertain to Putin's Russia no less than Brezhnev's Soviet Union: "'You are no match for them. You do not understand with whom you are dealing'" (19).[2]

Though the book gives their due to Jerusalem's tourist attractions, some of them off the beaten track, its main interest is in the people, their attitudes, what they say, and what they hold back. Bellow meets intellectuals, politicians, poets, scholars: the text becomes a gallery of speaking faces. In his position of listener he seems to be well aware that what he sees and hears are facets turned toward himself, with much of the soul remaining behind. In most cases, the face and the discourse addressing him are felt to express genuine positions; at other times, they seem to be audience-oriented, self-fashioning.

Bellow and his wife Alexandra, a mathematics professor who is lecturing at the Hebrew University during their stay, are hosted at the Mishkenot Sha'ananim in Jerusalem. Bellow translates the name of this guesthouse, a beloved project of Mayor Teddy Kollek, as "the dwellings of serenity" (5). It is one of the most picturesque Jerusalem landmarks. What he does not mention is that when the building was first erected on the initiative of Moses Montefiore, on a slope facing Mt. Zion across a valley, to offer residence to Jews outside the walls of Jerusalem, many of the "serene" still retreated within the walls for the night, in fear of bandit attacks. The location, which signifies the respect and recognition accorded to distinguished guests and which symbolizes a hilltop view of Israeli realities, also evokes a tension between sweet Levantine serenity and endemic anxieties about survival.

Indeed, survival – "the survival of the decent society created in Israel within a few decades" (25) – is one of the most insistently recurrent themes of the book. Bellow sees the distinctive perennial feature of Jewish life in that "you cannot take your right to live for granted. Others can; you cannot. This is not to say that everyone else is living pleasantly and well under a decent regime. No, it means only that the Jews, because they are Jews, have never been able to take the right to live as a natural right" (26). The Jewish state, for all the civilization that it has created, shares this predicament; by contrast, "when a bomb goes off in a West End restaurant the fundamental right of England to exist is not in dispute" (25). In his review of Bellow's book, Teddy Kollek, one of its heroes, writes that Bellow "is troubled by the military patrols in the streets, but he realizes that while the 'struggle for existence' everywhere else means a fight for a better life, with us here it means survival."³ In his 1967 reportage from Israel, Bellow had seen that Israelis had apparently decided "that they need not concern themselves with the great powers since the great powers had apparently decided to let the Arabs have their way."⁴ This sense of Israel being left to its own fate has waned only partly: variations on the theme of the country's survival recur in Bellow's numerous encounters, even at the dinner with the Armenian Archbishop in Jerusalem.

The "intelligent discussions" that take place on this and similar occasions are a historically and personally familiar genre. Bellow notes sadly that, "the discussants invariably impart their own intelligence to what they are discussing," whereas "historical studies show that what actually happened was devoid of anything like such intelligence." His comment that what is perpetuated by such discussions "is the ritual of civilized discussion itself" (8) resonates with his remark about the face of the young Hasidic man who sat next to him on the airplane and tried to persuade him to renounce non-kosher food: "He does not keep a civilized face. Thoughts and impulses other than civilized fill it – by no means inferior impulses and thoughts" (2). A true believer's passion need not be regarded as inferior to the civilized irony of the intellectual. In another connection Bellow will answer Yeats's "The Second Coming" by calling into question the belief that "passionate intensity is all on the side of wickedness" (60).

In this book, written before the Palestinian issue came to dominate concerns with the Middle East, the Palestinian perspective is limited to the statements of Abu Zuluf, editor of an East Jerusalem Arabic newspaper *El Kuds*, whom Bellow visits in his office and whom Teddy Kollek describes as a "pleasant and jovial ... six-foot plus millionaire."⁵ In Abu Zuluf's estimate, the Arab countries "are continually gaining strength while Israel becomes weaker," therefore Israel "'must come forward quickly with peace plans and initiate negotiations, show willingness to negotiate'" (36). When later, at tea in the house of the novelist David Shahar, Bellow recounts this point, he feels uneasy: "I am beginning to irritate [Shahar] with my American evenhandedness, my objectivity at his expense. It is so easy for outsiders to say that there are two sides to the question. What a terrible expression! I am beginning to detest it" (38).

After giving Bellow a historical retrospect on the Arab–Israeli conflict, the host grows passionate: "'They don't want our peace proposals. They don't want concessions, they want us destroyed!' Shahar shouts and slams the table" (38). The poet Dennis Silk, who is also present, turns his "exquisite face" downward to gaze at the table – the rules of civilized conversation have been broken. Bellow's tacit response is reminiscent of James Joyce's rejection of the "big words" that "make us so unhappy."[6] He feels that he cannot tell Shahar that "the consciousness of the West" will never permit Israel to be destroyed ... Such grand statements are no longer made; all our hyperbole is nowadays reserved for silence. We know that anything can happen" (38).

In hindsight, views associated with Abu Zuluf's and Shahar's positions will continue ascending and descending, sea-saw fashion, for several decades (they still mark the discourse on the two sides of the Israeli dove/hawk divide). This rhythm is uncannily foreshadowed in the book through alternation of their variants. Abu Zuluf's view finds support in, for instance, an article by the Hebrew University Professor Tzvi Lamm, which Bellow recounts (65–70); Shahar's views find uneasy indirect support in the poet Chaim Gouri's distress over the attitudes of an Arab family with whom he had become friends (49–50). Prime Minister Yitzak Rabin is still inclined to the latter view, still remote from the position that will lead him to Oslo accords and that will make him a victim of assassination in 1995. Notably, neither of these views is extreme – Bellow distances himself, for instance, both from Noam Chomsky's view of Israel as an instrument of Western imperialism and from Yuval Ne'eman's rejection of the concept of Israel's dependence on the United States (171–175). The perspective that he regards as better balanced than most others is that of Professor Yehoshafat Harkabi, who

> concedes that the Arabs have been wronged, but .... insists upon the moral meaning of Israel's existence .... The Zionists were not deliberately unjust, the Arabs were not guiltless. To rectify the evil as the Arabs would wish it rectified would mean the destruction of Israel. Arab refugees must be relieved and compensated, but Israel will not commit suicide for their sake. By now the Arabs see themselves returning in blood and fire, and Israel will not agree to bleed and burn. A sweeping denial of Arab grievances is, however, an obstacle to peace. (157–158)

In his review of *To Jerusalem and Back*, Teddy Kollek (whose extensive portrait, presented in instalments in the book, combines admiration with an almost imperceptible touch of irony) notes that, as an outsider, Bellow has difficulty estimating "which views are widely held and which are maverick, or which are likely to be acted upon."[7] Yet the status of opinions as mainstream or marginal and as operative or dangling would keep fluctuating for decades. However it might be, Bellow sometimes does point to views which, he believes, are not likely to be translated into practice. An attempt to bridge the gap is reflected on in the wake of his reading of an article by Harkabi, which suggests that "Arab and Israeli scholars should cooperate in studying the conflict" but admits that this may be "an inordinate faith in the power of rationality." For Bellow, this is also "Jewish faith or Jewish longing or even Jewish transcendentalism" (92). This remark, however, is placed considerably earlier than the record of Harkabi's oral statements quoted above, as if to reduce its potential for subverting them.

Meantime, Bellow puts little trust in what he sees as the fatigued and despairing "humanistic civilized moral imagination" (58). At one of the more luxurious moments in his Israeli experience, he has an apocalyptic vision:

> Suddenly this temperate Mediterranean day and the orange groves and the workers steering their bikes and the children's playground flutter like illustrated paper. What is there to keep them from blowing away? (64)

This, however, may well be the influence of a pre-prandial glass of Stolichnaya. In the next section it turns out that Bellow is in need of a massage to relieve "muscular tensions" (64) – a literal detail with symbolic connotations. He will also get a respite from "the butcher problems on politics" (80) on a morning spent with the poets Harold Schimmel and Dennis Silk.

Though some readers focus on the book's exploration of the author's identity, the concern with "what am I that I am here" (as of Matthew Arnold visiting the Chartreuse Convent) is not central in Bellow's account of this journey. Bellow goes to Israel in order to understand its world – by analogy with his Henry Jamesian view of America as "more a world than a country" (130) – rather than in order to understand himself. He tends to refer to himself as an American when he represents his stay in Israel, his sense of his American cultural affiliation apparently increasing in his interactions with his cousins who had recently immigrated from the Soviet Union, where they had known unspeakable suffering, especially under the German occupation. By contrast, in the passages dealing with his return to the USA, via England, he tends to see himself as a Jew.[8] In both cases, the complexity of his identity creates a touch not so much of alienation as of defamiliarization – an artistic stance appropriate to his seeing himself, first and foremost, as a writer.

De-emphasizing problems of identity does not diminish the reflectiveness of the book. Though extrapolation and inference are often regarded as marks of a superior intellect, Bellow is wary of the hastiness of generalization and judgment, especially since some of his interlocutors have a limited tolerance "for vague views and inexact formulations" (105). He abstains from judgmental bottom lines, even at the price of disappointing those readers who expect a leading novelist of ideas to sort out "the Arab-Israeli muddle"[9] for them, instead of offering to complicate the way one thinks about Israel, its vitality, its tensions, and its griefs. In reference to Sartre as a proponent of the view that more is to be demanded of Israel than of other countries, Bellow notes that "in taking positions or advocating actions that may cost people their lives one should be as clear as possible about historical facts" (123); otherwise, much "intelligence can be invested in ignorance when the need for illusion is deep" (127).

The issue of Israeli attitudes to American Jewish identity is shifted from Bellow himself to the puzzling case of Henry Kissinger. While Bellow is in Jerusalem, people are discussing an open letter published by Joseph Alsop which, among other things, suggests that Kissinger's role is underappreciated by Israeli public opinion. Bellow notes that Kissinger is "widely believed to have delayed sending help during the Yom Kippur War because he wanted the Egyptians to enjoy a limited victory and recover self-esteem. In the end, so goes the story, it was Defense Secretary James R. Schlesinger who went to Nixon and pressed him to fly supplies immediately to Israel" (102). Kissinger is also believed to have negotiated a would-be premature cease-fire behind the back of the Israeli cabinet, a cease-fire that made the ultimate Israeli victory less striking. Though "[a]nother week's fighting would have cost a thousand more Israeli lives, as Abba Eban sensibly said," Kissinger tends to remain unforgiven: "What in Kissinger is called 'betrayal' might, in a non-Jewish secretary of state, be accepted with a shrug as diplomacy – one of the normal forms of perfidy, that is" (102).

As to Alsop, "very much the New England aristocrat" (103) who, judging by what Bellow hears from Yitzhak Rabin, had not been "altogether in favor of a Jewish state in Palestine" and changed his mind later, some of his erstwhile attitudes seem to be betrayed by lexical choices that irk Bellow. The section about Alsop and Kissinger is concluded by a rhetorical question: "[t]he fact that Israel is dependent on the United States is plain enough. What is it that tempts an American publicist to make what everyone can see so cruelly explicit?" (103–104).

Throughout the book, Bellow is concerned with the quality of his own attitudes and thoughts. Both admiration and condescension are responses that he strives, consistently – but not always successfully – to avoid. A twelve-year-old Russian-immigrant violinist who is auditioning with Isaac Sterne and Alexander Schneider almost reconciles him to "the detested" Mendelssohn Concerto: "I try to smile at his fiddler's affectations but my face refuses to obey. I can only think, How did I ever learn to smile such a cheap smile. I'm well rid of it, then, and I sit listening" (74). He listens, respectfully, to the government minister Israel Galili, with whom he disagrees regarding Israeli attitudes to Palestinian grievances, but he cannot withhold admiration from Shimon

Peres, "too superior a politician to be drawn into a dispute of this nature over lunch." Mr. Peres, who "has really come to discuss literature" with a fellow writer, "carries an aura," somewhat like the Kennedy brothers. As if in order not to get carried away, Bellow attempts to convey this feature through the trope of diet – it is as if these people have been nourished by "liver, kidneys, and potent glands," only to withdraw this man-is-what-he-eats touch ("for Leopold Bloom, who ate these with relish, did not dazzle Dublin with his vitality") and concede that their shine is that of a sense of power. Yet the metaphor of "organ meats" (69) qualifies the admiration.

Israeli reality confounds neat distinctions between causes and consequences, intentions and effects, as well as criteria for judgment. Is Israel a "democratic exception" (14) in the Middle East, or the arena of a tug of war between intentions to build a "just society" and assorted bigotries? Is it a long-sought haven for the Jews from all over the world or, as a Harvard professor suggests to Bellow, a concentration of the Jews conveniently assembled for a second Holocaust (an idea that obsesses a character in Philip Roth's *Operation Shylock*[10])? "And what is it that has led the Jews to place themselves, after the greatest disaster of their history, in a danger zone?" asks Bellow (15), partly in tune with Elie Kedurie's unease with the entrance of the Jews into politics through construction of the nation-state. Part of the answer is given several pages earlier, when on a walk in the Hinnom valley underneath Mishkenot, David Shahar mentions that one can be sure that "the Prophet Jeremiah passed this way. Right where we are standing" (11): by implication, the danger zone is where Jewish history is anchored.[11] Yet the effect of placing the question after the answer amounts to a partial subversion of the answer. And when David Shahar is quoted as saying "Where there is no paradox there is no life" (15), one may wonder whether this is an insight that supports his intellectual stamina or a sound-bite that only staves off doubts. Judging by the way Bellow seems to be gradually warming up to the Jewish state,[12] not despite but because of the paradoxes to which he is exposed by his "reality instructors,"[13] the former assessment is more fully applicable.

Bellow's own positions are likewise tested against reality.[14] Mentioning, with reference to A. B. Yehoshua's book of interviews, the inability of Israelis to "break free of the moment, forget the moment" in the current history and politics, Bellow posits the need "[n]ot to submit to what societies and governments consider to be important" (21), and to allow, instead, "human feelings, human experience, the human form and face" to recover "their proper place – the foreground" (22). Yet the section that immediately follows is devoted to Bellow's friend John Auerbach. This Holocaust survivor is living an active practical and intellectual life while always grieving for his son, whose helicopter had crashed on the way back from a military action: in Israel, the human experience, in the foreground of everyday consciousness and of the artistic text, is inseparable from history and politics. Bellow becomes aware of Israeli citizens' addiction to the news on the media, and interprets it as an aspect of having

> to work so hard on so many levels . . . . In less than thirty years the Israelis have produced a modern country – doorknobs and hinges, plumbing fixtures, electrical supplies, chamber music, airplanes, teacups . . . . All resources, all faculties are strained. Unremitting thought about the world situation parallels the defense effort. These people are actively, individually involved in universal history. I don't see how they can bear it. (46)

For Bellow, this fascinating feature of living in Israel is thus also alienating because he suspects – wrongly – that it dampens individual creativity (reviewing the book, Irving Howe refers, hyperbolically, to "a murderous barrage on the nerves" that Bellow senses, as it were, on his trip). Judging by the number of scholars whom Bellow encounters,[15] he appreciates the work done in the humanities in Israel, but, though he meets Meyer Weisgal, one of the founders of the Weizmann Institute of Science, he does not foresee the vigorous development of Israeli science and high-tech engineering at the turn of the millennium. In this book, the Israeli economy is still based on fruit, flowers, and the polishing of diamonds.

Bellow inscribes his book into a specific strand of the American thought: its precursors are, in particular, two nineteenth-century representations of journeys to Jerusalem – Melville's *Clarel* and Mark Twain's *The Innocents Abroad*, which refute the Puritan Zionism of the seventeenth century that viewed America as a promised land and denied the material, geographical meaning of Zion.[16] Bellow records sometimes thinking that "there are two Israels. The real one is territorially insignificant. The other, the mental Israel, is immense, a country inestimably important, playing a major role in the world, as broad as all history – and perhaps as deep as sleep" (131). It seems, however, that this thought too is mutable, a wave that periodically rises and subsides among other ripples of reflection.

Significantly, however, this wave begins to assemble mainly in the sections that pertain to the author's last days in Israel, before returning to the USA. It is against the background of these days that Bellow places his reading of and his talks with Jacob Leib Talmon, a tormented thinker underneath his surface of gentle professorial propriety. Talmon believes that with the destruction of the Jewish intellectual vanguard during the Holocaust – "Zionists, liberal democrats, highly trained and accomplished" – along with their secular institutions, the synagogue was left as a unifying factor in Jewish life, leading to the "success of clericalism in Israel" (134). In the free-indirect-speech record of their further conversation, Bellow's thoughts seem to merge with Talmon's. They return to the worries about survival and, critically, to the view that more is demanded of Israel than of other nations. Now, forty years later, the remarks may be read as prophetic:

> While Israel fought for life, debates weighed her sins and especially the problem of Palestinians. In this disorderly century refugees have fled from many countries. In India, in Africa, in Europe, millions of human beings have been put to flight, transported, enslaved, stampeded over the borders, left to starve, but only the case of the Palestinians is held permanently open. Where Israel is concerned, the world swells with moral consciousness. ... What Switzerland is to winter holidays and the Dalmatian coast to summer tourists, Israel and the Palestinians are to the West's need for justice – a sort of moral resort area.
>
> (135–136)

It is the territorial conquest of 1967 and the settlement of the West Bank (still incipient in 1975) that is viewed as the main factor in the endangered status of Israel. Bellow does not withhold a note of admiration for the descendants of the Gush Etzion colony farming the land on which their fathers had been slaughtered in 1948, yet he distinguishes these settlers from the early Zionists who "were satisfied with a sanctuary and did not try to recover the Promised Land" (131–132).

Bellow partly endorses Melville's and Twain's vision of the land as bleak and desert-like, though he mentions its reclamation by the Jewish settlement. What he does not seem to experience is the mysterious sense of homecoming to which many Russian-Jewish immigrants to Israel testify, even while they still do not speak Hebrew. Though at some points, e.g. in the orchards of John Auerbach's seaside kibbutz, Bellow feels the Levantine sensuousness of the air and the sun and is "only slightly heavyhearted" (62), it seems that his non-Jewish wife Alexandra is more positively responsive to the ambiance than himself.

On leaving Israel, Bellow continues his pursuit of understanding. In London he purchases books to further his study of the history of the Middle East. Distance means living down his direct experience, as well as zooming out to study the broader contexts, including the twentieth-century history of Israel's Arab neighbors. The genre of Bellow's "Personal Account" thus comes to combine that of the memoir-in-conversations with that of the memoir-in-books: the positions expressed in works by Elie Kedurie, Jakov Lind, Lev Navrozov, A. B. Yehoshua, George Steiner, Mikhail Agursky, and others join the vortex of ideas. The art of this non-fictional work is a matter not only of style but also of collocations and juxtapositions. Bellow joins into one section the story of his being attended on by the barber of Jerusalem's King David hotel, who is an admirer of Hubert H. Humphrey, and the memory of circulating at a White House banquet in honor of Harold Wilson, where Humphrey was present.[17] Whereas the episode with the hairdresser is a new take on the elderly barber topos,[18] the White House part of the section is a masterpiece account of circulating among celebrities, structured (like most of the book, but in a more condensed way) on a convergence-and-distancing pattern. One cannot say that the encounter with an ordinary person is the more meaningful of the two events, but it ends in a haircut and a memory of communication in Ladino, whereas the banquet leaves the speaker with an almost physical sense of "the phenomenon described by neurologists as an insult to the brain" (33).

Back in the USA, Bellow – the "I" of the book – continues meeting people to hear their perspectives on Israel. This is an innovative approach to *nostos* – Chicago is neither a familiar setting rendered dull by the recent exotics nor an embracing comfort zone. Rather, it is a platform for further thought and study. The last sections of the book bring into relief the ambiguity of its narrative structure: it is not always clear which of Bellow's views are ex-tempore responses to his Jerusalem experience and which are retrospective conceptualizations. One's hold on one's opinions may, in any case, be uneven – as in the case of Professor Shlomo Avineri, whose all too lenient views on the repressive Soviet Union are, Bellow believes, experimental – "in another mood, he may take a different line" (44). Bellow himself, mindful of Soviet labor camps no less than of the Arab–Israeli conflict, attempts to maintain some consistency of attitudes while seeking to keep them complex and nuanced, but he feels that "[i]nstead of coming to clarity," while navigating among discourses, "one is infected with disorder" (175). The ambiguity of time-layers replicates this effect: it is not always clear what Bellow said "then" and what he thinks "now." For instance, when he characterizes Hubert Humphrey as a person "who learns by talking," who "knows the right thing when he sees it, or when he says it," who "picks up a good many intelligent opinions," and may be making his own creative contribution "by debate, repetition, embellishment, and editing" (43), it is not clear whether this portrait replicates what he told Abba Eban on their drive downtown from the Knesset or whether it is constructed at the time of composition. To some extent, the remarks on Humphrey are self-referential: Bellow himself likewise learns not just by listening and reading but also – and perhaps mainly – by writing. The book does not so much express formed views as work toward their formation.

The views remain uncodified, however. In the end Bellow has not achieved intellectual comfort and has not had the emotional knots of his experience massaged away. The book ends on a note of sadness, with a conclusion in which nothing is really concluded. This indeterminacy is an artistically suitable response to what he has absorbed of Israel's irrepressible tensions, whether, as he thinks, detrimental or, on the contrary, favorable to individual creativity.

Notes

1. As Willis Salomon notes, in Bellow's novels, the "focus on personal depth involves the idea of 'soul,' which, for Bellow, resonates both in individual characters and in the 'character' of culture – one of Bellow's career-long preoccupations, and one usually viewed as being in historical decline." ("Saul Bellow on the Soul: Character and the Spirit of Culture in *Humboldt's Gift* and *Ravelstein*," *Partial Answers* 14.1 [2016]: 127–128.)
2. The parenthetic page references are to Saul Bellow, *To Jerusalem and Back: A Personal Account* (London: Secker & Warburg, 1976.)
3. Teddy Kollek, "To Jerusalem and Back by Saul Bellow," *The New Republic* (November 20, 1976): 37.
4. Saul Bellow, "Israel: The Six-Day War," *It All Adds Up*, p. 206.
5. Kollek "To Jerusalem and Back by Saul Bellow," 36.
6. James Joyce, *Ulysses* (Harmondsworth: Penguin, 2000), p. 38.
7. Kollek "To Jerusalem and Back by Saul Bellow," 36. In addition, Kollek is critical of Bellow's Chicago colleague's opinion of Israel's political prospects, quoted at length at the end of *To Jerusalem and Back*. One might add that Bellow also misnames the national-religious stream in Israeli society as the "ultra-Orthodox" (165).
8. Christine Bird discusses this contrast as part of the book's concern with a *return* journey; see "The Return Journey in *To Jerusalem and Back*," *MELUS* 6.4 (1979): 52.
9. Steven David Lavine, "On the Road to Jerusalem: Bellow Now," *Studies in American Jewish Literature* 3.1 (1977): 1. Though Lavine grants "Bellow's decency, humility, and honesty in refusing to opt for some simplistic solution," he goes on to say that "even the almost willfully wrong-headed analyses of Mailer's journalistic works have more potential to excite and enlighten" (2).
10. For a comparison of *To Jerusalem and Back* and Roth's 1994 *Operation Shylock* (as well as Roth's *Portnoy's Complaint* and *Counterlife*), see Sophia Lehmann, "Exodus and Homeland: The Representation of Israel in Saul Bellow's *To Jerusalem and Back* and Philip Roth's *Operation Shylock*," *Religion and Literature* 30.3 (1998): 77–96.
11. In Washington, Kissinger (whom Bellow believes to be taping the conversation to protect himself from misquotations), says to Bellow, "if only the Bible had been written in Uganda" (177), referring to the scheme (declined by the Zionist

Congress of 1905) of offering the Jewish people a homeland in a part of British-held Uganda.

12. See Lehmann, "Exodus and Homeland," 84–85.

13. Sarah Blacher Cohen, "Saul Bellow's Jerusalem," *Studies in American Jewish Literature* 5 (1979): 16.

14. What makes Irving Howe's 1976 review of *To Jerusalem and Back* somewhat unfair is his singling out ideas that jar on him without noting how they are attenuated, tested, and juxtaposed with opposite positions in the complex web of Bellow's book.

15. Incidentally, his farewell party is attended by, among others, "our friends the Daleskis" (138), that is, Prof. H. M. Daleski and his wife, the poet Shirley Kaufman.

16. On the self-inscription of Bellow's book in this American literary strand of ideas, see Cohen 1979 and Emily Miller Budick, "The Place of Israel in American Writing: Reflections on Saul Bellow's *To Jerusalem and Back*," *South Central Review* 8.1 (1991): 59–70.

17. Bellow's choice of intellectual events to collocate in the same sections is not dependent on the chronology of his encounters and might be an interesting subject of rhetorical analysis.

18. Cf., in particular, the barber-of-Kasbeam passage in Nabokov's *Lolita* (*The Annotated Lolita*, ed. Alfred Appel, New York: McGraw-Hill, 1970, p. 215).

12

SUKHBIR SINGH

Bellow's Non-Fiction: *It All Adds Up*

> The concern of tale-tellers and novelists is with the human essences
> neglected and forgotten by a distracted world.
> Saul Bellow

It All Adds Up: From the Dim Past to the Uncertain Future (1994) is
a collection of selected essays written by Saul Bellow on different occasions and for diverse purposes. They are in the varying nature of
articles, interviews, reminiscences, travel accounts, lectures, character
sketches, literary analyses, and obituaries, etc. There is therefore no
thematic unity among them, and it is also difficult to trace a regular
artistic or ideological thread running across these pieces. But, still, there
is something *secretly* common among them that only an astute reader
can apprehend. One senses while reading them horizontally – from the
first to the last – a downward, vertical pull toward the *hidden treasure*
that each essay conceals at its bottom. What promptly possesses the
reader is a compelling wish, a kind of mystical lure, to search for this
buried wealth of Bellow's views on several significant aspects of contemporary life such as arts, literature, politics, religion, race, science,
society, people, and places, etc. The essays simultaneously open up
a wide window to innumerable yet unknown or lesser-known facts of
Bellow's personal and literary lives: himself, his parents, family, friends,
his education, artistic apprenticeship, ideological leanings, rise to fame,
and slow maturing of his artistic talents to the winning of Nobel Prize in
1976. At the end, such knowledge leaves one sufficiently sensitized to
grasp the *Bellow mystique*, which has kept his readers endlessly
enthralled in the last several decades. The anthology thus offers
a master key to the long locked vaults beneath Bellow's vast fictional
edifice. "Clearly it [the collection] is meant," Christopher Lehman-
Haupt observes, "to take us through the labyrinth of its author's creative impulses to the door of his art. But where do we go from there
besides back to his fiction?"[1]

The Bellow Mystique

Before we plunge into the text of *It All Adds Up*, it would only be appropriate to first contextualize the collection within the overall gamut of Bellow's artistic concerns. Bellow has been widely hailed as a devout humanist by both students and scholars alike. For Bellow, it is wrong to believe that contemporary man is condemned to lead a "dreadful life"; the only thing he "can be in this world is human."[2] He therefore consistently preoccupies himself in his novels with the plight of common men and women amidst pervasive evil, egocentricity, complexity, and chaos in today's world. Irrespective of their gender, class, color, country, and economic status, Bellow projects them as *fundamentally human* in all their goodness and grotesqueries. In the process, he glosses those qualities that we all share in common and in which we are bound together in an inexorable bond. In doing so, Bellow assimilates the isolated people, such as Joseph in his first novel, *Dangling Man* (1944) and Wilhelm in *Seize the Day* (1956), into a common world of fellow beings and thereby responds to his own pertinent query: "When will we see new and higher forms of individuality purged of old sickness and corrected by a deeper awareness of what all men have in common?"[3] It is curious to note that in Bellow's statements here in the essays and elsewhere in his novels, two words strike the reader most prominently: "deep" or "deeper," and "high" or "higher." These two together characterize Bellow's basic approach to human life in terms of its *deeper* substance (primal) and *higher* truths (transcendental). Bellow's approach actually is that of an *essentialist* – he tirelessly probes the bottomless depths of the "common human nature" in search of the innate *essences* which resonate with divinity and relate us to a higher reality. Like Tommy Wilhelm in *Seize the Day*, Bellow is a "sucker" of the "deeper things of life"; like Artur Sammler in *Mr. Sammler's Planet* (1970), "a depth man"; and like Charlie Citrine in *Humboldt's Gift* (1975), a seeker of "higher wakefulness." In his interview with Jo Brans, Bellow notably displays his *down-reaching* perception of an astute anthropologist, saying that

> people live by something far deeper than the head culture [education and ideas]; they couldn't live if they didn't. They couldn't survive if they didn't. What a woman does for her children, what a man does for his family, what people most tenaciously cling to, these things are not adequately explained by Oedipus complexes, libidos, class struggles, or existential individualism – whatever you like.[4]

Bellow offers an explanation to such silent secrets in his fiction by seeking the original, eternal, invariable, and transcendental in man and matter. But his quest for higher truths and deeper realities does not remain confined to his fiction alone; it carries on with equal zeal in his non-fictional prose as well. This pursuit is indeed the central unifying factor among the divergent essays in *It All Adds Up*: it holds them together like beads on a string and links the anthology with Bellow's best fictional books. John Brown therefore aptly remarks, "Closely linked with Bellow's fiction, they [the essays] reveal the richness and the variety and occasionally the contradictions and discursiveness, of the outstanding novelist of his brilliant generation."[5]

It All Adds Up

Bellow's passion for a dip into the deep interiorities of life consistently characterizes each essay in the anthology. Whether he talks about men of great eminence in arts, literature, and public life, or treats surging crowds on the imperial streets of Paris, France, and stinking dirt on the dingy roads of Shawneetown, Illinois, his eagle eyes are singularly set on the unseen and unknown below or above or beyond the apparent glamour and gloom of the material surroundings. These eminent men appear to Bellow as "intervention of invisible purposes" in the apparent affairs of the phenomenal world (3). The cities are to him a passing pageant of the material life which carries en route what is superficial or ephemeral and leaves behind what is fundamental, deep-rooted, below the remains. While sketching some of the celebrated artists and politicians in the anthology, Bellow peeps beyond their "superfluous externals" and "somnambulistic histrionics" to see the "radical mysteries of our being" unveiled in the spontaneous expressions of their elemental selves (12). For instance, he hears from behind Mozart's troubled self the calm music of his soul which gives the listener "an orderly and also an emotional exit – an endlessly rich and exalted release" by the tonal expression of "essences inseparable from what we call our 'higher life'" (3). Despite his clownery and spoofing, Roosevelt "*looked* the great man, sent Americans the message that beyond pretending and theatricality there was a further range, in which one's deeper nature could continue to live, its truth undamaged" (27; emphasis in original). Similarly, in Khrushchev, Bellow senses, beyond the dictator's comic buffoonery and abusive outbursts, an "essential Russian" who "wears his instincts on his sleeve" and freely "releases his deepest feelings" in full public view (36–37). Bellow's yearning for depth is so compelling that he at times comically becomes an intruder into *kitchens*, voyeur of *bedrooms*, and a surveyor of *latrines*. When he briefly halts at the Hilton hotel in Ramallah during his journalistic travel through war-torn Israel (201–217, italics added), he strays into the kitchen to fathom its interiority and enlarge his culinary awareness as a fond lover of good food:

"I get into the kitchen – always drawn to kitchens – and admire the great saucepans and cleavers, grinders, the chopping block a piece of tree trunk with the bark still on it" (213). And, a little further, when the local residents at the Kalandia camp invite him and other journalists "into their houses with elaborate courtesy," he helplessly peeps into the inner compartments, not sparing even the most forbidden ones – the bedrooms and latrines: "The tiny, *sunken*, windowless rooms have a few scraps of carpet, a stool, a bedroll, a piece of broken mirror. I look into the latrine – the cement floors with slots for the feet are washed down. There is water" (214; emphasis mine). On another occasion, amid the "humanized" surroundings of far-off Tuscany, Bellow senses the soil carrying "the centuries lightly, and ancient buildings and ruins do not produce gloomy feelings. The Romanesque interiors in fact are a good cure for heaviness" (253). Similarly, the near-at-hand "rubble" of his ancestral residence on Le Moyne Street in Chicago turns him "inward, to look for what *endures*. Give Chicago half a chance, and it will turn you into a philosopher" (245; emphasis added).

It All Adds Up is a rich repository of Bellow's core convictions about a vast variety of subjects – they all individually and collectively bear the stamp of his overwhelming passion for the elemental, imperishable, and transcendental. The ensuing part of this chapter will display Bellow's insatiable appetite for interiority in his views on four fundamental facets of his creative mystique, i.e., *Art*, *Artist*, *Self*, and *Soul*. These beliefs act as basic ingredients in the shaping of Bellow's fictional literature and in the conduct of his personal life.

Art

Bellow repeatedly expresses his views on the compelling necessity of art through the many essays and interviews in *It All Adds Up*. For him, a "world *without* art" would be "a world corrupted – a condition far more desperate than any envisioned by the most pessimistic ecologists" (77). In Bellow's view, art is not for art's sake or an end in itself, as believed by many; it is an effective means to a human cause – deep exploration into the "radical mysteries of being" and moral elevation of humanity to "higher consciousness." In today's "distracted" world, where "survival anxiety has become permanent with us and public unrest has set into our souls,"[6] mankind faces a frightful challenge to its long-conserved sanity and morality. In Bellow's opinion, art can act as "the community's medicine for the worst disease of mind, the corruption of consciousness"[7] by offering "compensation for the hopelessness or meanness of existence" (61). Therefore, he calls upon his fellow artists to follow Shakespeare, Cervantes, and Tolstoy by excavating those human qualities in their art that did exist earlier but slowly got buried beneath the spiritual debris of a decadent society in the last two centuries. He exhorts them to learn from Flaubert, who believed that "the writer by means of imagery and style must supply the human qualities that the exterior world lacked" (61). These elemental qualities need to be supplemented by contemporary artists and experienced by the reader in their art: Art finds in the "universe, in matter as well as in the facts of life, what was fundamental, enduring, essential" (88). Actually, Bellow and his other young friends *felt* before they began to write that "something had not found full expression ['fundamental, enduring, essential'], and this was the intuition that made solitary young men and women so obstinate in their pursuit of art" (127). They persistently probed deep into the subterraneous regions of the lonely self to lay bare those primal mysteries of human nature that bestowed human status only upon us among all species in the universe. Their expression of the "unexpressed," such as in Joyce Cary's works, reassures the bewildered reader that "there are powerful and original natures to be found still, that genius exists, that striving is not necessarily monomania, happiness not extinct, hope not unjustified."[8]

Due to the shrinkage of moral space in today's world, the common man has suffered an unusual suppression of his primal essence. But, it is not so completely eliminated as to never be experienced again: "This essence reveals and then conceals itself. When it goes away it leaves us again in doubt. But our connection remains with the depths from which these glimpses come" (97). These "glimpses" (Proust's "true impressions" and Joyce's "epiphanies") need to be captured and turned into an inextinguishable glow in art for the moral enlightenment of the man on the street: "One of his [writer's] legacies from Romanticism is a sensitivity to banality and ugliness, in which originates much of the small change of modern fiction – the teeth that are crooked, the soiled underclothes, the clerk with carbuncles. From this comes a conventional unearned wretchedness, a bitterness about existence, which is mere fashion" (63). The novelist should overcome his "abhorrence of ordinary" existence because "With simple peoples we can nail down the meaning of life" (303). What Bellow implies here is that common people are closer to their real selves, are more capable of deeper and higher realizations than others, and they can fast recover the elemental states on being cleansed of their false illusions. For instance, Asa Leventhal, an ordinary Jewish clerk in Bellow's *The Victim* (1947), receives at the end an epiphanic intimation from "a depth of life" about his inexorable human kinship with all "outcasts" of the world. The intuition reverts him to the state of primal innocence, wondering over "who runs things?" The artist, therefore, should focus on the common struggle of people – to their great strife for the protection of soul that is taking place at the center of the human spectacle today. Bellow believes that

> Out of the struggle at the center has come an immense, painful longing for a broader, more flexible, fuller, more coherent, more comprehensive account of what we human beings are, who we are, and what this life is for. At the center, humankind struggles with collective powers for its freedom, the individual struggles with dehumanization for the possession of his soul.   (96)

Tolstoy enters this center to capture the struggle alive in *Anna Karenina* (1877), and, therefore, Dostoevsky remarks, "'in the very center of that insolent and petty life there appeared a great and eternal living truth, at once illuminating everything. These petty, insignificant and deceitful beings suddenly became genuine and truthful people worthy of being called men'" (68). Other novelists, too, can freely enter the center of this ordeal if they so wish and harness the power of their art to record intimations of the "higher truth": "The power of a work of art," Bellow informs, "is such that it induces a temporary suspension of activities. It leads to contemplative states, to wonderful and, to my mind, sacred states of the soul" (84). There the reader blissfully transcends the barriers of his creaturely bondage and floats freely in the higher domains of transcendental consciousness. Bellow believes that "art has something to do with the achievement of stillness in the midst of chaos. A stillness which characterizes prayer ... an arrest of attention in the midst of distraction."[9] The reader experiences such stillness, the silencing of "will and desire," in Sammler's serene state of mind at Elya Gruner's death bed and Herzog's clairvoyant repose in the police station at the end.

Artist

Bellow's idea of the artist is closely aligned with his view of art as illustrated above. For him, an artist is not an angel from the distant heavens, but a common man of the mundane world. However, the artist's task is surely *uncommon* – to bestow artistic grandeur upon what otherwise appears as bland, boring, drab, dull, and damaged. He raises the mundane to metaphysical heights and imparts deeper meaning to the apparently meaningless things by the redemptive power of his art. It begins, in Bellow's view, with the artist's exploration into the lowest layers of his own lonely self:

> To begin with, the artist had only himself; he descended within himself, and in the lonely regions to which he descended he found "the terms of his appeal." He appealed, said Conrad, "to that part of our being which is a gift, not an acquisition, to the capacity for delight and wonder ... our sense of pity and pain, to the latent feeling of fellowship with all creation – and to the subtle but

invincible conviction of solidarity that knits together the loneliness of innumerable hearts ... which binds together all humanity – the dead to the living and
living to the unborn." (88–89)

Likewise, subsequent artists too can plumb deep into the subliminal regions
of their characters' distraught selves to excavate and express the immutable
truths of life in their works. By arresting these inner realities, which fall
beyond all human travails and temptations, the artist would liberate both
his art and his audience from the cultural fixities and ideological orthodoxies.

Bellow insistently draws the reader's attention toward those emancipative
facts of life that have remained submerged within the darker recesses of the
distracted modern self: "We are much more limber, versatile, better articulated, there is much more to us – we all feel it" (95–96). Hence, contemporary
artists should "appeal to that part of our being which is a gift under the
wreckage of many systems. The collapse of those systems may bring a blessed
and necessary release from formulations, from misleading conceptions of
being and consciousness" (96). Under the debris of these reductive systems lie
the unfettering essences ever untainted by the man-made laws and legisla-
tions. With the help of his art, imagery, style, and "serenity of form," the
artist should penetrate below the rubble to search for the underlying and
unidentified facts of life; he should pierce beyond "what pride, passion,
intelligence, and habit erect on all sides – the seeming realities of this
world. There is another reality, the genuine one, of which we lose sight.
This other reality is always sending us hints, which, without art, we can't
receive" (93). A passionate and perceptive writer records these hints to enter
himself and his readers into the "quiet zone" of aesthetic bliss (93). He or she
attempts "to describe the pleasure that comes from recognition or rediscovery of certain essences permanently associated with human life. These
essences are restored to our consciousness by persons who are described as
artists" (168). According to Bellow, these essences are the source of people's
hunger, and it is the artist's duty to satisfy such "deepest human needs" (78):
"In our times, those essences are forced to endure strange torments and
privations. There are moments when they appear to be lost beyond recovery.
But then we hear or read something that exhumes them, even gives them
a soiled, tattered resurrection. ... they revive for us moments of emotional
completeness and overflowing comprehension, they unearth buried
essences" (168). Bellow sets an example to follow in his "classic" novella,
Seize the Day, where the protagonist Tommy Wilhelm finally sheds his
"pretender soul" and extends his "real soul" to "a larger body" of common
people on Broadway. The anonymous crowd forces him into a nearby funeral parlor where he weeps from the depths of his heart over the dead body of

an unknown person. Wilhelm sinks "deeper than sorrow," descends into the "quiet zone," where the sublime "sea-like music" fills his famished ears.

Self

Several contemporary novelists, and those modernist novelists in the past, have most irrationally dispensed with the romantic notion of the uniqueness of the human self: "Those writers who wish to meet the demand for information," Bellow comments, "have perhaps been successful as social historians, but they have neglected the higher forms of imagination" (67). Of course, now "the human being is not what he commonly thought a century ago. The question nevertheless remains. He is something. What is he?"[10] In his essay on "Recent American Fiction" (1963), Bellow stoutly contradicts the stances of novelists such as James Jones, Philip Roth, and John Updike who fail to find an appropriate answer to the moral and cultural maladies of contemporary man and merely succeed in offering a "self devoid of depths."[11] Such novelists of "sensibility," Bellow maintains, have failed to answer this question and have offered at best "a thin fare" in this direction (67). He retorts rather sharply: writers who cannot offer justification for human existence need not waste their intellectual energy in writing books because the "wish for death is powerful and silent. It respects actions; it has no need of words."[12] He takes it upon himself to answer the above question in his fiction as well as non-fiction. In Bellow's opinion, superior human qualities and "greatness can still be seen by us" (59). It is simply that

> A modern mass society has no open place for such qualities, no vocabulary for them, and no ceremony (except in the churches) that makes them public. So they remain private and are mingled with other private things that vex us or of which we feel ashamed. But they are not lost. ... This society, with its titanic products, conditions but cannot absolutely denature us. It forces certain elements of the genius of our species to go into hiding. (59–60)

However, the expression of these concealed human attributes depends upon the way one approaches one's predicament:

> This "being human" is our very own show. All that mankind is said to be, pro and contra, comes from mankind itself. Everything that we can possibly conceive is made into fact, and it all comes out of bottomless reservoirs of our invention and fantasy. Everything has to be tried out. Funnily enough, the same mind that takes in "Dallas" or rap music is also accessible to Homer and Shakespeare. (13)

Thus "we have transhistorical powers. The source of these powers is in our curious nature" (14). To facilitate a free flow of these "central energies," Bellow touches the innermost primal cords of his characters' essential selves persistently in collision with the hostile cultural and historical forces (93).

Thus, there appears in all his works

> a primordial person, he is not made by his education, nor by cultural or historical circumstances. He precedes culture and history. .... This means that there is something invariable, ultimately unchangeable, native to the soul. A variety of powers arrive whose aim is to alter, to educate, to condition us. If a man gives himself over to total alteration I consider him to have lost his soul. If he resists these worldly powers, forces of his own can come into play.[13]

Moses in Bellow's *Herzog* (1964) stoutly refuses "to be a victim" – he survives an intense emotional and intellectual turmoil in his private life and finally returns to a "primal point of balance."[14] Eugene Henderson in *Henderson the Rain King* (1959) too puts up a valiant fight against his spiritual chaos, and at the end returns from dark Africa bubbling with pristine energy and eager to live a new life. In the past, man helplessly endured the catastrophic afflictions of historical processes in the forms of fierce wars, bloody revolutions, and mass murders. Hence, most writers of the period – such as Mann, Gide, Kafka, Joyce, Woolf, Lawrence, and Hemingway – declared the death of the human self in their works and sent out a disturbing message of imminent universal doom. Their novels, therefore, were peopled by sick men, sexually sterile youth, "moral pygmies, emotionally regressive adults, and intellectual flyweights; altogether they seem far beyond plain man's courage as their philosophies are beyond his understanding – and interest, too, for that matter."[15] But, Bellow declines to comply with their pessimistic ideologies and projects a buoyant image of man in his novels, especially from *The Adventures of Augie March* (1953) onwards. Hereafter, Bellow eloquently defends "the sense of positive human potential against the great mass of leveling, negative appraisals the events of this century encourage."[16] Bellow's exalted image of man can be deemed as a later version of Dostoevsky's "higher individualism, to which the desire for fraternal love is natural, an individualism that is self-effacing and sacrificial" (42–43). His sense of such lofty self originates from his belief that

> When complications increase, the desire for essentials increases too. The unending cycle of crises that began with the First World War has formed a kind of person, one who has lived through strange and terrible things and in whom there is an observable shrinkage of prejudices, a casting off of disappointing ideologies, an ability to live with many kinds of madness, and an

immense desire for certain durable human goods – truth, for instance; freedom; wisdom. (93)

From the unprecedented disasters a new human self has once again arisen like a phoenix:

> He is in many respects narrow and poor, blind in heart, weak, mean, intoxi-cated, confused in spirit – stupid ... But the leap towards the marvelous is a possibility he still considers nevertheless. In fact, he is well qualified by his peculiar experiences to try jumping. He dreams of being the rap, outwitting the doom prepared for him by history. Often he seems prepared to assert that he is a new kind of human being, whose condition calls for original expression, and he is ready to take a flier, go for the higher truth. (135)

Soul

Bellow's penchant for discussions of the soul emanated from his birth in a spiritually informed and morally conscious Jewish family in Montreal, Canada (321). He therefore got early in life an idea about the higher reality. The Bellow children studied Hebrew and read *The Old Testament* with curious interest. Bellow "felt very cozy with God, the primal parent, and by the time I was up to the Patriarchs (I was five or six years old), I felt they were very much like members of my family. I couldn't readily distinguish between a parent and the heroic ancestors – Abraham, Isaac, and Jacob, and the sons of Jacob, especially Joseph" (287). And such familiarity further intensified after he spent six months on the children's ward of a tuberculosis sanatorium in his seventh year. There, "A missionary lady gave me a *New Testament* for children. I read that. I was very moved by the life of Jesus, and I recognized him as a fellow Jew. I think the hospital drove a lot of that home to me. Because I'd never been away from my parents before" (288). The young Bellow saw children dying every day on his ward, and their empty beds reminded him of his own turn to die soon: "I got out of bed occasionally; they used to hang your chart at the foot of the bed. I would read my chart, and I knew it was very unpromising" (289). But, he finally "got away with it" and felt indebted to "*some entity* for the privilege of surviving" (289; emphasis added). He realized deep within him that "it had been by permission of some *high authority*. ... Some kind of central connec-tion, in the telephonic sense" (290; emphasis mine).

Bellow's early reading in the scriptures and his later escape from death thus sensitized him toward the higher power, the Super-soul. Later, he identifies it through Sammler as a "splash" of "God's own spirit," the "richest thing" all creatures "share in common." But, Bellow slowly sensed that these higher things were in danger of extinction due to the "diffusion" of the very "essence of being" in modern mass society: "I was made aware in adolescence that there were higher things and that these high things were under siege, were in trouble – their ground was diminishing" (155). However, Bellow was not wholly pessimistic about their survival; he firmly believed that these higher things had descended into the depths of our soul, and they always found an unconscious expression in our everyday behavior: people "live by something quite unknown to themselves, some kind of moral intuition which they can't apparently get rid of but they rely upon without acknowledgment. With many of us this does not even rise to the consciousness."[17] Though it is a "taboo" to talk about soul these days, true artists do have a soul; they are all mutually connected by their common appeal to it (77):

> When you open a novel – and I mean of course the real thing – you enter into a state of intimacy with its writer. You hear a voice or, more significantly, an individual tone under the words. This tone you, the reader, will identify not so much by a name, the name of the author, as by a distinct and unique human quality. It seems to issue from the bosom, from a place beneath the breastbone. It is more musical than verbal, and it is the characteristic signature of a person, of a soul.   (168)

This unambiguously proves that some artists are still "stuck" with "what is left of the soul and its mysteries" (113). The "powers of soul," the staple subjects of Shakespeare, Handel, and Mozart, indeed have no relevance amid a climate of hate and nihilism today. But, writers here and there "still stake their lives on the existence of these forces. About this, intellectuals have little or nothing to say" (113). For Bellow, intellectuals are mere "Reality Teachers"; they generate abstract ideas which have "nothing to do with [the] most significant intentions and actions" of the common people (135).

Thus, their philosophical formulations alienate people from the true forms of life and create the thickets of synthetic selves around their original ones. These theories therefore obstruct the free expression of peoples' real soul and render them vulnerable to the sudden exigencies of life. "Some of these explosive modern manifestations," Bellow warns, "are exactly proportionate to the degree of poisoned autonomy, egocentricity, isolation, self-imprisonment that the modern soul experiences."[18] But the contemporary man has known from his complex and varied experiences of life how to come out unscathed from the intricate maze of the "ideas and doctrines" that have dominated the present century. Bellow affirms,

> Anyone who has lived attentively through five decades of this epoch has had centuries of history thrust upon him, ages of mental experience. He is (or can

be) skeptical, cant-free, heedful of his own intuitions. He has seen orthodoxies come and go, and he has learned that he must trust the communications coming from his own soul – stipulating that his soul should know the dry taste of objectivity. (135)

It sounds rather farcical that "We 'square' ourselves with our ideas, but in time we recognize that the unacknowledged soul has somehow saved us from the worst effect of those ideas" (135). By now man is capable of "lightening" himself, taking his own decisions, and making his own judgments based on his deeper illumination or intuitions. And, by the "light of one's own judgment, and in one's own style, and with one's own powers, one sees the naked soul. When *oneself* has come *out*, many things become visible" (137; emphasis in original). As soon as Charlie Citrine in *Humboldt's Gift* has come out of the "nagging rush" of ideological confusions and spiritual chaos, he sees the "spring" coming ahead – the stirring of his sleepy soul into a "higher wakefulness."

Bellow endeavors to excavate the hidden essences from the inmost depths of man's soul for the sole purpose of restoring his lost romantic image and freeing him from the enslavement of false ideological formulations. The inner essences are of primal nature and therefore they do not adhere to those cultural or psychological entrapments that obstruct or impede their spontaneous flow in everyday life. Bellow displays this sense of the inner essence in his novels by confronting his protagonists with emotionally or physically challenging situations where their social constraints drop down like loose garments and they revert to the elemental states, allowing their deeper impulses to find unrestrained expression. And Bellow persistently aims at higher truths to suggest to ordinary people possible avenues for the preservation of their soul. At the end of their breathless struggle, Bellow's protagonists enter a "quiet zone" of bliss, leaving behind all the grandeur, glitter, and grief of the world. By the coalescence of the lower essences and higher truths in his novels, Bellow attempts to create "a new man," who can survive undamaged by the dint of his deeper vitality and higher spirituality in today's distracted world. *It All Adds Up* offers a fine justification for Bellow's lifelong efforts in this direction.

Notes

1. Christopher Lehmann-Haupt, "Books of the Times: Who Is Saul Bellow? And Who Isn't Saul Bellow," *New York Times* (April 11, 1994): 15C.

2. Saul Bellow, *It All Adds Up: From the Dim Past to the Uncertain Future* (New York: Viking, 1994), p. 63. Subsequent citations indicated in the text with page numbers are to this edition.
3. Saul Bellow, "Bunuel's Unsparing Vision," *Horizon*," 2 (November 1962): 112.
4. Jo Brans, "Interview with Saul Bellow," *Southwest Review*, 62, No. 1 (Winter 1977): 8.
5. John L. Brown, "A Review of *It All Adds Up*," *World Literature Today*, 69, No. 1 (Winter 1995): 148.
6. Saul Bellow, "A World Too Much with Us," *Critical Inquiry*, 2, No. 1 (Autumn 1975): 7.
7. Saul Bellow, "Culture Now: Some Animadversions, Some Laughs," *Modern Occasions*, 1, No. 2 (Winter 1971): 178.
8. Saul Bellow, "A Personal Record: A Review of Joyce Cary's *Except the Lord*," *The New Republic* (February 22, 1954): 20.
9. Gordon L. Harper, "Saul Bellow: An Interview," *The Paris Review*, 36 (Winter 1966): 65–66.
10. Saul Bellow, "Some Notes on Recent American Fiction," *Encounter*, 21, No. 5 (November 1963): 29.
11. Ibid.
12. Saul Bellow, "The Writer as Moralist," *The Atlantic Monthly*, 211 (March 1963): 62.
13. Matthew C. Roudane, "An Interview with Saul Bellow," *Contemporary Literature*, 25, No. 3 (Fall 1984): 276.
14. Saul Bellow, "Foreword" to Allan Bloom's *The Closing of the American Mind* (New York: Simon & Schuster, 1987), p. 16.
15. Julian N. Hartt, *The Lost Image of Man* (Baton Rouge: Louisiana State University Press, 1963), p. 12.
16. Robert Solotaroff, "The Personal Essay and Saul Bellow's *It All Adds Up*," *Studies in American Jewish Literature*, 18 (1999): 39.
17. Henrietta Buckmaster, "The Writer's Obligation: Returning to the Center," *The Christian Science Monitor* (March 1, 1978), p. 24.
18. Saul Bellow, "Writers and Morals," quoted from the unpublished essay in the Saul Bellow papers at the Joseph Regenstein Library, University of Chicago, IL.

13

DAVID BRAUNER

Bellow's Short Fiction

In an article in the *Guardian* trailing the first volume of his monumental biography of Bellow, Zachary Leader declared: "Ten years after his death . . . Bellow's reputation remains undiminished."[1] This is debatable, if not misleading. In the last monograph on Bellow, published in 1992, Peter Hyland was able credibly to describe Bellow as "the major post-war American novelist,"[2] but since then his reputation has declined, both critically and in terms of popular profile. In a review of Leader's biography, Lee Siegel pointed out that "many people under the age of 50 have barely heard of Bellow, if at all."[3] Siegel sees this as partly the consequence of the "magisterial generalizations about history and culture" in his work, which alienated a postmodernist generation "suspicious of intellectual abstractions and doubtful of the authority behind them," and partly the consequence of the furore provoked by Bellow's reactionary remarks in the 1980s about attempts to expand the literary canon ("Who is the Tolstoy of the Zulus? The Proust of the Papuans? I'd be happy to read them"), from which, he says, "[h]is reputation never recovered" ("Wrestling With Saul Bellow").

In this essay, I will argue that his reputation might most effectively be rehabilitated by a reconsideration of his short fiction, which is formally more radical and richly complex than has been generally acknowledged. I will also suggest that in their insistent self-reflexivity, their interrogation of subjectivity, and their subtle, shifting, ironic point of view, many of Bellow's short stories demonstrate an unexpected affinity, if not with the postmodernism of his peers, then with a later generation of writers whom we might call post-postmodernists, so that it is ripe for rediscovery by a new generation of readers.

Even at the zenith of his fame, Bellow's short fiction tended to receive short shrift. In the only full-length study of Bellow's short fiction, published in 1996, Marianne Friedrich observed that "criticism of Bellow's short fiction has been remarkably limited," and this is still true today.[4] Whereas many of his novels, particularly *The Adventures of Augie March* (1953), *Herzog*

159

(1966), and *Humboldt's Gift* (1976), won major literary prizes and generated critical acclaim, his short stories remained relatively neglected. "Like most novelists," Bellow regarded his short stories as "welcome interludes" from the serious business of novel-writing, according to James Atlas.[5] Atlas himself colludes with this marginalization of the short fiction, implicitly privileging the novel form by calling Bellow a novelist here and elsewhere and by devoting very little space in his biography to the short stories.[6] When he does refer to them, he tends to damn them with faint praise, observing of his first collection, *Mosby's Memoirs and Other Stories* (1968), that "it wasn't major Bellow," a judgment he reinforces by citing Bellow's own self-deprecating comments to Robert Penn Warren: "Two or three of the stories [in *Mosby*] meet a good standard, one does not, and another is only a toy" (*Bellow*, 372). Bellow's second biographer, Zachary Leader, ostensibly has a much higher opinion of the short fiction: "When asked which of Bellow's works to start with ... I often say the *Collected Stories* (2001), which contains several of his novellas, including *The Bellarosa Connection* (1989), a brilliant meditation on the psychic impact of the Holocaust, in Europe, America and Israel."[7] Yet Leader's endorsement of the short fiction is equivocal: by drawing attention to Bellow's longer short fiction – to the novellas rather than the short stories – he implicitly reinforces the traditional hierarchy of form in which longer fiction is more prestigious than shorter. Moreover, in singling out *The Bellarosa Connection* for praise because of its engagement with the legacy of the Holocaust, Leader suggests that its status depends more on the gravitas of its subject-matter than on any formal characteristics.[8] There are dissenting voices. In their reviews of *Him with His Foot in His Mouth* (1984), Robert Adams suggests that "short stories may be more congenial to Bellow's gift than novels,"[9] and Martin Amis claims that the collection demonstrates Bellow at "the height of his ... powers," each story displaying "the same consistency of brilliance and vigour,"[10] while Friedrich's detailed study of the short fiction makes a powerful case for the stories to be seen not as adjuncts to or digressions from the novels, but "independently as unique and complex works of art" (*Character and Narration in the Short Fiction of Saul Bellow*, 3). Overall, however, Adam Mars-Jones's view that Bellow is one of those "novelists who have no affinity with the short story" remains the prevailing one ("Bellow Par").[11]

Bellow himself seems to have felt ambivalent about the place of the short fiction in his oeuvre. On the one hand, he professed not to prioritize the short story form, confiding in a letter to his would-be biographer Mark Harris that he "wrote few stories and ... used them as 'scale models' for bigger jobs" and offering only a rather half-hearted defense of *Mosby*: "I don't think it's all bad, however."[12] On the other hand, he also expressed a particular pride in his stories and novellas, observing that they were written "at the top of my form" ("'I got a scheme!'") and boasting of having written "Mosby's Memoirs" "on six successive mornings ... in a state of all but intolerable excitement," the "words com[ing] readily" as if he were "striking them with a mallet" (*Saul Bellow Letters*, 287). The exuberant enthusiasm of this description is reminiscent of his account of the composition of *The Adventures of Augie March*, when he found himself writing with "reckless spontaneity" and "feeling the excitement of discovery";[13] this is, I think, no coincidence, since "Mosby" represents a pivotal moment in the evolution of Bellow's poetics of the short story form in much the same way as *Augie* does for his poetics of the novel.

Bellow's claim that he "wrote few stories" is actually somewhat misleading. He began his career as a short story writer, publishing two stories ("Two Morning Monologues" and "The Mexican General") before the appearance of his first novel, *Dangling Man* (1944), and he continued to publish stories throughout his career. As the title of his first published piece of fiction suggests, voice and the representation of (self-)consciousness was of vital importance to Bellow's short fiction from the start. However, although a number of his early stories were "monologues" of one sort or another, most of the pieces in his first collection are ostensibly conventional third-person narratives. Yet on closer inspection, the stories in *Mosby* fall into two distinct camps. The four stories that were written and originally published in the 1950s – "Looking for Mr. Green," "The Gonzaga Manuscripts," "A Father-To-Be," and "Leaving the Yellow House" – conform to the traditional model of the short story, proceeding chronologically, establishing a predicament for the protagonist, before moving to a crisis and a resolution, if not a revelation, at the end. The other two stories in the collection – "The Old System" and "Mosby's Memoirs" – were written a decade after the last of the earlier stories and are arguably closer in form, content, and tone to the stories of Bellow's second collection, *Him with His Foot in His Mouth*, than to their companion pieces in *Mosby*. These stories are not stories at all in the conventional sense of the term; they proceed through what Philip Roth, writing about the narrative structure of *Portnoy's Complaint* (1969) – which itself owed a debt to Bellow's novel *Herzog* – referred to as "blocks of consciousness, chunks of material of varying shapes and sizes piled atop one another and held together by association rather than chronology."[14] They not only follow the trajectory of their protagonists' thoughts and memories, they follow their protagonists' thoughts *about* their thoughts, their memories *of* their memories.

The opening sentence of "The Old System" – "It was a thoughtful day for Dr Braun"[15] – contains in microcosm many of the characteristics of the story that follows. The formal identification of the protagonist, by surname and honorific – which anticipates the naming of the protagonists of "Mosby" ("Mr Mosby – Dr Mosby, really," [*Mosby*, 157]) and the novel that Bellow was writing at the same time as these stories, *Mr. Sammler's Planet* (1970) – seems to imply a distance between narrator and character. This sense of detachment is amplified by the unconventional diction: by the use of "thoughtful" as an adjectival modifier for "day" rather than for Braun himself, which seems to deprive him of agency, and by the ambiguity of "for," which could be read either as a preposition (meaning "Braun spent much of this day in thought") or as an adverb (altering the meaning of the sentence to either "Dr Braun spent more time thinking on this day than he usually did," or even, albeit improbably, "Given Dr Braun's usual aversion to thinking, this day might be described as a thoughtful one"). As the paragraph proceeds, however, the narrative point of view seems to fluctuate with disorientating frequency:

> The feeling of necessary existence might be the aggressive, instinctive vitality we share with a dog or an ape. The difference being in the power of the mind or spirit to declare *I am*. Plus the inevitable inference *I am not*. Dr Braun was no more pleased with being than with its opposite. For him an age of equilibrium seemed to be coming in. How nice!   (*Mosby*, 43, emphases in original)

The first sentence here seems to be focalized through Dr Braun; to be effectively paraphrasing his own thoughts, or at least, as the use of the first-person plural implies, to be articulating a position in which the points of view of narrator and protagonist coincide. This impression is reinforced by the intellectual and grammatical short-hand of the two sentences that follow (they are technically sub-clauses rather than sentences in their own right, and they allude to the ontological debates at the heart of much twentieth-century philosophy), but at the same time complicated by their insistence on the subjectivity of consciousness. The recurrence of the third-person reference to Dr. Braun in the following sentence seems to reassert a distance between narrator and protagonist, a distance that is made explicit by the specific attribution of the sentiments in the next sentence to Braun's peculiar perspective ("For him") and by the irony of the final comment ("How nice!"), which seems to imply a narrative judgment of Braun's vision as at best naively utopian and at worst complacently self-serving. Yet there is a further potential complication here. For one way of explaining the sudden shifts in narrative point of view might be to infer that the narrator of "The Old System" is in fact Braun himself, "speaking of himself in the third person as Henry Adams had done in *The Education of Henry Adams*," as the narrator of "Mosby" says of Mosby's modus operandi in his memoirs (*Mosby*, 165).

Seen in this light, then, what had seemed like narrative distance might just as easily be read as Dr. Braun's pedantically self-conscious manner of referring to himself, or even as a self-parodic version of himself as excessively fastidious. These ambiguities deepen with the reflections in the second paragraph that "civilized man today cultivated an unhealthy self-detachment" and has "learned from art the art of amusing self-observation and objectivity" (44), reflections which beg the question of whether Braun is including himself in his analysis and, if he is, whether that makes him more or less disingenuous. It is in the third paragraph, however, that we encounter perhaps the finest example of the new mode of self-reflexive (self-)narration of (self-)consciousness that Bellow had discovered.

> He opened a fresh can of coffee, much enjoyed the fragrance from the punctured can. Only an instant, but not to be missed. Next he sliced bread for the toaster, got out the butter, chewed an orange; and he was admiring long icicles on the huge red, circular roof tank of the laundry across the alley, the clear sky, when he discovered that a sentiment was approaching. This was not true. He did not love anyone steadily. But unsteadily he loved, he guessed, at an average rate. (*Mosby*, 45)

Here each action, each sensation, each flicker of cogitation, is refracted through the lens of self-observation, a process that simultaneously invokes the objectivity of ironic self-detachment and insists on the inescapability of subjectivity. The protagonist's absorption in the immediate stimuli of the quotidian world ("He ... enjoyed the fragrance [of coffee] ... chewed an orange") is mediated through his rarefied, self-absorbed consciousness, apprehended in the very moment of experience ("he was admiring ... he discovered that a sentiment was approaching ... The sentiment, as he drank his coffee"), so that this experience becomes the experience of reflecting on experience. Furthermore, even this compulsive self-reflexivity is itself subject to the refinement of the recognition of its own provisionality, so that his discovery "that a sentiment was approaching" is no sooner offered than it is withdrawn ("This was not true"). And because the referent of "this" is itself unclear (does it refer to the "discovery" of the sentiment or to the sentiment itself, or both?), the qualification is not a clarification but, rather, another complication.

The manner in which jaded skepticism about "unhealthy self-detachment" – which manifests itself in "the art of amusing self-observation and objectivity" – co-exists here with ironic self-detachment places Bellow in the company of some unexpected bedfellows. In a frequently cited essay, "E Unibus Pluram: Television and US Fiction," David Foster Wallace articulated his impatience with what he saw as a lazy irony that he felt had become the hallmark of postmodernism. For Wallace, this kind of irony, accompanied by a reflex ridicule, had become "the agents of a great despair and stasis in US culture" that posed "terrifically vexing problems" for novelists.[16] Wallace and contemporaries such as Dave Eggers and Jonathan Franzen responded to these problems by writing maximalist novels[17] that invest in what Adam Kelly calls "the new sincerity"[18], while at the same time demonstrating an ironic awareness of their own self-deconstructive tendencies. Wallace calls for his peers to risk accusations of "sentimentality" and "softness" ("E Unibus Pluram," 171) by rejecting self-consciousness, but in his own fiction he is invariably self-conscious about any attempt to reject self-consciousness and constantly wary of sentimentality, just as Bellow's narrator, in the passage from "The Old System" above, rigorously regulates and scrutinizes his own "sentiment" rather than unselfconsciously surrendering to it. In this, in the unapologetically cerebral, metaphysical lyricism of their prose, and in their predilection for representing ideas both as "a comic conceit and a heartfelt belief"[19] – treating them ironically and sincerely, in other words – Wallace and Bellow occupy common ground.[20]

Whereas Wallace in *Infinite Jest* (1996) and Dave Eggers in *A Heartbreaking Work of Staggering Genius* (2000) engage in an ongoing commentary on their own work through the copious use of endnotes and footnotes, respectively, and the intrusive literary allusions in Jonathan Franzen's *The Twenty-Seventh City* (1988) suggest a similarly acute, exacerbated form of self-consciousness, Bellow's short stories are punctuated by qualifications, parentheses, and afterthoughts, resulting in fiction that appears to be constantly *in process*, revising and re-revising, compulsively second-guessing itself. This self-correcting self-reflexivity is particularly conspicuous in "Mosby's Memoirs." This is how the story introduces its protagonist: "Mr Mosby – Dr Mosby, really; erudite, maybe even profound; thought much, accomplished much – had made some of the most interesting mistakes a man could make in the twentieth century" (157). At each stage of its evolution, this sentence doubles back on itself: firstly, Mosby's title is pedantically corrected; then the initial adjective applied to him ("erudite") is tentatively refined ("maybe even profound"); and finally what begins as a description of habitual cogitation ("thought much") becomes an assertion of success ("accomplished much") before being displaced by an emphasis on his failures ("had made some of the most interesting mistakes a man could make in the twentieth century") that paradoxically presents them as further evidence of his significance as a world-historical individual, a Hegelian concept with which many of Bellow's later stories engage.[21] As in "The Old System," so here the narrative point of view is hard to locate. Is the word "interesting" being used ironically (as in the Chinese proverb "We live in interesting times")? Is the belated allusion to Mosby's PhD a sincere acknowledgment of his intellectual distinction or a sly dig at his preciosity? As they were in "The Old System," these questions are related to the larger question of whether Mosby is the narrator of his story, which would make any satire at his expense self-satire. Similar questions are raised when Mosby is summed up again a few pages later:

> The only absolute democrat in America (perhaps in the world – although who can know what there is in the world, among so many billions of minds and souls) was Willis Mosby. Notwithstanding his terse, dry, intolerant style of conversation (more precisely, examination), his lank dignity of person, his aristocratic bones. (162)

Here we have another variation in the way that Mosby is referred to: one that appears less formal because there is no title and his first name is included, but whose syntax retains an awkward self-consciousness. Rejecting the conventional declarative form ("Willis Mosby was ..."), the main verb and subject of the sentence are withheld until the end ("... was Willis Mosby"). The archaic word-order once again highlights the self-correcting process of the narrator's thoughts. The sentence begins with an absurdly hyperbolic assertion about Mosby's political convictions ("The only absolute democrat in America") which threatens to deconstruct itself (since "absolute" is an adjective usually associated with dictatorship rather than democracy, "absolute democrat" is potentially oxymoronic) before introducing a parenthetical after-thought which extends the scope of the claim for Mosby's exceptional status even further ("in the world") while at the same time qualifying it (through the use of "perhaps" and the sub-clause beginning "although"). The next sentence (which is technically not a sentence at all, but a subordinate clause) characterizes Mosby's conversation in terms that implicitly undermine the democratic credentials that have just been extolled, while at the same time echoing them, since "absolute" is, in certain contexts, a synonym for "intolerant." Once again, this view is no sooner articulated than it is revised ("conversation" being rejected for the more "precise" term "examination") in such a way as to suggest that Mosby's belief in democracy does not extend to his social intercourse. This impression of imperious disdain for the views of others (the very antithesis of "absolute democracy," if "absolute" is taken to signify "complete commitment to") is confirmed by the final adjective applied to Mosby here ("aristocratic"), which implies a belief in precisely the class-based hierarchy that democracy was designed to render redundant. Once again, the extent to which the overall tone of this passage is (self-)regarding and/or (self-)satirical depends not just on the ambiguities of the diction and syntax of Bellow's discourse, but on the identity of the narrator.

The possibility that this narrator is Mosby himself is raised not just by the revelation that Mosby refers to himself in the third person in his memoirs, but also by the interjection which follows a long passage paraphrasing part of those memoirs: "Mosby, writing these reflections in a blue-green color of ink which might have been extracted from the landscape" (167). Here, the use of a comma rather than (as might have been expected) the word "was" at the start of the sentence ("Mosby, writing") is suggestive of a collapsing of time between the composition of the story "Mosby's Memoirs" and the composition of those memoirs within the frame of the story. This, in turn, might be read metafictionally, as a suggestion that the account of Mosby writing his memoirs *is*, in fact, the manuscript of his memoirs: that "Mosby's Memoirs" are Mosby's memoirs, with Mosby its author and protagonist. Further evidence for such a reading might be found in the narrator's comment on the penultimate episode of his account of Mosby's relationship with Lustgarten, an account which, although it begins as a digression designed to "lighten the dense texture of his memoirs" (184), becomes the central focus of "Mosby's Memoirs": "The end? Not quite. There was a coda: the thing had quite good form" (178). The diction here anticipates Mosby's final thoughts on himself – "himself, Mosby, also a separate creation, a finished product ... He had completed himself in this ... form" (184). Characteristically, the point of view here is ambiguous: Mosby's reflections on the "form" that he has given both to Lustgarten and to himself might be read as examples of free indirect discourse, but the repetition of the word "form," the emphasis on self-representation ("He had completed himself"), and the blurring of the lines between Mosby's memoirs and "Mosby's Memoirs" throughout the story all support the notion that narrator and protagonist are one and the same. Moreover, if, as I have been suggesting, this story and "The Old System" represent a new direction for Bellow's short fiction – if we read these stories as early examples of a "form" that Bellow perfected in the stories of his second collection, *Him with His Foot in His Mouth* – then the conflation of third-person objectivity and first-person subjectivity that we find in these stories looks like a deliberate strategy, an experimental prototype for what I believe is Bellow's masterpiece: "Cousins."

In his review of the *Collected Stories*, Adam Mars-Jones singles out "The Old System" and "Mosby's Memoirs" for particular criticism, calling the latter "weakly constructed" and complaining that the "handling of point of view" in the former is "awkward" since "Bellow has his central character, Dr Samuel Braun, pass on conversations of which he can have no knowledge" ("Bellow Par"). Yet Mars-Jones has missed the point: in these stories Bellow is deliberately rejecting the conventional construction of the short story (so that Mosby's self-satisfied reflection on the "good form" of his Lustgarten narrative is ironic) and subverting received wisdom about how to handle point of view. For Mars-Jones, Braun is superfluous, a redundant narrative encumbrance: "there seems no reason to have him in the story at all, since his only activity is to brood over the tragic estrangement between his cousins, Isaac and Tina" ("Bellow Par"). For Bellow, however, what matters is not the story of the feuding cousins, but how Braun recalls, relates and responds to it. "The Old System" is the story of Braun's "thoughtful day," his reflections on his reflections, the form he gives to the "crude circus of feelings" (*Mosby*, 82) that parades through his consciousness. It is no coincidence that the story closes, as does "Mosby's Memoirs," with the thoughts of the narrating consciousness on the "particular forms" that the story's central characters (Braun's cousins) have taken (*Mosby*, 83) and with the intimation of mortality that accompanies "the close black darkness when the short day ended" (*Mosby*, 83). This somber contemplation of mortality (and eternity, since the very last words of the story allude to the "great begetting spasm" [*Mosby*, 83] that initiated all life, according to the big bang theory) has its analogue in the final moments of "Mosby's Memoirs," which might also be the final moments of Mosby himself, in which the protagonist finds himself struggling to breathe in the "shade" of the tomb of an ancient Zapotec temple (*Mosby*, 181).

The endings of both these stories anticipate the denouement of "Cousins," in which Ijah Brodsky, the narrator and protagonist, arrives early for a rendezvous with his dying cousin Scholem, an intellectual-turned-cabbie, at a seventeenth-century "great dome" in Paris, the venue for an international conference of taxi drivers.[22] Whiling away the time before the delegates arrive, Brodsky visits the crypt of the Chapelle Saint-Jerome and when he emerges, finally to encounter the "emaciated" form of his cousin, he has a funny turn, feeling abruptly "robbed of all strength" and "bizarrely weak in the legs," before being led away by Scholem's sister (*Him*, 293, 294). Brodsky interprets his feelings of fragility as a kind of karmic memento mori:

> Doesn't existence lay too much on us? I had remembered, observed, studied the cousins, and these studies seemed to fix my own essence and to keep me as I had been. I had failed to include myself among them, and suddenly I was billed for this oversight. (294)

Here Brodsky explicitly draws attention to the same structural anomaly that Mars-Jones identified in "The Old System": namely, that through its focus on the lives of other characters (cousins, in both cases), "Cousins" marginalizes the figure who is ostensibly its protagonist. Whereas "The Old System" and "Mosby's Memoirs" were third-person narratives, and "Cousins" is told in the first person, all three stories disrupt or dissolve altogether the conventional distinctions between these points of view in order to interrogate the very nature of subjectivity. Although Brodsky claims to have omitted himself from his memories, observations and studies (note the characteristic Bellovian list, refining itself as it proceeds), the very fact of this observation and the movement in this passage between the first- and third-person pronouns ("us," "I," "me," "myself," "them," "I") suggests that Brodsky both is, and is not, one of the cousins referred to in the title of the story.

This dual perspective, in which Brodsky is both the narrator of a series of character sketches of his cousins and the recorder of the process of narrating his own cousinhood, is central to the story. Brodsky vacillates between using the first person and referring to himself in the third person throughout the story, sometimes in the same sentence ("I wanted to dispel the mystery – scatter the myth of Ijah Brodsky" [*Him*, 229]), but his interrogation of his own subjectivity is unrelenting. He indicts himself for his arcane academic interests ("I do feel the disgrace of being identified as an intellectual" [*Him*, 230]), for his susceptibility to sentimentality ("You've always been soft about cousins," his ex-wife tells him [*Him*, 286]) and, above all, for his shortcomings as a narrator. Repeatedly, Brodsky pulls himself up in the middle of an anecdote to draw attention to his tendency to digress – "But never mind these preoccupations" (232); "But never mind that" (*Him*, 238); "That's neither here nor there" (*Him*, 259) – or to claim, unconvincingly, that he's "not digressing at all" (*Him*, 282), or to apologize for his "irritating" "habit" of providing "more information than" his readers will have "any use for" (*Him*, 240).

Cumulatively, this self-reflexive self-satire amounts to an implicit defense of Bellow's methodology in "Cousins" and throughout *Him*; a narrative mode that focuses on what Brodksy calls "the minute particulars," privileging the "unnecessarily circumstantial" (*Him*, 266) details of the process of consciousness rather than those that might be deemed "necessary" (in Mars-Jones's terms) for a conventionally well-constructed story. "Cousins" exemplifies the polarizing characteristics of Bellow's short fiction. To readers such as Mars-Jones it is likely to appear rambling, repetitive, digressive, plotless, pretentious, self-indulgent, sentimental, narcissistic, and nostalgic. To readers attuned to the "new sincerity" of post-post-modernist fiction, it is likely to be appreciated for its freewheeling, vivid, bold, generously open-ended representation of a consciousness in constant motion, for the richness of its prose, crammed full of brilliant phrases and images, and for its unapologetic investment in both the cerebral and the emotional. In these stories the minute particulars, the unnecessarily circumstantial, the inconsequential, the incidental, the superfluous, the marginal, the ephemeral, the digressive, become central, essential, indispensable. Formally innovative and thematically subversive, the best of Bellow's short fiction rejects the traditional virtues of the short story – economy, clarity, revelation – in favor of an ambiguous, expansive, self-reflexive interrogation of how subjectivity is constituted and constitutes itself.

Notes

1. Zachary Leader, "'I got a scheme!' – the moment Saul Bellow found his voice," *The Guardian* (April 17, 2015). www.theguardian.com/books/2015/apr/17/i-got-a-scheme-the-moment-saul-bellow-found-his-voice, accessed September 26, 2015.
2. Peter Hyland, *Saul Bellow* (Houndmills, Basingstoke: Macmillan, 1992), p. 2.
3. Lee Siegel, "Wrestling With Saul Bellow: A New Biography Renews the Fight Over the Author's Reputation" (review of Zachary Leader, *Saul Bellow*), *Vulture* (March 22, 2015). www.vulture.com/2015/03/saul-bellow-biography .html, accessed October 4, 2015.
4. Marianne Friedrich, *Character and Narration in the Short Fiction of Saul Bellow* (New York: Peter Lang, 1996), p. 3.
5. James Atlas, *Bellow: A Biography* (London: Faber & Faber, 2000), p. 272.
6. In the index of Atlas's 686-page biography there is, for example, only one entry for "Mosby's Memoirs," and four each for "The Old System" and "Cousins."
7. Leader, "'I got a scheme!'.
8. The online version of Leader's essay also features a link to a feature entitled "Five Essential Saul Bellow Novels," with no mention of the stories, long or short. I have decided to confine my discussion in this chapter to stories from the two collections of stories that Bellow published and to exclude the novellas – *Seize the Day* (1956), *The Bellarosa Connection* (1989), and *A Theft* (1989) – that were published as books in their own right, as well as the republication of these last two together with the story "Something to Remember Me By" as *Something to Remember Me By: Three Tales* (1991).
9. Robert M. Adams, "Winter's Tales" (review of *Him with His Foot in His Mouth*), *New York Review of Books*, 30 (July 19, 1984): 28–29, 29.
10. Martin Amis, *The Moronic Inferno and Other Visits to America* (London: Jonathan Cape, 1986), pp. 11, 10.
11. Adam Mars-Jones, "Bellow Par" (review of Saul Bellow, *The Collected Stories*), *The Observer* (December 30, 2001). www.theguardian.com/books/2001/dec/30/ fiction.saulbellow, accessed November 6, 2015.
12. Benjamin Taylor, *Saul Bellow Letters* (New York: Viking, 2010), p. 283.

13. Saul Bellow, "The Art of Fiction" (interview with Gordon Lloyd Harper), *The Paris Review*, 36 (1966): 51–73, 55.
14. George Plimpton, "Philip Roth's Exact Intent" (interview with Philip Roth), in *Conversations with Philip Roth*, ed. George Searles (Jackson: University Press of Mississippi, 1992): 35–40, 35.
15. Saul Bellow, *Mosby's Memoirs and Other Stories* (Harmondsworth: Penguin, 1988 [1968]), p. 43. Subsequent references to the collection will be abbreviated to *Mosby* while the title-story itself will be referred to as "Mosby."
16. David Foster Wallace, "E Unibus Pluram: Television and U.S. Fiction," *Review of Contemporary Fiction*, 13.2 (Summer 1993): 151–194, 171.
17. Many of the characteristics associated with this form – excess, redundancy, digressiveness – are also to be found in Bellow's short fiction.
18. Adam Kelly, "David Foster Wallace and the New Sincerity in American Fiction," in *Consider David Foster Wallace: Critical Essays*, ed. David Hering (Austin: SSMG Press, 2010): 131–146. In this essay Kelly explores the extent to which Wallace's notion represents "a reworking of the concept [of sincerity] as a complex and radical response to contemporary conditions" (p. 131).
19. Jonathan Raban, "Divine Drudgery" (review of several books by David Foster Wallace), *The New York Times* (May 12, 2011). www.nybooks.com /articles/2011/05/12/divine-drudgery/, accessed November 5, 2015.
20. Consider D. T. Max's description of Wallace's fiction, which could just as easily be applied to Bellow's: "His novels were overstuffed with facts, humor, digressions ... He conjured the world in ... sentences that mixed formal diction and street slang ... his prose slid forward with a controlled lack of control that mimed thought itself"; D. T. Max, "The Unfinished," *The New Yorker* (March 9, 2009). www.newyorker .com/magazine/2009/03/09/the-unfinished, accessed November 15, 2015.
21. As well as Mosby, who "had expected a high post-war appointment" [in the U.S. government]" (*Mosby* 160) and who cites Hegel's view of history later in the story (*Mosby*, 171), and Dr. Braun, who is "*first* in his field" (*Mosby*, 45: italics in original), Shawmut, the protagonist of "Him with His Foot in His Mouth," is a famous musicologist; Victor Wulpy in "What Kind of Day Did You Have?" is "a world-class intellectual" (*Him with His Foot in His Mouth*, 63); the eponymous hero of "Zetland: A Character Witness" is a child prodigy who wins "prizes in poetry, essay contests" at college (*Him with His Foot in His Mouth*, 174); and Ijah Brodsky, the narrator of "Cousins," is a "genius" (226) former eminent lawyer and "public personality" (*Him with His Foot in His Mouth*, 227) now revered for his understanding of money markets.
22. Saul Bellow, *Him with His Foot in His Mouth* (Harmondsworth: Penguin, 1985 [1984]), p. 290. All subsequent references to the collection will be abbreviated to *Him*.

14

LEAH GARRETT

The Late Bellow: *Ravelstein* and the Novel of Ideas

Saul Bellow's last novel, *Ravelstein* (2000), is a moving rumination on the final months of Bellow's close friendship with the well-known philosopher and cultural critic, Allan Bloom.[1] In the novel, Allan Bloom is the eponymous character Ravelstein, and Bellow the narrator Chick, soul mates whose friendship is profoundly important to both. As elderly Jewish intellectuals living in the Hyde Park neighborhood of the University of Chicago, they have a complicated and longstanding relationship. Through their friendship we learn about their attitudes toward aging, love, death, and Jewishness. Ravelstein has requested that Chick write his memoir after his death and that in it he be truthful about Ravelstein, underlining that he be "as hard on me as you like (13)." The novel describes Chick's impressions and memories of Ravelstein in their last few months together as Ravelstein dies of HIV/ AIDS.

Ravelstein is written in the first-person voice of Chick recounting their final months together and interspersed with loving memories of their long friendship. While seemingly a straightforward narrative, Chick in fact often repeats the same recollections from different angles, giving us a range of perspectives on the same situation. For instance, Chick regularly brings up the time when Ravelstein drank a Coca-Cola at a fancy faculty lunch and was derided by the host. For Ravelstein it was evidence that "she wasn't going to let any *kike* behave so badly at her table" (38). These leitmotifs serve to highlight particular aspects of their relationship, and to show the moments when Chick is struggling to fully accept some of Ravelstein's ideas, such as Ravelstein's view that anti-Semitism is an undercurrent of faculty life at the University of Chicago. Since there are no clear chapter breaks, the novel reads as a series of free-flowing thoughts, and the repetitions add to the effect that this book is being generated as a kind of real-time monologue about the relationship. Here the primary objective is an honest rendition of two men – the subject, Ravelstein, and the artist, Chick – and the repetitions point toward the artist's obsessions. The oral account also suggests the legacy of psychoanalysis and talking therapies, where ideas about the self and other are expressed through a free-flowing stream of consciousness.

Ravelstein/Bloom, according to Chick/Bellow's portrait of him, is a larger than life figure with great passions and numerous contradictory impulses: "A man of idiosyncrasies and kinks, of gobbling greed for penny candies or illegal Havana cigars, was himself a Homeric prodigy" (57). In real life Bloom is the author of *The Closing of the American Mind* (1987), a bestselling, pointed attack on left-wing cultural relativism that argued that after the 1960s, American universities embraced liberal ideologies in their teaching practices that negated the great, moral ideas of the Western canon. Privately, he is homosexual, which stands him against the trends of conservative sexuality espoused by leading ideologues of the time. A well-read thinker, particularly enamored of Plato, Ravelstein at the same time loves crass, dirty humor and jokes. Bellow's stand-in, Chick, is a less famous version of himself, employed like Ravelstein at the University of Chicago, and in the final stages of an unhappy marriage to his third wife, Vela, based on Bellow's real-life marriage to Alexandra Tulcea.

As in real life, Bellow initially has problems writing his memoir about Bloom. On vacation with his new wife Janice (here named Rosamund), Bellow takes a holiday trip to St. Martin, where Chick/Bellow nearly dies from poisoning related to eating a toxin-filled Red Snapper fish. Suffering from acute poisoning, he has a series of hallucinations while tottering between life and death in a Boston Hospital. Under the loving care of Janice/Rosamund he slowly recovers, and, upon returning to the world of the living, he feels that he is finally ready to write Ravelstein's memoir. At this point the novel ends.

As with Bellow's earlier novels *Herzog* and *Humboldt's Gift*, this is a novel of ideas that describes the relationship between the lived world and the intellectual one. This is epitomized in the relationship between Ravelstein and Chick, whose exchanges are manifested in witty conversations, deep thoughts, and the appreciation of one another's intellect. For Chick, Ravelstein is a figure who he can tell everything and anything to: "I was free to confess to Ravelstein what I couldn't tell anyone else, to describe my weakness, my corrupt shameful secrets, and the cover-ups that drain your strength" (95). Also, Ravelstein is always truthful with him and forces him to look honestly at himself: "His severity did me good. I didn't have it in me at my time of life to change, but it was an excellent thing, I thought, to have my faults and failings pointed out by someone who cared about me (98)." Bellow wrote *Ravelstein* after he had won the Nobel Prize for literature and was being feted as one of the most important literary figures in the world; it must have been deeply gratifying to Bellow to have a friend who treated him as a flawed human being with whom he could "shoot the shit" about anything. Reciprocally, Ravelstein finds in Chick someone who is always honest with him, and a figure with a dry, humorous take on the world. Generally, Bellow draws Bloom/Chick as the more interesting, lively character of the duo.

Because the novel mostly takes place during the final months of Ravelstein's life, discussions about the meaning of life and death regularly arise, enabling the novel to be a thoughtful meditation on the role of sickness and death in the modern era. Since both men are deep thinkers – Ravelstein approaching matters of life and death as a philosopher and Chick as an artist – they struggle to understand the relationship between their intellectual interests and their declining health. Readers of the novel are therefore spectators to the conversations and discussions of two great minds on matters of central, existential importance.

Ravelstein embraces all aspects of his life with intense gusto. Having rejected his family and reinvented himself after a difficult childhood, Ravelstein now encourages his circle of admiring graduate students to do the same and to lead similarly authentic, passionate lives: "He hated his family and never tired of weaning his gifted students from their backgrounds" (50). Following Bellow/Chick's suggestion that he write a book about his teaching philosophies, which subsequently becomes an unexpected best seller (in real life Saul Bellow wrote its foreword), Bloom/Ravelstein is now a Conservative star with direct access to the leading figures of the era, such as Margaret Thatcher and the Reagan administration. Moreover, because Ravelstein used Chick's agent to negotiate the book deal, he has made a huge amount of money, allowing Ravelstein to indulge his love for the finer things in life, such as natty designer clothes, antiques, good food, and trips to Paris. Chick regularly reminds the reader that he is responsible for Ravelstein's success, saying on numerous occasion things such as "By following my suggestion Ravelstein had become very rich" (40). Because of these assertions, Bellow later received the preposterous accusation that he was jealous of how successful Bloom had become and to retaliate he decided to "out" him.[2]

The contrast between Ravelstein's intellectual interests and his more base desires is symbolized by his repeat encounters with the pop icon Michael Jackson at his Paris hotel (a real-life occurrence). These meetings delight Ravelstein greatly and epitomize what Chick finds so intriguing about him: he has equal love for the crass and the elevated, pop culture and philosophy. Ravelstein's greatest interest of all, however, is matters of the heart, and he is deeply involved with the relationships of those around him since for him "passionate love was his perennial interest" (27). Like Socrates, Ravelstein embodies the two spheres of the mind and the heart, the intellect and Eros, making him a fascinating figure both to Chick and to the novel's readers.

While Bellow had written other novels about his good friends, such as the American poet Delmore Schwartz, who plays a central role in *Humboldt's Gift*, because *Ravelstein* is a Roman-á-clef that discusses Bloom's death by AIDS, it brought Bellow censure for "outing" a prominent conservative academic. I would argue that any accusations of betrayal show the deep fears of the accusers about homosexuality and express their own shame about the topic. Ravelstein/Bloom is portrayed throughout the novel in a loving and generous manner, with his quirks presented as unique aspects that merely make him more interesting. It is therefore understandable that Bellow was very surprised by the criticism he received for what he thought was a loving literary gift to a good friend. The only negative description of Ravelstein's lifestyle in the book is when Chick says of Ravelstein's contraction of AIDS: "poor Ravelstein, destroyed by his reckless sex habits" (189). Yet I would suggest that rather than this being a condemnation of homosexuality, it is instead a challenge to Ravelstein's hypocritical propagation of a pure love that does not give in to sensual impulses.

Although Bellow was criticized at the time for his own cultural conservatism, his rendition of the love between Ravelstein and his young boyfriend, Nikki, is empathetic and kind, portraying Nikki as a fierce protector of the dying Ravelstein, and his intellectual and spiritual equal. Chick, by contrast, is in an ugly, empty, and mean relationship with an aloof and cold but brilliant physicist, Vela (in real life, Bellow's wife was a mathematician). Ravelstein continually derides Vela and constantly challenges Chick to free himself of her. During the course of the novel Vela ends their unhappy marriage, and Chick falls in love with Ravelstein's graduate student, Rosamund (based on Bellow's last wife, Janice). When Chick becomes sick, we see Rosamund become his most loving caretaker, as had been the case with Ravelstein and Nikki.

Even though at the time it was not year clear if in real life Allan Bloom succumbed to AIDS or to a different disease, for the sake of the novel AIDS made narrative sense because Ravelstein's main obsession in life is the manifestations of love and passion, and AIDS, a disease passed through intimate sexual contact, is the ideal symbol for the tensions that Ravelstein feels about matters of the intellect and Eros. Also, AIDS stands as a challenge to the love between Ravelstein and Nikki, suggesting that their relationship is not monogamous and therefore Ravelstein is pulled by desires not related to love but to sexuality. His death by AIDS, moreover, signifies the gap between his public embrace by conservatives and his private life as a gay man, since in this period AIDS was still a largely taboo subject, especially in Conservative, Republican circles.

Ravelstein and Chick's friendship unfolds in two stages. In the first part of the book, when Ravelstein is still alive, they are one another's primary intellectual partner, sharing their lives and beliefs, challenging one another, and appreciating and loving each other unconditionally. As Chick says of the pair, "we were close friends, none closer" (14). In the second part of the book, narrated after Ravelstein's death, Chick's love shifts to a new focus: that of his developing relationship with Rosamund. With Ravelstein gone, Rosamund becomes Chick's intellectual and spiritual soul mate. Yet where the best efforts of Chick and others cannot stop death's advance for Ravelstein, for Chick, Rosamund successfully saves his life, both literally and figuratively.

The love between Ravelstein and Chick, and later Chick and Rosamund, is selfless and deep, and it makes little difference that in one case sex is involved while in another it is platonic. This blurring of lines between heterosexual, homosexual, and platonic love is symbolized by the name "Chick." "Chick" connotes not only a baby bird, but in Yiddish/English a "boytshik": a word combining the English "boy" with the Yiddish diminutive "tshik" to mean a young man. In American and British English, "chick" is slang word for a young woman. Chick is therefore a combination of these things; he is Ravelstein's "chick," his younger partner and significant other. Ravelstein has taught Chick the rudiments of a healthy, adult, honest relationship, which he can now transfer to Rosamund. It is in fact Rosamund who actualizes all the theories that Ravelstein has held about true, passionate, selfless love, and who shows Chick that this notion is real and has been responsible for literally saving his life: "Rosamund kept me from dying ... Rosamund had studied love – Rousseauan romantic love and the Platonic Eros as well, with Ravelstein-but she knew far more about it than either her teacher or her husband" (231). The novel is thus a love letter from Bellow to his closest male friend, Bloom, and to his beloved final wife, Janice.

However, Rosamund/Janice is portrayed in such an idealized manner as the selfless helpmate, it suggests that, in this case, Bellow the husband (whose wife was due to give birth at the same time as the book's publication) overcame Bellow the artist, because her portrait lacks the complexity of all his other characters. His real-time love for Janice Bellow overtakes his ability to render her character, Rosamund, in anything less than an idealized light. It also makes his character, Chick, appear as a man able to experience the type of perfect love that Ravelstein idealizes but cannot have. Yet it also suggests that Ravelstein's and Chick's conceptions of ideal love are different, with Ravelstein able to contemplate a more complex, non-monogamous type of love than Chick can.

The novel concludes with the words "You don't easily give up a creature like Ravelstein to death" (233). Where Rosamund has saved Chick's life in the here and now, Chick will revive Ravelstein's life in his written memoir. Yet it was only by experiencing first hand intense and extreme sickness that Chick could fully appreciate and describe what Ravelstein had gone through in his final days. Intentionally or not, these scenes in *Ravelstein* illuminate important discussions of the time by the major cultural critic, Susan Sontag, in her 1989 book *AIDS and Its Metaphors*, which was a follow-up to her earlier work *Illness as Metaphor*. Sontag's writings challenged the stigmatization in the United States of sick patients generally and AIDS patients specifically. In Bellow's novel, by having Chick experience a near-death illness and, by so doing, undergo similar suffering to Ravelstein, Chick/Bellow metaphorically takes onto himself the stigmatized disease of AIDS and humanizes it.

Upon finishing *Ravelstein*, the reader is left unsure if the novel is the memoir Ravelstein has requested or if that is to be written at some later date. Or perhaps the novel and the anticipated memoir together make up the documents of Ravelstein's life. Since the real location where Ravelstein lives after his death is in the memories and thoughts of others, by writing this type of novel/memoir about him, and showing the impact Bloom made upon Bellow, *Ravelstein* is a true testimony and embodiment of what a memoir should be: an expression of love realized and lost when a beloved dies. The novel, therefore, is Bellow's beautiful gift to his dearest friend. Through the process of undergoing a similar near-death experience, and then writing the memoir, Chick frees himself to fully love and appreciate his wife Janice and to embrace his life rather than retreat from it. This shift is not described or detailed overtly, but is instead suggested through numerous subtle hints. Yet, by writing the memoir Bellow is also able to reinvent certain parts of his own history and paint himself in a more positive light. For instance, although his marriage to Alexandra Tulcea ended because of mutual affairs, in *Ravelstein* she is the only one who cheats and he is the innocent cuckold.

A basic pillar of the friendship between Ravelstein and Chick is their Jewish identity, and through the course of the novel Ravelstein teaches Chick how to be a more authentic Jew. In all instances, Ravelstein reads the world as a Jew, asking "And what about the Jewish side of the thing?" (9). He never shies away from exposing the anti-Semitism lurking just below the surface of academic and cultural life. Ravelstein's Jewishness is another one of his contradictory personality quirks as it feeds his love of crass, "borsht belt" type humor, which stands in opposition to his highbrow interests in Western philosophy: "Because he loved to talk, to think while talking, to lean backward while the bath of ideas overflowed – he instructed, examined, debated, put down errors, celebrated first principles, mixing his Greek with a running translation and stammering madly, laughing as he embroidered his exposition with Jewish jokes" (100). For most of the book, Ravelstein's Jewishness is American in tone, not only with its embrace of that type of humor, but also in its continual awareness of the anti-Semitism in American academic life. In the final third of the book, as Ravelstein is near death, his Jewishness expands to include religiosity and a belief that it can help him to understand and deal with his impending death. He even encourages Chick and Rosamund to attend synagogue services for the coming High Holidays (which they do). Throughout Ravelstein's life, like the pull between Eros and intellect, Ravelstein found "Jerusalem and Athens were the twin sources of civilization" (15). And in the final days of his life "it was the Jews he wanted to talk about, not the Greeks" (175). He turns to Judaism to help prepare himself for the questions he has about the soul in death: "It was unusual for him these days, in any conversation, to mention even Plato or Thucydides. He was full of Scripture now. He talked about religion and the difficult project of being man in the fullest sense, of becoming man and nothing but man" (178). Judaism brings Ravelstein comfort and he seeks the same for Chick, who is anxious about his own death.

The other aspect of Jewishness evident in the novel, besides American Jewishness and Judaism, is the focus on the impact of the Holocaust on Jewish postwar identity. The shadow of the Holocaust is strong and Ravelstein requires that Chick navigate the world in such a way as to admit that he is a Jew in a world that has recently sought to extinguish them all. Chick discusses this with Rosamund:

> Of course that's what this conversation is circling – what it means to the Jews that so many others, millions, of others, willed their death . . . As Ravelstein saw it I refused to do the unpleasant work of thinking it all through . . . Well, I had a Jewish life to lead in the American language, and that's not a language that's helpful with dark thoughts. (167)

The idea that Chick will ignore the realities of anti-Semitism in order to maintain a peaceful American life plays out in the first part of the novel when Ravelstein constantly challenges Chick about his acceptance of his wife Vela's friendship with a Romanian couple, the Grielescus. According to Ravelstein, the dignified, European, classy husband, the Jungian scholar Radu, has a dark history as a member of the fascist group the Iron Guard, who were active antisemites, and he had also been a cultural officer when the

Nazis were in control of Romania. Where Vela views the couple as educated, polite Europeans whose friendship she cultivates to express her own elite status, Ravelstein rips this apart, showing Chick that her friendship is rooted in her denial of their anti-Semitism. And even worse, Chick is accountable by also having a friendship with them. When Ravelstein is dying he forces Chick to accept his culpability for a friendship with a man who was aligned with groups that skinned people alive after hanging them on meat hooks: "And your Radu has written books, endless books, about myth. So what do you want with mythology, anyway, Chick? Do you expect to be tapped one of these days and be told that you have now become an elder of Zion? Just give a thought now and then to those people on the meat hooks" (128–129).

Ravelstein's challenge to Chick is to reject the elite, polite status and to accept himself as an outsider Jew who is challenging the decorum of silence on anti-Semitism. When Chick's marriage ends with Vela, in part because Ravelstein has let Chick know about the affair she has been having, it frees up Chick to fully embrace his Jewish status and to conduct a new relationship with a fellow Jew, Rosamund. Their idealized relationship is free of the anxiety of anti-Semitism that Ravelstein has laid bare in Chick's previous marriage to Vela, and it suggests that this new love is more authentic and true because it respects Chick's Jewishness. Perhaps the most important way that the friendship between the men impacts on Chick is that it subtly pushes him to embrace his Jewish identity rather than sublimating it to be a more acceptable un-hyphenated American.

Reception and Controversy

Much of the "controversy" over the novel was generated by an April 2000 *New York Times* article by D. T. Max with the inflammatory title "With Friends Like Saul Bellow."[3] The essay insinuates bad intentions from Bellow in myriad ways. For instance, it begins with a description of the journalist D. T. Max watching a videotape of Bloom's and Bellow's attendance at Bellow's birthday party ten years previously and asks of Bellow, who is filmed looking at Bloom: "Is he sizing him up, getting ready to pin him to the glass?"[4] The essay then proceeds to interview a few of Bellow's embittered ex-friends, who imply Bellow's ill-will, as well as an unnamed person who suggests that "Bellow's motive was unarticulated jealousy."[5] As Max views it: "In *Ravelstein*, the instinct to use fiction for revenge gets free play."[6] This essay, in the most central of intellectual mediums, the *New York Times*, created the notion that *Ravelstein* was a piece of "revenge fiction" by the cranky, jealous Bellow. While writing the essay Max was able to interview Bellow, who told Max of his great admiration and friendship with Bloom:

"There are few people who are trained in their souls, so to speak, to do something extraordinary, and I think Bloom was such a person." However, Bellow added, he had "erred" "in misjudging people's sensitivities about homosexuality and AIDS." For this, "he said he now felt sorry about having exposed Bloom."[7]

The "controversy" hurt Bellow greatly. After the interview for the *New York Times*, he wrote a private letter to the British novelist Martin Amis expressing his honest views on the whole affair and expressing regret for his acceptance of culpability with the *New York Times*:

> I'd never written anything like *Ravelstein* before, and the mixture of fact and fiction has gotten out of hand ... I was not prepared to hear a leper's bell ring at the crossroads of affection and eccentric charm. It seems that many people knew the truth about Allan. If not the pure truth then the bendable, versatile kind that academic politics is familiar with. So I found myself challenged by fanatical people. I discovered very soon that Allan had enemies who were preparing to reveal that he had died of AIDS. At this point I lost my head; when *The New York Times* telephoned to have it out with me I fell apart – I was unable to outsmart the journalists. So here I am, the author of a tribute which has been transformed into one of those civilized disasters no one can be prepared for.[8]

Bellow was clearly surprised by the stinging indictment of him as a betrayer of Allan Bloom, and his letter to Amis expresses how difficult he found these accusations.

Besides this example from the *New York Times*, the novel received wide praise from a range of critics around the world, many surprised that a man in his eighties was able to still produce such masterly and deep writing. The novel also brought out impassioned views focusing on the Roman-á-clef format and if/how this was a novel versus a memoir. Two prominent figures rose to Bellow's defense in light of the "controversy" about the book, although arguing their points from opposite sides of the spectrum. The American novelist Cynthia Ozick wrote a compelling essay for the *New Republic*, "Throwing Away the Clef," admonishing all those who read *Ravelstein* as a Roman-á-clef since this reduced its complexities to simplistic analysis of the biographical aspects, thereby overlooking the artistry of the work: "It is important to repudiate the tag of Roman-á-clef not only because it is careless and rampant, but because it reduces and despoils the afflatus – and the freedom – of the literary imagination."[9] She argues that *Ravelstein* is first and foremost a great work of art and ridicules all the reductionists.

The prominent conservative critic Norman Podheritz wrote a piece for *Commentary* that argued that Ozick herself was also being reductionist by assuming that a Roman-á-clef or memoir or biography was somehow of lesser stature than a "literary novel" since for Podheritz "it is no insult or denigration of *Ravelstein* to read it as a memoir."[10] Podheritz, moreover, challenges those who read Bellow's portrayal of Ravelstein/Bloom as a negative figure: shallow, materialistic, and unable to repress his sexual urges. Rather, "for Saul Bellow, the richness of Allan Bloom's blood (and mind) was thickened by his entanglement with what some dismiss as the grosser things of this world. There is also in Bellow's eyes a kind of greatness – as spiritual as it is material – in the extremity of Bloom's extravagance."[11] For both Ozick and Podheritz, fiercely protective of the legacy of Saul Bellow, they challenge, from different angles, those who "misread" *Ravelstein* as some kind of subconscious attack on Allan Bloom, and point out the great artistry of the novel against the simplistic and misguided attacks of some critics.

Sarah Blecher Cohen wrote one of the most compelling considerations of the novel, arguing forcefully that *Ravelstein* was one of Bellows "most comic novels" and pointing out the layers of humor and satire that critics had missed in their intense focus on the question of whether or not the work was biographical.[12] For Blacher Cohen, Ravelstein embodies Bellow's "comic Jewish man," with rich speech patterns overflowing with Yiddish rhythms and humor, whose relationship with Chick enables both men to laugh at their impending deaths.[13]

That *Ravelstein* could call forth such impassioned responses from a range of great critics suggests Bellow's success at blurring the genre lines of the novel/memoir/biography/Roman-á- clef and his triumph at creating two characters that challenge assumptions about what defines both greatness and virtue.

Notes

1. Saul Bellow, *Ravelstein* (New York: Viking, 2000).
2. D. T. Max, "With Friends Like Saul Bellow," *The New York Times Magazine* (April 16, 2000): 75.
3. Ibid., pp. 70–76. For an essay aiming to get at the real truth of *Ravelstein*, it is surprising how much the author gets wrong about the novel, including misnaming the narrator, Chick, as Chickie.
4. Ibid., p. 72.
5. Ibid., p. 75.
6. Ibid.
7. Ibid., p. 76.

8. Letter by Saul Bellow to Martin Amis in *Saul Bellow's Letters*, ed. Benjamin Taylor (New York: Viking, 2010), pp. 547–548.

9. Cynthia Ozick, "Throwing Away the Clef," *The New Republic* (May 22, 2000): 29.

10. Norman Podhoretz, "Bellow at 85, Roth at 67," *Commentary*, 110.1 (July 2000): 42.

11. Ibid., p. 43.

12. Sarah Blecher Cohen, "Saul Bellow's *Ravelstein* and the Graying of American Humor," *Saul Bellow Journal*, 18.2 (2000): 40.

13. Ibid., p. 47.

GUIDE TO FURTHER READING

Primary Works

Novels and Longer Fiction

A Theft. New York: Penguin, 1989.
The Actual. New York: Viking, 1997.
The Adventures of Augie March. New York: Viking, 1953.
The Bellarosa Connection. New York: Penguin, 1989.
Dangling Man. New York: Vanguard, 1944.
The Dean's December. New York: Harper & Row, 1982.
Henderson the Rain King. New York: Viking, 1959.
Herzog. New York: Viking, 1964.
Humboldt's Gift. New York: Viking, 1975.
More Die of Heartbreak. New York: William Morrow, 1987.
Mr. Sammler's Planet. New York: Viking, 1970.
Ravelstein. New York: Viking, 2000.
Seize the Day. New York: Viking, 1956.
The Victim. New York: Vanguard, 1947.

Story Collections

Collected Stories. New York: Viking, 2001.
Him with His Foot in His Mouth and Other Stories. New York: Harper & Row, 1984.
Mosby's Memoirs and Other Stories. New York: Viking, 1968.
Something to Remember Me By: Three Tales. New York: Viking, 1991.

Essays, Letters, Memoirs, and Interviews with Saul Bellow

"A Half Life: An Autobiography in Ideas." Interview. *Bostonia* (November–December, 1990), Part One: 37–46.
"A Jewish Writer in America." *The New York Review of Books*, LVIII.16 (October 27, 2011): 26–28.
"A Second Half Life: An Autobiography in Ideas." Interview. *Bostonia* (January–February, 1991), Part Two: 34–39.

"A Second Half Life." *It All Adds Up: From the Dim Past to the Uncertain Future*. New York: Viking, 1994, pp. 314–327.

"A Talk with Saul Bellow." Interview with Joseph Epstein. *New York Times Book Review* (December 5, 1976): 93.

"A World Too Much with Us." *Critical Inquiry*, 2.1 (Autumn 1975): 1–9.

"An Interview with Saul Bellow." Interview with Matthew C. Roudane. *Contemporary Literature*, 25.3 (Fall 1984): 265–80.

"Bunuel's Unsparing Vision." *Horizon*, 2 (November 1962): 110–112.

"Chicago: The City That Was, the City That Is." In *It All Adds Up*. New York: Viking, 1994, pp. 240–245.

Conversations with Saul Bellow. Eds. Gloria L. Cronin and Ben Siegel. Jackson: University Press of Mississippi, 1994.

"Culture Now: Some Animadversions, Some Laughs." *Modern Occasions*, 1.2 (Winter 1971): 162–178.

"Deep Readers of the World, Beware!" *New York Times* (Feb. 15, 1959): 1–3.

"Distractions of a Fiction Writer." *The Living Novel: A Symposium*. Ed. Granville Hicks. New York: Macmillan, 1957.

"Foreword" to Allan Bloom's *The Closing of the American Mind*. New York: Simon & Schuster, 1987, pp. 11–18.

"How I Wrote Augie March's Story." *New York Times Book Review* (January 31, 1954): BR3.

"I Got a Scheme!: The Words of Saul Bellow." *The New Yorker*, 81 (April 25, 2005): 72–85.

"In Memory of Bernard Malamud." In *Letters*: 435–436.

"In Memory of Ralph Ellison." In *Letters*: 505–506.

"Interview with Saul Bellow." Interview with Jo Brans. *Southwest Review*, 62.1, (Winter 1977): 1–31.

It All Adds Up: From the Dim Past to the Uncertain Future. New York: Viking, 1994.

"John Berryman, Friend." *New York Times Book Review* (May 27, 1973): 263–264.

"Literature and Culture: An Interview with Saul Bellow." *Salmagundi*, 30 (1975): 6–23.

"Man Underground: On Ralph Ellison." In *There Is Simply Too Much to Think About*: 60–64.

"New York: World Famous Impossibility." In *It All Adds Up*. New York: Viking, 1994, pp., 217–220.

"'Off the Couch by Christmas' Saul Bellow on His New Novel." Interview with Melvyn Bragg. *The Listener* (November 20, 1975): 675–676.

"Saul Bellow: An Interview." Interview with Gordon L. Harper. *The Paris Review*, 36 (Winter 1966): 48–73.

Saul Bellow: Letters. Ed. Benjamin Taylor. New York: Viking, 2010.

"Some Notes on Recent American Fiction." *Encounter*, 21.5 (November 1963): 22–29.

"The Art of Fiction" (interview with Gordon Lloyd Harper), *The Paris Review*, 36 (1966): 51–73.

"The Writer as Moralist." *The Atlantic Monthly*, 211 (March 1963): 58–62.

There Is Simply Too Much to Think About: Collected Nonfiction. Ed. Benjamin Taylor. New York: Viking, 2015.

To Jerusalem and Back: A Personal Account. New York: Viking, 1976.

Secondary Works

Biography

Atlas, James. *Bellow: A Biography*. New York, Random House, 2000.
Leader, Zachary. *The Life of Saul Bellow: To Fame and Fortune, 1915–1964*. New York: Alfred A. Knopf, 2015.

Collections of Essays

Bloom, Harold, ed. *Saul Bellow*. New York: Chelsea House, 1988.
Chavkin, Allan, ed. *Critical Insights: Saul Bellow*. Pasadena/Hackensack: Salem Press, 2012.
Cronin, Gloria and Lee Trepanier, eds. *A Political Companion to Saul Bellow*. Lexington: University Press of Kentucky, 2013.
Goldman, L. H., Gloria L. Cronin, and Ada Aharoni, eds. *Saul Bellow: A Mosaic*. New York: Peter Lang, 1992.
Searles, George, ed. *Conversations with Philip Roth*. Jackson: University Press of Mississippi, 1992.

Books

Amis, Martin. *The Moronic Inferno and Other Visits to America*. London: Jonathan Cape, 1986.
Bellow, Greg. *Saul Bellow's Heart: A Son's Memoir*. New York: Bloomsbury, 2013.
Bradbury, Malcolm. *Saul Bellow*. London & New York: Methuen, 1982.
Buell, Lawrence. *The Dream of the Great American Novel*. Cambridge, MA: Harvard University Press, 2014.
Clayton, John J. *Saul Bellow: In Defense of Man*. Bloomington: Indiana University Press, 1979.
Codde, Philippe. *The Jewish American Novel*. West Lafayette: Purdue University Press, 2007.
Cohen, Sarah Blacher. *Saul Bellow's Enigmatic Laughter*. Urbana: University of Illinois Press, 1974.
Cronin, Gloria L. *A Room of His Own: In Search of the Feminine in the Novels of Saul Bellow*. Syracuse University Press, 2001.
Eichelberger, Julia. *Prophets of Recognition: Ideology and the Individual in Novels by Ralph Ellison, Toni Morrison, Saul Bellow, and Eudora Welty*. Baton Rouge: Louisiana State University Press, 1999.
Friedrich, Marianne. *Character and Narration in the Short Fiction of Saul Bellow*. New York: Peter Lang, 1996.
Fuchs, Daniel. *Saul Bellow: Vision and Revision*. Durham: Duke University Press, 1984.
Galloway, David. *The Absurd Hero in American Fiction: Updike, Styron, Bellow, Salinger*. Austin: University of Texas Press, 1981.
Glenday, Michael K. *Saul Bellow and the Decline of Humanism*. Basingstoke: Macmillan, 1990.

Guttmann, Allen. *The Jewish Writer in America: Assimilation and the Crisis of Identity*. New York: Oxford University Press, 1971.

Hassan, Ihab. *Radical Innocence: Studies in the Contemporary American Novel*. Princeton: Princeton University Press, 1961.

Hyland, Peter. *Saul Bellow*. New York: St. Martin's Press, 1992.

Kremer, S. Lillian. *Witness Through the Imagination: Jewish-American Holocaust Literature*. Detroit: Wayne State University Press, 1989.

Leader, Zachary. *The Life of Saul Bellow: To Fame and Fortune, 1915–1964*. New York: Knopf, 2015.

Malin, Irving. *Saul Bellow and the Critics*. New York: New York University Press, 1967.

  Saul Bellow's Fiction. Carbondale: Southern Illinois University Press, 1969.

Malin, Irving and Irwin Stark, eds. *Breakthrough: A Treasury of Contemporary American-Jewish Literature*. Philadelphia: The Jewish Publication Society of America, 1964.

Miller, Ruth. *Saul Bellow: A Biography of the Imagination*. New York: St. Martin's Press, 1991.

Milton, John. *Paradise Lost*. William Kerrigan, John Rumrich, and Stephen M. Fallon, eds. *The Complete Poetry and Essential Prose of John Milton*. New York: Modern Library, 2007, pp. 283–630.

Newman, Judy. *Saul Bellow and History*. London: Macmillan, 1984.

Opdahl, Keith. *The Novels of Saul Bellow: An Introduction*. University Park: Pennsylvania State University Press, 1967.

Paul, Pamela. *By the Book: Writers on Literature and the Literary Life from The New York Times Book Review*. New York: Henry Holt, 2014.

Pifer, Ellen. *Saul Bellow Against the Grain*. Philadelphia: University of Pennsylvania Press, 1990.

Pinsker, Sanford. *The Schlemiel as Metaphor*. Carbondale: Southern Illinois University Press, 1991.

Said, Edward. *Orientalism*. Harmondsworth: Penguin Books, 1995.

Shechner, Mark. *After the Revolution: Studies in the Contemporary Jewish America Imagination*. Indianapolis: Indiana University Press, 1987.

Taylor, Benjamin. *Saul Bellow Letters*. New York: Viking, 2010.

Wilson, Jonathan. *On Bellow's Planet: Readings from the Dark Side*. Rutherford: Farleigh Dickinson University Press, 1985.

Chapters in Books

Aarons, Victoria. "'Washed Up on the Shores of Truth': Saul Bellow's Post-Holocaust America," in *A Political Companion to Saul Bellow*, eds. Gloria L. Cronin and Lee Trepanier, Lexington: University Press of Kentucky, 2013: 129–152.

  "Saul Bellow," in *The Cambridge Companion to American Novelists*, ed. Timothy Parrish. Cambridge: Cambridge University Press, 2012: 230–240.

Amis, Martin. "The American Eagle: *The Adventures of Augie March* by Saul Bellow," in *The War Against Cliché: Essays and Reviews, 1971–2000*. New York: Hyperion, 2001: 447–469.

Berger, Alan L. "Remembering and Forgetting: The Holocaust and Jewish-American Culture in Saul Bellow's *The Bellarosa Connection*," in *Small Planets: Saul Bellow and the Art of Short Fiction*, eds. Gloria Cronin and Gerhard Bach. East Lansing: Michigan State University Press, 2000: 315–328.

Fuchs, Daniel. "Identity and the Postwar Temper in American Jewish Fiction," in *A Concise Companion to Postwar American Literature and Culture*, ed. Josephine G. Hendin. Malden: Blackwell, 2004: 238–262.

Gordon, Andrew. "Saul Bellow's 1968 Speech at San Francisco State University," in *A Political Companion to Saul Bellow*, eds. by Gloria Cronin and Lee Trepanier. Lexington: University Press of Kentucky, 2013: 153–166.

Kelly, Adam. "David Foster Wallace and the New Sincerity in American Fiction," in *Consider David Foster Wallace: Critical Essays*, ed. David Hering. Austin: SSMG Press, 2010: 131–146.

Kiernan, Robert. "*The Dean's December* (1982)," in *Critical Insights: Saul Bellow*, ed. by Allan Chavkin. Pasadena: Salem Press, 2012: 249–266.

Kremer, S. Lillian. "Saul Bellow," in *Holocaust Literature: An Encyclopedia of Writers and Their Work*, Volume I, ed. S. Lillian Kremer. New York: Routledge, 2003: 124–134.

Ozick, Cynthia. "Introduction," in Saul Bellow, *Seize the Day* (rpt. 1956; New York: Penguin, 2001): ix–xxiv.

Plimpton, George. "Philip Roth's Exact Intent" (interview with Philip Roth), in *Conversations with Philip Roth*, ed. George Searles. Jackson, Mississippi: University Press of Mississippi, 1992: 35–40.

Quayum, M. A, "*The Dean's December*," in *Saul Bellow and American Transcendentalism*. New York: Peter Lang, 2004: 221–269.

Rodrigues, Eusebio. "Koheleth in Chicago: The Quest for the Real in 'Looking for Mr. Green,'" in *Critical Insights: Saul Bellow*, ed. Allan Chavkin. Pasadena: Salem Press, 2012: 312–320.

Siegel, Ben. "The Visionary Exuberance of Saul Bellow's *The Adventures of Augie March*," in *A Companion to the American Novel*, ed. Alfred Bendixen Malden: John Wiley & Sons, 2015: 554–569.

Smith, Carol. "The Jewish Atlantic: The Deployment of Blackness in Saul Bellow," in *A Political Companion to Saul Bellow*, eds. Gloria Cronin and Lee Trepanier. Lexington: University Press of Kentucky, 2013: 101–127.

Steers, Nian "Successor to Faulkner," in *Conversations with Saul Bellow*, eds. Gloria Cronin and Ben Siegel. Jackson: University Press of Mississippi, 1995: 28–36.

Articles

Aarons, Victoria (ed.), "Foreword: Saul Bellow's Urban Landscapes." *Saul Bellow Journal*, 26.1–2 (Winter/Fall 2013): v–vii.

"'Not Enough Air to Breathe': The Victim in Saul Bellow's Post-Holocaust America." *Saul Bellow Journal*, 23.1–2 (Fall 2007/Winter 2008): 23–36.

Acocella, Joan. "Augie March Books." *The New Yorker*, 79.29 (October 6, 2003): 113–117.

Adams, Robert M. "Winter's Tales" (review of *Him with His Foot in His Mouth*). *The New York Review of Books*, 30 (July 19, 1984): 28–29.

Aharoni, Ada. "Bellow and Existentialism." *Saul Bellow Journal*, 2.2 (1983): 42–54.

Axelrod, Steven G. "The Jewishness of Bellow's Henderson." *American Literature*, 47.3 (November 1975): 439–443.

Bartz, Fredrica K. "The Role of Rudoph Steiner in the Dreams of *Humboldt's Gift*." *Ball State University Forum*, 24.1 (1983): 27–29.

Bilton, Alan. "The Colored City: Saul Bellow's Chicago and Images of Blackness." *Saul Bellow Journal*, 16.2–17.1-2 (2001): 104–128.

Bird, Christine M. "The Return Journey in *To Jerusalem and Back*." *MELUS*, 6.4 (1979): 51–57.

Birindelli, Roberto. "Tamkin's Folly: Myths Old and New in Seize the Day by Saul Bellow." *Saul Bellow Journal*, 7.2 (Summer 1988): 35–48.

Booth, Sherryl. "'Living your own experience': The Role of Communities in Saul Bellow's *The Dean's December*." *Saul Bellow Journal*, 10.1 (1991): 13–24.

Bradbury, Malcolm. "Saul Bellow's *The Victim*." *The Critical Quarterly*, 5.2 (1963): 19–128.

Brown, John L. "A Review of *It All Adds Up*." *World Literature Today*, 69.1, (Winter 1995): 148–149.

Budick, Emily Miller. "The Place of Israel in American Writing: Reflections on Saul Bellow's *To Jerusalem and Back*." *South Central Review*, 8.1 (1991): 59–70.

Cappell, Ezra. "Sorting the Vital from the Useless: Holocaust Memory in Saul Bellow's *The Bellarosa Connection*." *Saul Bellow Journal*, 23.1-2 (Fall 2007/ Winter 2008): 75–76.

Chavkin, Allan. "Bellow and English Romanticism." *Studies in the Literary Imagination*, 17.2 (1984): 7–18.

"Recovering the World That Is Buried Under the Debris of False Description." *Saul Bellow Journal*, 1.2 (1982): 47–57.

"*The Dean's December* and Blake's *the Ghost of Abel*." *Saul Bellow Journal*, 13.1 (1995): 22–26.

"The Feminism of *The Dean's December*." *Studies in American Jewish Literature*, 3, *Jewish Women Writers and Women in Jewish Literature* (1983): 113–127.

Chavkin, Allan and Nancy Feyl Chavkin. "Bellow's Dire Prophecy." *Centennial Review*, 33.2 (1989): 93–107.

Cohen, Mark. "'A Recognizable Jewish Type': Saul Bellow's Dr. Tamkin and Valentine Gersbach as Jewish Social History." *Modern Judaism* 27.3 (2007):350–373.

Cohen, Sarah Blacher. "Comedy and Guilt in *Humboldt's Gift*." *Modern Fiction Studies*, 25.1 (Spring 1979): 47–57.

"Saul Bellow's Jerusalem." *Studies in American Jewish Literature*, 5 (1979): 16–23.

"Saul Bellow's *Ravelstein* and the Graying of American Humor." *Saul Bellow Journal*, 18.2 (2002): 40–49.

Cronin, Gloria L. "Art vs. Anarchy: Citrine's Transcendental." *Indian Journal of American Studies*, 15.1 (1985): 33–43.

De Bellis, Jack. *The John Updike Encyclopedia*. Westport: Greenwood Press, 2000.

Fiedler, Leslie. "The Breakthrough: The American Jewish Novelist and the Fictional Image of the Jew." *Midstream*, 4 (1958): 15–35.

"Saul Bellow." *Prairie Schooner*, 31 (1957): 103–110.

Foster, John B. "'Show Me the Zulu Tolstoy': A Russian Classic Between 'First' and 'Third' Worlds." *The Slavic and East European Journal*, 45.2 (Summer 2001): 260–274.

Frank, Elizabeth. "On Bellow's Seize the Day: Sunk Though He Be Beneath the Wat'ry Floor." *Salmagundi*, 106–107 (Spring/Summer 1995): 75–79.

Hall, Joe. "*The Dean's December:* A Separate Account of a Separate Account." *Saul Bellow Journal*, 5.2 (1986): 22–31.

Hitchens, Christopher. "The Great American Augie." *The Wilson Quarterly*, 25.1 (2001): 22–29.

Howe, Irving. "People on the Edge of History: Saul Bellow's Vivid Report on Israel." *New York Times* (October 17, 1976). www.nytimes.com/books/00/04/23/specials/bellow-jerusalem.html, accessed October 14, 2015.

Kazin, Alfred. "In Search of Light" (review of *Seize The Day*). *The New York Times* (Nov. 18, 1956): 278.

Keller, Julia. "'Adventures of Augie March' is new One Book, One Chicago pick." *Chicago Tribune* (August 17, 2011). http://articles.chicagotribune.com/2011-08-17/entertainment/chi-belows-augie-march-one-book-one-chicago-pick-20110817_1_augie-march-saul-bellow-somber-city.

Kollek, Teddy. "To Jerusalem and Back by Saul Bellow." *The New Republic* (November 20, 1976): 36–37.

Kremer, S. Lillian. "Cities on His Mind: Urban Landscapes of Saul Bellow's Fiction." *Saul Bellow Journal*, 26.1–2 (Winter/Fall 2013): 1–20.

Kuzma, Faye. "'We Flew On': Flights of Imagination in *Humboldt's Gift*." *Michigan Academician*, 25.2 (1993): 159–177.

Lavine, Steven David "On the Road to Jerusalem: Bellow Now." *Studies in American Jewish Literature*, 3.1 (1977): 1–6.

Leader, Zachary. "I got a scheme!" – the moment Saul Bellow found his voice." *The Guardian* (April 17, 2015). www.theguardian.com/books/2015/apr/17/i-got-a-scheme-the-moment-saul-bellow-found-his-voice, accessed 9/26/15.

Lehmann, Sophia. "Exodus and Homeland: The Representation of Israel in Saul Bellow's *To Jerusalem and Back* and Philip Roth's *Operation Shylock*." *Religion and Literature*, 30.3 (1998): 77–96.

Lehmann-Haupt, Christopher. "Books of the Times; Who Is Saul Bellow? And Who Isn't Saul Bellow." *New York Times* (April 11, 1994): 15C.

Marovitz, Sanford. "The Emersonian Lesson of *Humboldt's Gift*." *Saul Bellow Journal*, 14.1 (Winter 1996): 84–95.

Mars-Jones, Adam. "Bellow Par" (review of Saul Bellow, *The Collected Stories*). *The Observer* (December 30, 2001). www.theguardian.com/books/2001/dec/30/fiction.saulbellow, accessed 10/6/2015.

Max, D.T. "The Unfinished." *The New Yorker* (March 9, 2009). http://www.newyorker.com/magazine/2009/03/09/the-unfinished, accessed 11/15/2015.

"With Friends Like Saul Bellow." *The New York Times Magazine* (April 16, 2000): 70–76.

Menand, Louis. "Young Saul: The Subject of Bellow's Fiction." *The New Yorker*, 91.12 (May 11, 2015): 71–77.

Michelson, Bruce. "The Idea of Henderson." *Twentieth Century Literature*, 27.4 (Winter 1981): 309–324.

Mikics, David. "Bellow's Augie at Sixty." *The Yale Review*, 102 (2014): 30–42.

Newman, Judie. "Saul Bellow, *Humboldt's Gift:* The Comedy of History." *Durham University Journal,* 72 (1979): 79–87.

Ozick, Cynthia. "Lasting Man." *The New Republic* (February 10, 2011): 13–25.

"Throwing Away the Clef." *The New Republic* (May 22, 2000): 27–31.

Parrish, Timothy. "The Urban Soul: Bellow's Rewriting of the City of Dreiser." *Saul Bellow Journal,* 26.1–2 (Winter/Fall 2013): 153–172.

Podhoretz, Norman. "Bellow at 85, Roth at 67." *Commentary,* 110.1 (July 2000): 35–43.

"The Language of Life." *Commentary,* 15 (January 1953): 378–282.

Porter, Gilbert M. "Is the Going Up Worth the Coming Down? Transcendental Dualism in Bellow's Fiction." *Studies in the Literary Imagination,* 17.2 (Fall 1984): 19–37.

Raban, Jonathan. "Divine Drudgery" (review of several books by David Foster Wallace), *The New York Times* (May 12, 2011). www.nybooks.com/articles/2011/05/12/divine-drudgery/, accessed 5/11/2015.

Rahv, Philip. "Bellow the Brain King." *New York Herald Tribune Book Week* (September 20, 1964): 1, 14, 16.

Ranta, Jerrald. "Time in Bellow's Seize the Day." *Essays in Literature,* 22 (Fall 1995): 300–315.

Rodriques, Eusebio L. "Beyond All Philosophies: The Dynamic Vision of Saul Bellow." *Studies in the Literary Imagination,* 17.2 (Fall 1984): 97–110.

"Bellow's Africa." *American Literature,* 43.2 (May 1971): 242–256.

Roth, Philip. "Acceptance Speech by Philip Roth for the Saul Bellow Award." PEN America (May 31, 2007). www.pen.org/nonfiction/acceptance-speech-philip-roth-saul-bellow-award.

Roudané, Matthew C. "An Interview with Saul Bellow." *Contemporary Literature,* 25.3 (Autumn 1984): 265–280.

Salomon, Willis. "Saul Bellow on the Soul: Character and the Spirit of Culture in *Humboldt's Gift* and *Ravelstein,*" *Partial Answers,* 14.1 (2016): 127–140.

Sánchez-Canales, Gustavo. "'A tale of two cities': A Comparative Analysis of James Joyce's Dublin and Saul Bellow's Chicago." *Saul Bellow Journal,* 26.1–2 (Winter/Fall 2013): 127–151.

"The Romantic Spirit in Saul Bellow's *The Dean's December.*" *Estudios Ingleses de la Universidad Complutense,* 11 (2003): 111–122.

Schwartz, Delmore. Review of *The Adventures of Augie March. Partisan Review,* 21.1 (1954): 112–113.

Shulman, Robert. "The Style of Bellow's Comedy." *PMLA,* 83.1 (1968): 109–117.

Siegel, Ben. "Artists and Opportunists in Saul Bellow's *Humboldt's Gift.*" *Contemporary Literature,* 19.2 (1978): 143–164.

Siegel, Lee. "Wrestling With Saul Bellow: A New Biography Renews the Fight Over the Author's Reputation" (review of Zachary Leader, *Saul Bellow*). *Vulture* (March 22, 2015). www.vulture.com/2015/03/saul-bellow-biography.html.

Smith, Herbert J. "*Humboldt's Gift* and Rudolf Steiner." *Centennial Review,* 22.4 (1978): 479–489.

Solotaroff, Robert. "The Personal Essay and Saul Bellow's *It All Adds Up.*" *Studies in American Jewish Literature,* 18 (1999): 35–40.

Spivey, Ted R. "Death, Love, and the Rebirth of Language in Saul Bellow's Fiction." *Saul Bellow Journal,* 4.1 (1985): 5–18.

Stanger, James. "The Power of Vision: Blake's System and Bellow's Project in *Mr. Sammler's Planet.*" *Saul Bellow Journal*, 12.2 (1994): 17–36.

Strand, Eric. "Lighting Out for the Global Territory: Postwar Revisions of Cultural Anthropology and Jewish American Identity in Bellow's *Henderson the Rain King.*" *ELH*, 80 (2013): 287–316.

Wallace, David Foster. "E Unibus Pluram: Television and U.S. Fiction," *Review of Contemporary Fiction*, 13.2 (Summer 1993): 151–194.

Weinstein, Anne. "*The Dean's December:* Bellow's Plea for the Humanities and Humanity." *Saul Bellow Journal*, 2.2 (1983): 30–41.

Weinstein, Mark. "Bellow's Imagination-Instructors." *Saul Bellow Journal*, 2:1 (Fall/Winter): 19–21.

"Charles Citrine: Bellow's Holy Fool." *Saul Bellow Journal*, 3:1 (Fall/Winter 1983): 28–37.

Yetman, Michael G. "Who Would Not Sing for Humboldt?" *ELH*, 48.4 (1981): 935–951.

INDEX

Cambridge Companions to...

AUTHORS

TOPICS